D0571423

THE MITCHELL BEAZLEY
POCKET GUIDE TO

FRENCH
REGIONAL
W · I · N · E · S

ROGER VOSS

MITCHELL BEAZLEY

The Pocket Guide to French Regional Wines was edited and
designed by Mitchell Beazley International Limited, Artists
House, 14–15 Manette Street, London W1V 5LB

British Library Cataloguing in Publication Data
Voss, Roger
    The Mitchell Beazley pocket guide to
    French regional wines.
    1. Wine and wine making – France
    I. Title
    641.2'2'0944   TP553

ISBN 0 85533 667 6

The author and publishers will be grateful for any
information which will assist them in keeping future
editions up to date. Although all reasonable care has been
taken in the preparation of this book neither the publishers
nor the author can accept any liability for any consequences
arising from the use thereof or from the information
contained herein.

Maps by Sue Sharples
Typeset by Servis Filmsetting Ltd, Manchester, England
Printed and bound in Hong Kong by Mandarin Offset.

Editor Alison Franks
Designer Paul Drayson, Heather Jackson ·
Production Androulla Wakefield
Senior Executive Editor Chris Foulkes
Senior Executive Art Editor Roger Walton

CONTENTS

France produces a fifth of the world's wine. Her vineyards cover a million hectares of land – 9.3 percent of the total farmland under cultivation – stretching from Alsace and Lorraine in the northeast down to the deep southwest of the Basque country. Over 14% of each harvest – nine million hectolitres – leaves France to be drunk round the world.

I have started off with this clutch of statistics to illustrate something of the hold wine has on France, and to show how important French wine is to the rest of the world (which seems to have a permanent love affair with the wines of France). For the British, for instance, until very recently, wine seemed to stop with the top three French areas of Bordeaux, Burgundy and Champagne, and producers in the United States, South Africa and Australia for a long time seemed compelled to base their wines on French originals.

We all thought we knew everything about French wine. We could recite châteaux in Bordeaux and name great Champagne houses. Areas of Burgundy gave their names to oceans of wine that had never seen French soil.

But what we knew was only the tip of an iceberg. Vast tracts of vineyards, some producing wines every bit as good as the three classic areas, were ignored or dismissed. In wine merchants' lists and in restaurants, everything was categorized as "the rest of France".

This book is about the rest of France. It has been written because at last we have come to begin to understand something of the treasure trove we have been missing.

We started by discovering regions like Sancerre and Pouilly-Fumé – and so appreciated the refreshing pleasure of the Sauvignon grape. British wine bars suddenly realized that in Muscadet they had a wine that was ideally suited to simple quaffing.

Then, in the classic areas, the price of wine started to rise – and went on rising. That was just the impetus needed to start us tracking down the other wines France had to offer. The superb Syrah wines of the northern Rhône have been rediscovered, initially because we could not afford red Burgundy, but afterwards because of their own inherent quality. Alsace has filled a gap in a world thirsty for white wine, with good-quality, sometimes great, utterly reliable drinking pleasure. The South-west has turned up some almost forgotten vineyards which recognition is bringing back to fascinating life. We have not yet discovered the sweet white wines of the Loire – but we surely will.

Which leaves the south of France, land of the great European wine lake. It is here that we find the other reason why a book like this can be written today. All the areas I have mentioned so far have been making quality wines for a long time – it is just that we needed the spur of high prices in the classic regions to make us buy. But in the south, quality was not the criterion – it was quantity.

12–13% of the world's wine production comes from the area we know as the Midi – covered by the two provinces of Languedoc and Roussillon. The flat plains by the Mediterranean Sea are themselves another sea – of vines. Much of it has been fairly undrinkable at best, disgusting at worst. But the vine has provided a livelihood for farmers whose land seemed unable to produce anything else.

Developments in agriculture have begun to change that. It is possible to grow cereals and other crops on this seemingly intractable land. Vines can be pushed back to the hills behind the plains where they can begin to show a touch of quality. And we can all benefit with a supply of wines that, while they reach no great heights, give us enjoyable everyday drinking.

New equipment has helped to improve quality as well – all over France. Farmers, supposedly resistant to change, seem to have been very happy to install stainless steel fermenting tanks, temperature control equipment, and smart bottling lines – aided, inevitably, by generous grants from the European Commission and the French Government. In the vineyard, new clones have been developed to give quality as well as quantity.

And France, which only a few years ago was regarded as the model for California and Australia, has at last realized that she has something to learn from those wine regions. Frenchmen and women are now studying viticulture and oenology – learning about what happens in the vineyard and the winery. They are not just depending on centuries of observation, but benefiting from research and development in universities and colleges.

A new generation of French winemakers is beginning to take charge of the vineyards and the cellars. They are willing to break with tradition if it is too restrictive – and they are equally willing to go back to the roots of winemaking which have sometimes been obscured by centuries of accretions.

If all this paints a picture that seems all light and no dark, there are certainly areas where enlightenment has hardly reached. Cooperatives, which control 40% of French wine, have often done much to keep an area on its viticultural feet. But in many cases they have a long way to go to emulate the quality of individual private estates. Many cooperatives still seem to equate high alcohol with high quality and to pay their members accordingly. More should follow the example of those few which pay a premium for quality and even reject grapes that are not up to standard.

Today there is also a risk of standardization in wine. Those aristocrats of grape varieties – Cabernet Sauvignon, Chardonnay and their fellow nobs – are encroaching into the territory of some fine grape varieties, taking away individuality in the desire to copy styles of wine that are in great demand. Many grape varieties are almost endangered species in their own home vineyard.

It would be sad if, just as we rediscovered the vast wealth of styles and the range of character that France can produce, all those qualities were to be put at risk just because it is easier to sell a wine if it calls itself Cabernet Sauvignon.

One of the pleasures of wine drinking, after all, is that there is seemingly infinite variety. France's wine variety is certainly wider than most. Let us hope that this variety can not only be preserved, but enhanced, as we begin to appreciate what comes out of "the rest of France."

This book is a region-by-region guide to Appellation Contrôlée (AC) wines and Vins Délimité de Qualité Supérieure (VDQS), and the people who produce them, in all the wine growing regions of France, apart from Bordeaux, Burgundy and Champagne (which are dealt with in companion volumes). It does not deal, except in passing, with Vins de Pays. Nor does it cover the island of Corsica.

Each region is treated in the same way. There is an introduction, setting out the general styles and character of the wines that come from that region, and giving some indication of the character of the countryside. This general introduction is followed by detailed notes on each of the AC and VDQS areas within the main region. These notes contain information on the colours of the wines made (red, rosé and white), whether sparkling wine is made, and the grape varieties permitted. Where relevant, notes on the quality of currently available vintages (in 1987) are given.

Producer entries follow. These are arranged alphabetically by producer, within each AC or VDQS area. The AC and VDQS order is the same as in the introduction to each section. Where a producer or négociant makes more than one AC or VDQS wines, he or she will be listed under the area in which their cellars are situated or where their principal vineyard holding is.

Information contained in each producer entry is standardized as much as possible. The name of the producer is given first, followed by his or her address, including the Cedex code, essential when writing to France. Details of the vineyards owned followed, where relevant including information about the holdings in each AC or VDQS area. This in turn is followed by the production given in terms of 75cl bottles. This figure only refers to wine bottled by the producer – any sold in bulk is not included. At the end of the entry, there are details of when the producer's tasting room is open. Often, the entry will indicate an appointment is required or preferred, but even when this is not stated, it is a courtesy to write to smaller producers in advance. Larger firms and cooperatives normally have tasting rooms which are open to the public.

Abbreviations
ha   – hectares
VP-R – vigneron proprietaire-recoltant, a producer who only makes wine from his or her own land and does not buy in grapes or wine.
N   – négociant, or wine merchant, who buys in grapes or wine which is then sold under the firm's own name. A négociant may also own land, in which case the code will read VP-R and N.
Coop – cooperative of producers. This code is followed by the number of members in the cooperative.

6

Drézery, St-Georges d'Orques, St-Saturnin, St-Chinian, Minervois, Fitou; Cabardès, Collioure, Côtes du Roussillon, Côtes du Roussillon Villages, Costières du Gard, Faugères, Corbières, Côtes de la Malapère.
Provence: Bandol, Bellet, Côtes de Provence, Palette, Coteaux Varois.
Rhône: Côtes du Rhône, Côtes du Rhône Villages, Châteauneuf-du-Pape, Coteaux du Tricastin, Gigondas, Lirac, Tavel, Coteaux du Pierrevert, Côtes du Lubéron.
Southwest: Côtes du Frontonnais.

Counoise
Midi: Costières du Gard, Coteaux du Languedoc.
Provence: Coteaux d'Aix en Provence, Coteaux des Baux en Provence.
Rhône: Côtes du Rhône, Châteauneuf-du-Pape, Côtes du Ventoux.

Courbu Noir
Southwest: Béarn.

Duras
Southwest: Gaillac.

Fer
Midi: Cabardès.
Southwest: Béarn, Bergerac, Côtes de Bergerac, Gaillac, Irouléguy, Madiran, Côtes du Marmandais, Tursan, Vins d'Entraygues et du Fel, Vins d'Estaing, Vins de Lavilledieu, Vins de Marcillac.

Folle Noire
Provence: Bellet.

Gamay
Loire: Châteaumeillant, Côtes d'Auvergne, Côtes du Forez, Coteaux Giennois, Côte Roannaise, Saint-Pourçain, Coteaux du Loir, Touraine, Touraine Villages, Touraine-Mesland, Coteaux du Vendômois, Cheverny, Valençay, Anjou, Anjou Gamay, Saumur Mousseux, Vins de Haut-Poitou, Coteaux d'Ancenis, Fiefs Vendéens.
Lorraine: Côtes de Toul, Vins de Moselle.
Rhône: Coteaux du Lyonnais, Châtillon-en-Diois, Côtes du Lubéron, Côtes du Vivarais.
Savoie: Vin de Savoie, Vin de Bugey.
Southwest: Côtes du Frontonnais, Gaillac, Côtes du Marmandais, Vins d'Entraygues et du Fel, Vins d'Estaing, Vins de Lavilledieu, Vins de Marcillac.

Grenache Noir
Provence: Bandol, Bellet, Cassis, Coteaux d'Aix en Provence, Coteaux des Baux en Provence, Côtes de Provence, Palette, Coteaux Varois.
Midi: Coteaux du Languedoc, Coteaux du Languedoc: Cabrières, Coteaux de Méjanelle, Coteaux de Vérargues, La Clape, Méjanelle, Montpeyroux, Pic-St-Loup, Quatourze, Coteaux de St-Christol, St-Drézery, St-Georges d'Orques, St-Saturnin, Costières du Gard, Faugères, St-Chinian, Minervois, Corbières, Fitou, Cabardès, Côtes de la Malapère, Collioure, Côtes du Roussillon, Côtes du Roussillon Villages, Frontignan VDN, Banyuls VDN, Maury VDN, Rivesaltes VDN.
Rhône: Côtes du Rhône, Côtes du Rhône Villages, Châteauneuf-du-Pape, Coteaux du Tricastin, Côtes du Ventoux, Gigondas, Lirac, Tavel, Coteaux du Pierrevert, Côtes du Lubéron, Rasteau VDN.

Grolleau (Groslot)
Loire: Anjou, Vins de Haut-Poitou, Coteaux du Loir, Rosé de Loire, Touraine, Touraine-Amboise, Saumur Mousseux, Touraine Azay le Rideau.

Jurançon Noir
Southwest: Cahors, Gaillac, Vins d'Entraygues et du Fel, Vins d'Estaing, Vins de Lavilledieu, Vins de Marcillac.

Ladoner Pelut
Midi: Côtes du Roussillon, Côtes du Roussillon Villages.

Malbec (Cot or Auxerrois)
Loire: Touraine, Touraine Villages, Touraine-Mesland, Anjou, Saumur

Mousseux, Coteaux du Loir.
Midi: Cabardès, Côtes de la Malapère.
Southwest: Bergerac, Cahors, Côtes de Bergerac, Côtes de Buzet, Côtes de Duras, Côtes du Frontonnais, Pecharmant, Côtes de Brulhois, Côtes du Marmandais.

Manseng Noir
Southwest: Béarn.

Merlot
Midi: Cabardès, Côtes de la Malapère.
Southwest: Bergerac, Cahors, Côtes de Bergerac, Côtes de Buzet, Côtes de Duras, Côtes du Frontonnais, Gaillac, Pecharmant, Côtes de Brulhois, Côtes du Marmandais, Côtes de Saint-Mont, Vins d'Entraygues et du Fel, Vins d'Estaing, Vins de Marcillac.

Mondeuse
Savoie: Vin de Savoie, Vin de Bugey.

Mourvèdre
Midi: Coteaux du Languedoc St-Saturnin, Costières du Gard, Coteaux du Languedoc, Corbières, Cabardès, Collioure, Côtes du Roussillon, Côtes du Roussillon Villages.
Provence: Bandol, Cassis, Coteaux d'Aix en Provence, Coteaux des Baux en Provence, Palette, Coteaux Varois.
Rhône: Côtes du Rhône, Côtes du Rhône Villages, Châteauneuf-du-Pape, Coteaux du Tricastin, Côtes du Ventoux, Gigondas, Lirac, Tavel, Côtes du Lubéron.

Muscardin
Rhône: Côtes du Rhône, Châteauneuf-du-Pape, Côtes du Ventoux.

Négrette
Southwest: Côtes du Frontonnais, Gaillac, Vins d'Entraygues et du Fel, Vins d'Estaing, Vins de Lavilledieu.

Pineau d'Aunis
Loire: Coteaux du Loir, Touraine, Coteaux du Vendômois, Anjou, Saumur, Saumur Mousseux, Fiefs Vendéens.

Pineau Menu (Arbois)
Loire: Touraine, Cheverny, Valençay.

Pinenc
Southwest: Béarn.

Pinot Meunier
Loire: Vins de l'Orleannais, Touraine.
Lorraine: Côtes de Toul.

Pinot Noir
Alsace: Alsace, Crémant d'Alsace.
Jura: Arbois, Arbois Pupillin, Côtes du Jura.
Loire: Ménétou-Salon, Reuilly, Sancerre, Coteaux du Giennois, Saint-Pourçain, Touraine, Coteaux du Vendômois, Saumur Mousseux, Vins de Haut-Poitou, Fiefs Vendéens.
Lorraine: Côtes de Toul, Vins de Moselle.
Rhône: Châtillon-en-Diois.
Savoie: Vin de Savoie, Vin de Bugey.
Southwest: Vins de l'Estaing, Vins d'Entraygues et du Fel.

Portugais Bleu
Southwest: Gaillac

Poulsard (Plousard)
Bugey: Vin de Bugey.
Jura: Arbois, Arbois Pupillin, Côtes du Jura, L'Etoile.

Syrah
Midi: Coteaux du Languedoc Montpeyroux and St-Saturnin, Costières du Gard, Corbières, Cabardès, Côtes de la Malapère, Collioure.
Provence: Bandol, Côtes de Provence, Coteaux Varois.
Rhône: Côtes du Rhône, Côtes du Rhône Villages, Cornas, Côte Rôtie,

Crozes-Hermitage, Hermitage, St-Joseph, Coteaux du Lyonnais, Châteauneuf-du-Pape, Chatillon-en-Diois, Coteaux du Tricastin, Côtes du Ventoux, Gigondas, Lirac, Tavel, Côtes du Lubéron.

Tannat
Southwest: Béarn, Cahors, Irouléguy, Madiran, Côtes du Brulhois, Côtes de Saint-Mont, Tursan.

Terret Noir
Midi: Coteaux du Languedoc La Clape, Coteaux de Languedoc, Costières du Gard, Corbières.
Rhône: Côtes du Rhône, Châteauneuf-du-Pape, Côtes de Ventoux.

Tibouren
Provence: Bandol, Côtes de Provence.

Trousseau
Jura: Arbois, Arbois Pupillin, Côtes du Jura.

Vaccarèse
Rhône: Côtes du Rhône, Châteauneuf-du-Pape, Côtes du Ventoux.

White

Aligoté
Savoie: Vin de Savoie, Vin de Bugey.

Altesse
Savoie: Roussette de Savoie, Vin de Savoie, Vin de Bugey, Vin de Bugey Mousseux.

Baroque
Southwest: Béarn, Irouléguy, Tursan.

Bourboulenc
Midi: Coteaux du Languedoc, Coteaux du Languedoc Coteaux de Méjanelle, Pic Saint Loup, Quatourze, Costières du Gard, Corbières.
Provence: Bandol, Bellet.
Rhône: Côtes du Rhône, Côtes du Rhône Villages, Châteauneuf-du-Pape, Coteaux du Tricastin, Côtes du Ventoux, Lirac, Tavel, Côtes du Lubéron, Côtes du Vivarais.

Chardonnay
Alsace: Crémant d'Alsace.
Jura: Côtes du Jura, Côtes du Jura Mousseux, L'Etoile.
Loire: Saint-Pourçain, Touraine, Coteaux du Vendômois, Cheverny, Valençay, Anjou, Saumur, Saumur Mousseux, Vins de Haut-Poitou, Fiefs Vendéens.
Midi: Blanquette de Limoux.
Provence: Bellet.
Rhône: Coteaux du Lyonnais. Châtillon-en-Diois, Côtes du Lubéron.
Savoie: Roussette de Savoie, Vin de Savoie, Vin de Bugey, Vin de Bugey Mousseux.

Chasselas
Alsace: Alsace.
Loire: Pouilly-sur-Loire.
Savoie: Crépy, Seyssel Mousseux, Vin de Savoie.

Chenin Blanc (Pineau de la Loire)
Loire: Jasnieres, Montlouis, Touraine, Touraine Villages, Touraine Azay-le-Rideau, Touraine-Mesland, Vouvray, Coteaux du Vendômois, Cheverny, Anjou, Anjou Coteaux de la Loire, Anjou Mousseux, Bonnezeaux, Coteaux de l'Aubance, Coteaux du Layon, Quarts-de-Chaume, Coteaux du Saumur, Coteaux du Layon Villages, Savennieres, Saumur, Saumur Mousseux, Vins de Haut-Poitou, Vins de Thouarsais, Coteaux du Loir, Coteaux d'Ancenis, Fiefs Vendéens.
Southwest: Bergerac Sec, Montravel, Saussignac, Vins d'Entraygues et du Fel, Vins d'Estaing.

Clairette
Provence: Bandol, Bellet, Cassis, Côtes de Provence, Palette, Coteaux Varois.

Midi: Clairette de Bellegarde, Coteaux du Languedoc, Coteaux du Languedoc: Coteaux du Méjanelle, La Clape, Pic Saint Loup, Quatourze, Costières du Gard, Clairette du Languedoc, Faugères, Picpoul de Pinet, Blanquette de Limoux, Corbières, Clairette de Languedoc VDN.
Rhône: Côtes du Rhône, Côtes du Rhône Villages, Châteauneuf-du-Pape, Clairette de Die, Clairette de Die Mousseux, Côtes du Ventoux, Côtes du Vivarais, Lirac, Tavel, Coteaux du Pierrevert, Côtes du Lubéron.

Courbu Blanc
Southwest: Béarn, Irouléguy, Jurançon, Jurançon Sec, Pacherenc du Vic-Bilh.

Len de l'El
Southwest: Gaillac, Gaillac Doux, Gaillac Mousseux, Gaillac Premières Côtes.

Grenache Blanc
Provence: Cassis, Coteaux d'Aix en Provence, Coteaux des Baux en Provence, Palette, Coteaux Varois.
Midi: Banyuls VDN.
Rhône: Côtes du Rhône, Côtes du Vivarais, Châteauneuf-du-Pape, Côtes du Ventoux, Côtes du Lubéron.

Grenache Gris
Midi: Banyuls VDN.

Gros Plant (Folle Blanche)
Loire: Gros Plant du Pays Nantais, Fiefs Vendéens.

Gewürztraminer
Alsace: Alsace, Alsace Grand Cru.

Jacquère
Savoie: Vin de Savoie, Vin de Bugey, Vin de Bugey Mousseux.

Jurançon Blanc
Southwest: Côtes de Saint-Mont.

Lauzat
Southwest: Béarn, Irouléguy.

Maccabeo
Midi: Banyuls VDN, Rivesaltes VDN.
Rhône: Lirac.

Malvoisie (Pineau Beurot)
Loire: Coteaux d'Ancenis.
Midi: Coteaux du Languedoc, Côtes du Roussillon, Banyuls VDN, Rivesaltes VDN.
Provence: Coteaux Varois.

Manseng, Gros
Southwest: Béarn, Irouléguy, Jurançon, Jurançon Sec, Pacherenc du Vic Bilh.

Manseng, Petit
Southwest: Béarn, Irouléguy, Jurançon, Jurançon Sec, Pacherenc du Vic Bilh.

Marsanne
Provence: Cassis.
Rhône: Côtes du Rhône, Crozes-Hermitage, Hermitage, Saint-Péray, Saint-Péray Mousseux, Coteaux du Tricastin, Côtes du Ventoux, Coteaux du Pierrevert, Côtes du Lubéron, Côtes du Vivarais.

Mauzac Blanc
Midi: Blanquette de Limoux.
Southwest: Côtes de Duras, Gaillac, Gaillac Premières Cotes, Gaillac Doux, Gaillac Mousseux, Vins d'Entraygues et du Fel, Vins d'Estaing, Vins de Lavilledieu.

Melon de Bourgogne (Muscadet)
Loire: Muscadet, Muscadet des Coteaux de la Loire, Muscadet de Sèvre et Maine.

Meslier
Southwest: Côtes de Saint-Mont.

Mondeuse Blanche
Savoie: Roussette de Savoie, Vin de Bugey, Vin de Bugey Mousseux.

Muscadelle
Southwest: Bergerac Sec, Côtes de Bergerac Moelleux, Côtes de Buzet, Côtes de Duras, Côtes de Montravel, Gaillac, Gaillac Premières Côtes, Gaillac Doux, Gaillac Mousseux, Haut Montravel, Monbazillac, Montravel, Rosette, Saussignac.

Muscat Blanc à Petits Grains
Alsace: Alsace, Alsace Grand Cru.
Midi: Muscat de Frontignan VDN, Muscat de Lunel VDN, Muscat de Mireval VDN, Muscat de St-Jean-de-Minervois VDN, Banyuls VDN, Muscat de Rivesaltes VDN.
Rhône: Clairette de Die Mousseux, Muscat de Beaumes de Venise VDN.

Muscat Ottonel
Alsace: Alsace, Alsace Grand Cru.

Ondenc
Southwest: Bergerac Sec, Côtes de Duras, Gaillac, Gaillac Premières Côtes, Gaillac Doux, Gaillac Mousseux, Montravel, Saussignac.

Picardan
Rhône: Châteauneuf-du-Pape.

Picpoul
Midi: Coteaux du Languedoc, Coteaux du Languedoc Coteaux de Méjanelle, Pic Saint Loup, Quatourze, Picpoul de Pinet, Corbières.
Rhône: Châteauneuf-du-Pape, Lirac, Tavel.
Southwest: Côtes de Saint-Mont, Vins de Lavilledieu.

Pineau d'Aunis
Loire: Coteaux du Loir, Touraine, Coteaux du Vendômois, Anjou, Saumur, Saumur Mousseux, Fiefs Vendéens.

Pineau Menu
Loire: Touraine, Cheverny, Valençay.

Pinot Auxerrois
Alsace: Alsace, Crémant d'Alsace.

Pinot Blanc/Klevner
Alsace: Alsace, Crémant d'Alsace.
Jura: Côtes du Jura, Côtes du Jura Mousseux.
Lorraine: Vins de Moselle.

Pinot Gris/Tokay Pinot Gris
Alsace: Alsace, Alsace Grand Cru.
Bugey: Vin de Bugey.
Loire: Reuilly, Touraine.
Lorraine: Vins de Moselle.

Riesling
Alsace: Alsace, Alsace Grand Cru.

Rolle
Provence: Bellet, Côtes de Provence.

Romorantin
Loire: Cheverny, Valençay.

Roussanne
Provence: Bellet.
Rhône: Côtes du Rhône, Côtes du Rhône Villages, Crozes-Hermitage, Hermitage, Saint-Péray, Saint-Péray Mousseux, Côtes du Vivarais, Côtes du Ventoux, Châteauneuf-du-Pape, Coteaux du Pierrevert.

Roussette
Savoie: Seyssel, Seyssel Mousseux, Vin de Savoie Ayse Mousseux, Vin de Savoie Mousseux.

Ruffiac
Southwest: Pacherenc du Vic-Bilh.

Sauvignon
Loire: Ménétou-Salon, Pouilly-Fumé, Quincy, Reuilly, Sancerre, Coteaux du Giennois, Touraine, Cheverny, Valençay, Anjou, Saumur, Saumur Mousseux, Vins de Haut-Poitou, Fiefs Vendéens.
Provence: Bandol, Cassis, Coteaux d'Aix en Provence, Coteaux des Baux en Provence.
Southwest: Béarn, Bergerac Sec, Côtes de Bergerac, Côtes de Bergerac Moelleux, Côtes de Buzet, Côtes de Duras, Côtes de Montravel, Gaillac, Gaillac Premières Côtes, Gaillac Mousseux, Haut Montravel, Irouléguy, Monbazillac, Montravel, Pacherenc du Vic-Bilh, Rosette, Saussignac, Côtes du Marmandais, Côtes de Saint-Mont.

Savagnin (Gringet)
Jura: Arbois, Arbois Mousseux, Arbois Pupillin, Château-Chalon, Côtes du Jura, L'Etoile.
Savoie: Vin de Savoie Ayse Mousseux, Vin de Savoie Mousseux.

Sémillon
Provence: Coteaux d'Aix en Provence, Coteaux des Baux en Provence, Côtes de Provence.
Southwest: Béarn, Bergerac Sec, Côtes de Bergerac Moelleux, Côtes de Buzet, Côtes de Duras, Côtes de Montravel, Gaillac, Gaillac Premières Côtes, Gaillac Doux, Gaillac Mousseux, Haut Montravel, Irouléguy, Monbazillac, Montravel, Pacherenc du Vic Bilh, Rosette, Saussignac, Côtes du Marmandais.

Sylvaner
Alsace: Alsace.
Lorraine: Vins de Moselle.

Terret Blanc
Midi: Picpoul de Pinet.

Tressalier
Loire: Saint-Pourçain.

Ugni Blanc
Provence: Bandol, Cassis, Coteaux d'Aix en Provence, Coteaux des Baux en Provence, Côtes de Provence, Palette, Coteaux Varois.
Rhône: Côtes du Rhône, Côtes du Lubéron, Côtes du Vivarais.
Southwest: Côtes de Duras, Montravel, Côtes du Marmandais.

Viognier
Rhône: Condrieu, Château Grillet, Côte Rôtie.

ALSACE
BAS-RHIN · HAUT-RHIN

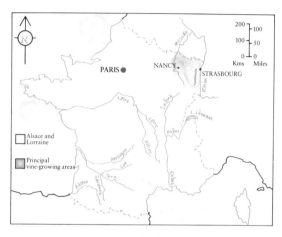

Alsace wines are often said to be Germanic wines made in a French way. But that, I feel, is to play up the German element of the equation and to play down the French. Because there is no doubt that – despite differences in history and philosophy – Alsace produces wines that could only be French.

Mind you, to listen to an Alsace grower talking on the telephone to a colleague in the next village, you could be forgiven for thinking you were on the east bank of the Rhine and not the west. Between themselves, Alsatians often speak a curious dialect which is much more German than French. As one grower put it "we think we're talking a dialect, but really we're talking German."

But that is hardly surprising. Alsace only became part of modern France in 1648 at the end of the Thirty Years' War. Before that, it had been part of the Holy Roman Empire or part of the Frankish kingdom of the Merovingians. Since then, its history has not been without troubles. Twice reoccupied by Germany (from 1870 to 1919 and from 1940 to 1945), it has been fought over as a prized border land for centuries. Now, it is French but European as well – the European Parliament meets in Strasbourg, the capital of Alsace.

Alsace is well to the north in terms of French vineyards and to the south in terms of German vineyards – level with south Baden and the Kaiserstuhl. But geography has been kinder to Alsace than history: the sheltering Vosges mountains run from north to south for virtually the whole length of Alsace parallel to the Rhine.

The vineyards lie in the eastern lee of the mountains, in a narrow strip that is never more than two miles wide. The Vosges protect the vines from rain – in Colmar in the central vineyards of Alsace the rainfall is the lowest in France apart from Perpignan in the deep south. The result is that for weeks on end in the summer, the skies of Alsace can be clear and blue, while a few miles away in the uplands of the Vosges it will be raining hard.

Alsace is picturesque wine country. The ribbon of vineyards is broken by small villages, full of tall, overhanging half-timbered houses, decorated in the summer with window boxes of flowers. Curious medieval signs indicate the cellars of wine producers who often invite visitors to taste their wines. Everyone seems to be connected in some way with wine.

The most northerly Alsace vineyards virtually touch the German border near the southern end of the Rheinpfalz. The vineyards of Rott and Cleebourg, dominated by their coopera-tive, have only recently been expanded and now have 120 hectares planted. Little of the wine, though, travels far beyond Strasbourg.

The main Alsace vineyard area begins 48 kilometres (30 miles) south, through the northern outcrops of the Vosges, where the village of Marlenheim marks the beginning of the Alsace wine road. From Marlenheim to Orschwiller, south of Sélestat, the vineyards are in the Bas-Rhin département (i.e. lower down the course of the River Rhine). While they have never achieved the fame of the vineyards further south, they give a definite character of their own to the wines: some would describe this northern Alsace wine as lighter, drier than the wine of the south. The rainfall here is certainly higher, because the Vosges are lower, and the grapes tend not to ripen so quickly or so completely. Much of the grapes for the sparkling Crémant d'Alsace (see below) tends to come from the Bas-Rhin vineyards. Famous wine villages in the Bas-Rhin include: Wangen, Barr, Goxwiller, Mittelbergheim, Itterswiller, Dambach-la-Ville, Kintzheim and Orschwiller.

At St-Hippolyte the Haut-Rhin département begins. The vineyards run the full length of this département, passing the famous villages of Riquewihr, Bergheim, Ribeauvillé, Kaysersberg, Eguisheim, Ammerschwihr, Huesseren-les-Châteaux, Rouffach, Guebwiller, Soultz and ending with the small vineyard concentration around Thann, just west of Mulhouse and the Swiss border. Here the Vosges are higher, the rainfall lower and the grapes ripen over a long growing period running into warm, dry autumns.

Négociants (merchants) dominate the Alsace wine trade, just as they did – until recently – in Burgundy. Many have been in the business for centuries. The reason is the same as it was in Burgundy – the vineyards are owned by many small growers with small holdings, who could not afford or did not wish to bottle and sell their own wine. Even now, there are 9,000 growers farming the 12,000 hectares of vineyard.

Cooperatives now take much of the produce as well – about 25%. Growers are beginning to bottle their own wine as they realise they can obtain high prices which cover their costs, so that now nearly 30% of the wine is bottled by growers, leaving 45% in the hands of the négociants, the balance going to cooperatives.

Inevitably with such northerly vineyards, it is white wines which dominate the viticulture. White and sparkling white wine make up 95% of production, and although Alsace growers like to produce their red wines at a tasting, when it comes to the meal it is bottles of Bordeaux which will be drunk.

Although vines have grown in Alsace probably since the Romans and certainly since the Merovingians in the eighth and ninth centuries, the development of the Alsace vineyard as we know it today is relatively new – dating from after the First World War. The appellation contrôlée system only reached Alsace in 1962.

When they were introduced, the new AC laws recognized a system of labelling which was unique in France – and certainly not one inherited from Germany. Until very recently (see below under Grand Crus), the whole Alsace vineyard – from the north by the border with Germany down to the Swiss border near Basle – was covered by only one appellation. Everything was AC Alsace.

On the labels, a system operates which will be familiar to Californian and Australian wine drinkers but which is still rare in the rest of France: the wines are labelled by variety with the name of the grape. The grape named had to make up 100% of the contents of the bottle. This applies to the bulk of wines exported from Alsace; back at home, Alsatians drink blended wines quite happily – sometimes calling them Edelzwicker, sometimes using a brand name.

Another revolution was adopted at the same time – revolutionary when compared with the rest of France. The AC rules stipulate that all Alsace AC wines have to be bottled in Alsace – not even elsewhere in France, let alone abroad. That has done more to give Alsace a reputation for reliability than anything else. As one consequence of this regulation, it is almost unknown to find a bad bottle of Alsace wine – bad, that is, in the sense of faulty.

Alsace grape varieties

The permitted grape varieties, with characteristics of the wine they produce, are as follows:

Chasselas: This used to be a widely planted vine, but is now down to about 3.5% of the vineyard. It is also grown in Savoie and Switzerland. In Alsace it only appears as part of an Edelzwicker blend. When tasted by itself, it has a smoky, herby taste with soft, low acid fruit.

Gewürztraminer: The grape that has brought more fame to Alsace than any other. It has a distinctive spicy, full, oily taste, high alcohol with sometimes a bitter finish and dryness even in the sweetest examples. It is the grape most frequently used in the late-picked Vendange Tardive and Sélection des Grains Nobles (see page 19) wines. Not a wine to drink in vast quantities, it is excellent with some of the rich Alsace cooking such as choucroute (pickled cabbage) and spicy sausages.

Pinot Blanc: This produces some of the most readily drinkable wines in Alsace. It is no surprise that it has been such a success in London wine bars: it is very quaffable on its own as it is relatively low in alcohol, very fresh, soft with a pleasing touch of acidity and not too pronounced a character. There are two forms of the Pinot Blanc in Alsace – the Pinot Blanc itself and the Pinot Auxerrois. The latter is generally regarded as producing the better-quality wine, but the two are normally blended and sold under the name Pinot Blanc – or further blended with other grapes and sold as Edelzwicker or a branded wine.

Muscat: The grape that in the south of France produces the sweet sparkling Clairette de Die and the Vins Doux Naturel like Muscat de Beaumes de Venise, in Alsace produces a wine that is a perfect combination between sweetness and lightness, dry yet with a honeyed tone, absolutely delicious as an apéritif wine. The trouble is that there is very little of it in Alsace: it is a difficult vine to grow so far north, so growers are reluctant to devote much of their vineyard space to a vine which only yields well in good years. As with the Pinot Blanc, there are two types of Muscat: the Muscat Blanc à Petits Grains (or Muscat d'Alsace) and the Muscat Ottonel. While the latter causes fewer growing problems, the former produces the finer wine.

Riesling: By general acclamation, the Riesling makes the finest wine in Alsace. The way it is treated here sums up the contrast and difference with Germany. In Alsace, the Riesling produces a wine that has medium alcohol, is bone dry with a flinty, steely taste, very fresh and often acidic when young, softening with maturity to give a superb wine with a petrolly taste when old. In very fine vintages, it is allowed to make sweeter wines which still retain a dryness and firmness no German wine is ever intended to achieve.

Sylvaner: Widely planted vine variety that produces a neutral, reliable wine that is attractive for quaffing, and is often used as a component of Edelzwicker blends. 20% of the Alsace vineyard is planted with this variety. It is especially popular in the northern Bas-Rhin vineyards where its early ripening and low acidity cope well with the cooler, wetter weather.

Tokay d'Alsace or Pinot Gris: A vine variety which has no links with the Tokay wine of Hungary (which is made with a different grape variety, the Furmint) but which has links with eastern Austria and western Hungary, as well as parts of northern Italy. The name Tokay, while formally banned by the EEC because of the confusion with the Hungarian wine, is still widely used – and in fact most producers now refer to the wine as Tokay Pinot Gris. It produces a full wine, one which many Alsatians call their favourite style, rich, soft, well balanced with much acidity, a touch of pepper, quite high in alcohol and with the ability to age over a long period. It is often drunk with *foie gras* which it certainly complements perfectly. If I am given the choice of Alsace wines, I am generally torn between a good Tokay and a good Riesling.

ACs

Virtually all the wine made in Alsace has AC status. Alsace produces 20% of all white AC wine in France – around 143 million bottles a year.

Alsace: This is the general AC to cover all the vineyards of Alsace. Any of the permitted grape varieties (see above) grown in any village in any AC vineyard can qualify for the appellation.

Alsace Grand Cru: A new AC, first introduced with the 1985 vintage. It covers certain specified vineyards for certain grape varieties. In other words, if Grand Cru vineyard X is designated as Grand Cru for Riesling, any Gewürztraminer in that vineyard will be simple AC Alsace. Grand Cru wines can be either 100% from one vineyard (which will be named on the label) or from a number of Grand Cru vineyards (when it will simply be called Alsace Grand Cru). All Alsace Grand Cru wines must be 100% from one grape variety, and only the four top grape Alsace varieties – Riesling, Gewürztraminer, Tokay and Muscat – can produce Grand Cru wines.

Like so many changes in AC laws anywhere in France, local

politics has played an important role in the Grand Cru designations. The négociant houses are not in favour of Grand Cru at all because it implies that single vineyard wines are better than wines blended from a number of top vineyards. The growers are all for Grand Cru (if they have Grand Cru land themselves) because it will increase the price they can charge. There was also much argument about the size of each designated Grand Cru. In the end it took 10 years for the first Grand Cru vineyards to be organized, and will probably take the same again for the second tranche of Grand Crus (see the second list).

The current (March 1987) list of Grand Cru vineyards (with their commune and the département), which takes in 10% of Alsace production, is as follows:

Altenberg de Bergbieten (Bergbieten, Bas-Rhin)
Altenberg de Bergheim (Bergheim, Haut-Rhin)
Brand (Turckheim, Haut-Rhin)
Eichberg (Eguisheim, Haut-Rhin)
Geisberg (Ribeauvillé, Haut-Rhin)
Gloeckelberg (Rodern and St-Hippolyte, Haut-Rhin)
Goldert (Gueberschwihr, Haut-Rhin)
Hatschbourg (Hattstatt and Voegtlinshoffen, Haut-Rhin)
Hengst (Wintzenheim, Haut-Rhin)
Kanzlerberg (Bergheim, Haut-Rhin)
Kastelberg (Andlau, Bas-Rhin)
Kessler (Guebwiller, Haut-Rhin)
Kirchberg de Barr (Barr, Bas-Rhin)
Kirchberg de Ribeauvillé (Ribeauvillé, Haut-Rhin)
Kitterlé (Guebwiller, Haut-Rhin)
Moenchberg (Andlau and Eichhoffen, Bas-Rhin)
Ollwiller (Wuenheim, Bas-Rhin)
Rangen (Thann and Vieux-Thann, Haut-Rhin)
Rosacker (Hunawihr, Haut-Rhin)
Saering (Guebwiller, Haut-Rhin)
Schlossberg (Kaysersberg and Kientzheim, Haut-Rhin)
Sommerberg (Niedermorschwihr and Katzenthal, Haut-Rhin)
Sonnenglanz (Beblenheim, Haut-Rhin)
Spiegel (Bergholtz and Guebwiller, Haut-Rhin)
Wiebelsberg (Andlau, Bas-Rhin)

There are currently another 22 vineyards which have been nominated by their villages for Grand Cru status. Producers are allowed to add the name Grand Cru to these vineyards even though the final decision has not been made. With these vineyards, production of Alsace Grand Cru will be 15% of total Alsace production.

Altenberg de Wolxheim (Wolxheim, Bas-Rhin)
Engelberg (Dahlenheim, Bas-Rhin)
Frankstein (Dambach-la-Ville, Bas-Rhin)
Froehn (Zellenberg, Haut-Rhin)
Mambourg (Sigolsheim, Haut-Rhin)
Mandelberg (Mittelwihr, Haut-Rhin)
Markrain (Bennwihr, Haut-Rhin)
Muenchberg (Nothalten, Bas-Rhin)
Osterberg (Ribeauvillé, Haut-Rhin)
Pfersigberg (Eguisheim, Haut-Rhin)
Pfingstberg (Orschwiller, Haut-Rhin)
Praelatenberg (Orschwiller, Bas-Rhin)
Schoenenbourg (Riquewihr, Haut-Rhin)

Sporen (Riquewihr, Haut-Rhin)
Steinert (Pfaffenheim, Haut-Rhin)
Steingruber (Wettolsheim, Haut-Rhin)
Steinklote (Marlenheim, Bas-Rhin)
Vorbourg (Rouffach and Westhalten, Haut-Rhin)
Wineck-Schlossberg (Katzenthal, Haut-Rhin)
Winzenberg (Blienschwiller, Bas-Rhin)
Zinnkoepfle (Westhalten and Soultzmatt, Haut-Rhin)
Zotzenberg (Mittelbergheim, Bas-Rhin)

Crémant d'Alsace: A *méthode champenoise* sparkling wine that can be made from grapes grown anywhere in the Alsace AC area. The appellation is fairly new and came in with the 1976 harvest. Permitted grape varieties for Crémant d'Alsace are: Pinot Blanc, Pinot Auxerrois, Pinot Noir, Pinot Gris, Riesling and Chardonnay. Most crémant is made from Pinot Blanc and Pinot Auxerrois.

Vendange Tardive and Sélection de Grains Nobles: Sweeter wines made either from bunches or selected berries which have particularly high sugar levels and levels of potential alcohol. To that extent they correspond to the German categories of Beerenauslese and Trockenbeerenauslese. The taste of noble rot (*pourriture noble*) is often found in these wines, which do not have to consist totally of grapes which have noble rot. While the terms have been around for some time, it was only in 1984 (referring to the 1983 vintage) that their use was regulated.

VDQS: Lorraine

Cotes de Toul: Red, rosé, gris and dry white wines from a small vineyard area around the city of Toul in the Meurthe-et-Moselle département. Most of the wine is Vin Gris, a pale rosé from Gamay. Pinot Noir and Pinot Meunier are also planted.

Vins de Moselle: Red and dry white wines from the département of Moselle. Red comes from Pinot Noir, Pinot Gris and Gamay. White from Pinot Blanc and Sylvaner.

Alsace: Bas-Rhin

Jean Pierre Bechtold et Fils

49 Rue Principale, 67310 Dahlenheim. Vineyards owned:
Grand Cru Engelberg 2ha; Alsace AC 12ha.
Produce: 70,000 bottles. VP-R.

Sylvaner, Pinot Blanc, Muscat, Riesling, Tokay Pinot Gris, Gewürztraminer and Pinot Noir are made by this traditional grower, who vinifies in wood. They have land in one of the new grand crus, Engelberg, planted with Riesling, Gewürztraminer and Tokay Pinot Gris. The firm also makes an Edelzwicker, a blend of Sylvaner, Pinot Auxerrois and Muscat. *Open: By appointment only.*

Vignobles Raymond Engel et Fils

1 Route du Vin, 67600 Orschwiller. Vineyards owned:
Grand Cru Praeletenberg 6ha; Alsace AC 9ha.
Produce: 150,000 bottles. VP-R.

The Grand Cru Praeletenberg vineyard supplies all four varietals – Gewürztraminer, Riesling, Tokay and Muscat, using the name Domaine des Prélats, while M. Engel's other vineyards also produce the complete range of wines. He makes a small amount of Crémant d'Alsace, and a Rouge d'Alsace.

The wines are normally aged briefly in wood before bottling.
The vineyards are in a fine situation at the foot of the Haut
Koenigsbourg castle. *Open: Mon–Fri 8am–noon; 3–7pm.*

Louis Gisselbrecht

67650 Dambach-la-Ville. Vineyards owned: Alsace AC 12ha.
Produce: 900,000 bottles. VP-R and N.

This firm produces a full range of wines in a modern style,
vinified in stainless steel. They are always attractively fresh and
drinkable, but without great depths. They are proudest of their
Riesling produced from their own vineyards in Dambach-la-
Ville. *Open: Appointment preferred.*

Willy Gisselbrecht et Fils

3a Route du Vin, 67650 Dambach-la-Ville. Vineyards
owned: Alsace AC 15ha.
Produce: 1.8 million bottles. VP-R and N.

A large négociant business, producing a range of good-quality
wines. They use a mixture of wood, glass-lined tanks and
stainless steel and follow traditional vinification methods.
Their philosophy is to bottle the wines quickly to cut the use of
sulphur down to a minimum. The range covers all the varietal
styles, plus Edelzwicker and Crémant d'Alsace. They also make
a small amount of Grand Cru Frankstein. Brand names used are
Willy Gisselbrecht and Antoine Heinrich. *Open: Mon–Fri
9am–noon; 2–6pm.*

Domaine André and Rémy Gresser

2 Rue de l'Ecole, 67140 Andlau. Vineyards owned: Grand
Cru Wiebelsberg 1ha; Grand Cru Moenchberg 0.4ha; Grand
Cru Kastelberg 0.2ha; Alsace AC 8.5ha.
Produce: 60,000 bottles. VP-R.

This small family vineyard was established in 1667, but they
have moved with the times. They now use stainless steel for
vinification, but still age in wood. The largest production is of
Sylvaner and Riesling, and their Grand Cru wines are all
Riesling. Some of the Wiebelsberg wine is from 65-year-old
vines. *Open: Mon–Fri 11am–7pm.*

Bernard Haegi

33 Rue de la Montagne, 67140 Mittelbergheim. Vineyards
owned: Grand Cru Zotzenberg 0.5ha; Alsace AC 5.5ha.
Produce: 40,000 bottles. VP-R.

The leading wine at this small firm is of Riesling, both Alsace
AC and Grand Cru Zotzenberg. The vinification is mainly in
wood, with some of the Pinot Noir being treated in stainless
steel to give extra colour. They also make a Crémant d'Alsace
from Pinot Noir and Pinot Blanc. *Open: By appointment only.*

Hering et Fils

67140 Barr. Vineyards owned: Kirchberg Grand Cru and
Alsace AC 8ha. *Produce: 90,000 bottles.* VP-R.

Apart from a holding in the Kirchberg Grand Cru, Pierre
Hering has vineyards in two other vineyards: Clos de la
Folie Marco (for Sylvaner) and Gaensbroennel (for
Gewürztraminer). His best wine is the Riesling from the
Kirchberg vineyard, but he makes a full range of wines (apart
from Tokay Pinot Gris). *Open: By appointment only.*

Pierre Kirschner

26 Rue Théophile Bader, 67650 Dambach-la-Ville.
Vineyards owned: Alsace AC 8ha.
Produce: 55,000 bottles. VP-R.

Riesling, Sylvaner and Gewürztraminer are the main varietals produced by this house, which was established in the last century. They regard the Riesling as their best wine, mainly from vineyards in Itterswiller and Scherwiller. *Open: By appointment only.*

Michel Laugel

102 Rue Général de Gaulle, 67520 Marlenheim. Vineyards owned: Alsace AC 6ha.
Produce: 6 million bottles. VP-R and N.

A large négociant firm which dominates the northern end of the Alsace vineyards. They have a small area of vines in Marlenheim, mainly planted with Pinot Noir, for which the village is famous. They produce a wide range, of which the most interesting is the selection of village wines. These are varietals made from vineyards in villages which are particularly famous for that grape variety: Riesling de Wolxheim, Gewürztraminer de Wangen, Pinot Noir de Marlenheim (a rosé) and Pinot Rouge de Marlenheim. They also produce Crémant d'Alsace. *Open: By appointment only.*

Frédéric Mochel

56 Rue Principale, 67310 Traenheim. Vineyards owned: Grand Cru Altenberg de Bergbieten 4ha; Alsace AC 4ha.
Produce: 80,000 bottles. VP-R.

M. Mochel produces Sylvaner, Pinot Blanc (locally called Klevner), Riesling, Muscat, Tokay Pinot Gris, Gewürztraminer and Pinot Noir from his vineyard in and around Traenheim. His methods are traditional. His Riesling Grand Cru Altenberg is his finest wine, and some of it forms a Cuvée Henriette, made from 30-year-old vines. *Open: 8am–noon; 2–4pm.*

Michel Nartz

40 Rue de la Paix, 67650 Dambach-la-Ville. Vineyards owned: Alsace AC 6ha. *Produce: 40,000 bottles.* VP-R.

This firm has been family-run for several generations. Wood vinification is used for most of the wines and M. Nartz's largest production is of Riesling – with which he certainly makes his best wine. He also makes a full range of varietals. *Open: By appointment only.*

Cave Vinicole d'Obernai Divinal

30 Rue du Général Leclerc, 67210 Obernai. Vineyards owned: Alsace AC 800ha. *Produce: 6 million bottles.* Coop.

A modern cooperative, founded in 1962, using stainless steel and producing a full range of Alsace wines. Brand names include Divinal and Fritz Kobus. They also make a Crémant d'Alsace. *Open: By appointment only.*

Caves Vinicole d'Orschwiller

67600 Orschwiller. Vineyards owned: Alsace AC 110ha.
Produce: 1.2 million bottles. Coop (141 members).

This cooperative produces the full range of varietal wines from vineyards around Sélestat and Ribeauvillé. They have two ranges – Moënchenbornes and Les Faîtières which is their top range. Quality is good generally, and the wines are fresh, fruity and light in style. *Open: Appointment preferred.*

Domaine Ostertag

87 Rue Finkwiller, 67680 Epfig. Vineyards owned: Grand Cru Muenchberg 1.2ha; Alsace AC 3ha.
Produce: 70,000 bottles. VP-R.

A small firm producing high quality wine, spoilt only by the head of a Pascal lamb on their label (Ostertag means Easter Day). They make the full range of varietals, but their finest wine is the Riesling Muenchberg which is well balanced, green, steely and full. A small amount of Gewürztraminer is made in good years, and they offer a Crémant d'Alsace. *Open: Appointment preferred.*

Alsace Seltz

21 Rue Principale, 67140 Mittelbergheim. Vineyards owned: Grand Cru Zotzenberg 3ha; Alsace AC 6ha.
Produce: 130,000 bottles. VP-R and N.

While the majority of production of this firm is from their own vineyards, they buy in some Sylvaner from the Zotzenberg vineyard (which cannot make Grand Cru wine), and produce one of the best Alsace Sylvaners I have tasted. They have a small amount of Riesling in the Brandluft vineyard, but their Grand Cru wine is all Gewürztraminer. Brand names are Alsace Seltz and Pierre Seltz. *Open: By appointment only.*

Louis Siffert Fils

16 Route du Vin, 67600 Orschwiller. Vineyards owned: Grand Cru Praeletenberg 2ha; Alsace AC 9ha.
Produce: 100,000 bottles. VP-R

An old-established (1792) family vineyard holding, specializing in Gewürztraminer and Riesling wines. They make half the wine in wood, half in stainless steel and blend the two. They make Gewürztraminer Vendange Tardive in good years. *Open: Mon–Sat 8am–noon; 2–7pm.*

Alsace Willm

BP 13, 32 Rue du Docteur Sultzer, 67140 Barr. Vineyards owned: Grand Cru Kirchberg 3ha; Alsace AC 17ha.
Produce: 500,000 bottles. VP-R and N.

The top wines from this medium-sized négociant firm are vinified in wood, while the standard range goes through stainless steel and early bottling. Apart from the usual Alsace range, labelled Alsace Willm, they make a Riesling Kirchberg and a Gewürztraminer from the Clos Gaensbroennel. The réserve wines are called Cuvée Emile Willm. They also make a range of Crémant d'Alsace including Crémant Prestige from réserve wines. The Cooperative of Eguisheim has bought an interest in the firm. *Open: Mon–Fri 8:30am–noon; 1:30–6pm.*

A. Zimmermann Fils

3 Grand Rue, 67600 Orschwiller. Vineyards owned: Alsace AC 12ha. *Produce: 100,000 bottles.* VP-R.

The vineyard, on the slopes of the Haut-Koenigsbourg château, has been in the Zimmermann family since 1693. They make all the varietal wines, with particular emphasis on Riesling, Gewürztraminer and Tokay Pinot Gris. Methods are traditional and wood is used. *Open: By appointment only.*

Alsace: Haut-Rhin

Caves Jean-Baptiste Adam

5 Rue de l'Aigle, 68770 Ammerschwihr. Vineyards owned: Grand Cru 4ha; Alsace AC 5.4ha.
Produce: 1 million bottles. VP-R and N.

The large merchant house of Adam has been in existence since 1614, and is now by far the largest producer in Ammerschwihr. Their small vineyard holding includes some land in the Kaefferkopf vineyard (the most famous in the village), from which they make Riesling and Gewürztraminer, Cuvée Jean Baptiste, which is a speciality of the house. Their Grand Cru holding is in the Sommerberg vineyard. They mix modern and traditional techniques to produce a standard range of quite acceptable quality. *Open: Appointment preferred.*

Cave Vinicole du Vieil Armand

1 Route de Cernay, 68360 Soultz. Vineyards owned: Grand Cru and Alsace AC 160ha.
Produce: 1 million bottles. Coop (150 members).

The usual range of Alsace wines includes some Grand Cru from the Ollwiller vineyard. Brand names include Château Ollwiller and Cuvée du Vieil Armand. The wine is bottled by the Cooperative of Eguisheim. *Open: 8am–noon; 2–6pm.*

Jean Jacques Baumann et Fils

43 Rue du Général de Gaulle, 68340 Riquewihr. Vineyards owned: Grand Cru 1.2ha; Alsace AC 7.8ha.
Produce: 80,000 bottles. VP-R.

A small-scale producer who nevertheless manages to make a large range of wines. These include Grand Cru wines from the two main Riquewihr vineyards: Schoenenbourg and Sporen. Methods combine traditional and modern. *Open: Appointment preferred.*

Cooperative Vinicole de Beblenheim et Environs

14 Rue de Hoen, 68980 Beblenheim. Vineyards owned: Grand Cru and Alsace AC 275ha.
Produce: 4 million bottles. Coop (200 members).

Newly-installed modern equipment at this large cooperative produces the usual range of varietal wines, including some Grand Crus from the Sonnenglanz vineyard. The standard is average, and their wines are drunk with pleasure but without too much seriousness. *Open: Mon–Sun 10am–noon; 2–6pm.*

J. Becker

4 Route d'Ostheim, Zellenberg, 68340 Riquewihr. Vineyards owned: Grand Cru 3.5ha; Alsace AC 8.6ha.
Produce: 400,000 bottles. VP-R and N.

One third of the production at this firm is from its own vineyards, two thirds is from grapes and wine brought in. They tend to a dry style of wine and are keen to produce wines which age well – 15-year-old Rieslings from this firm are often more appealing than 2-year-old wines. The intention is to vinify grapes from their own vineyards separately, and they make quite a range of single vineyard wines as well as the generic varietals. Their brand names are J. Becker and Gaston Beck. *Open: (Summer) Mon–Sun 8am–noon; 2–6pm. (Winter) Mon–Fri and Sat morning.*

Les Caves de Bennwihr

Rue de Général de Gaulle. 68630 Bennwihr. Vineyards owned: Alsace AC 350ha.
Produce: 3 million bottles. Coop (260 members).

The cooperative took over the re-planting of Bennwihr's vineyards which were devastated in the Second World War and now nearly every grower in the village is a member. They have modern equipment which allows them to make clean, simple wines which can be very pleasant to drink. Brand names they use include Les Caves Klug, Victor Preiss and Cuvée Hansi (for the Crémant d'Alsace). *Open: Mon–Fri 9–11am; 2–5pm.*

Léon Beyer

BP 1, 68420 Eguisheim. Vineyards owned: Alsace AC 20ha.
Produce: 700,000 bottles. VP-R and N.

A most respected firm, whose origins date back to 1580, making it one of the oldest in Alsace. Their wines cover the usual range of Alsace varietals, but they are particularly proud of their Riesling Cuvée des Écaillers and Cuvée Particulière, as well as their Gewürztraminer for which Eguisheim is noted. They also have a soft spot for their Rosé Pinot Noir – but I am less convinced about that. *Open: No.*

Paul Buecher et Fils (Domaine Ste Gertrude)

15 Rue Sainte Gertrude, Wettolsheim, 68000 Colmar.
Vineyards owned: Grand Cru and Alsace AC 20ha.
Produce: 200,000 bottles. VP-R.

This firm owns vineyards in eight communes which gives them, they believe, the possibility of producing blends which are very typical of Alsace. Their Grand Cru wine comes from the Hengst vineyard in Witzenheim. Their best wines are vinified in wood, while the standard range goes through stainless steel. *Open: Mon–Sun 8am–noon; 2–6pm.*

Dopff "Au Moulin"

68340 Riquewihr. Vineyards owned: Grand Cru 12.3ha;
Alsace AC 50ha. *Produce: 2.5 million bottles.* VP-R and N.

75% of the firm's grape requirements are bought in from 600 different growers. Production is on a large scale, covering the complete varietal range plus some Grand Cru wines from the Brand in Turckheim and the Sporen and Schoenenbourg in Riquewihr. Standards are maintained, though, and most Alsace wine drinkers will have enjoyed bottles from this firm. The "Au Moulin" was added to their name to avoid confusion with Dopff et Irion (see next entry). The families in the two firms are related but there are no business connections. *Open: Mon–Sat 8am–noon; 2–6pm.*

Dopff et Irion (Château de Riquewihr)

68340 Riquewihr. Vineyards owned: Grand Cru and Alsace
AC 27ha. *Produce: 2.8 million bottles.* VP-R and N.

The largest producer in Riquewihr, whose old premises occupy one side of the courtyard behind the Hotel de Ville. They have recently constructed immense warehouse and bottling facilities on the edge of the village. Most of their production is done in stainless steel, after pressing with modern pneumatic presses rather than the Vaslin press seen mostly in Alsace. Their wines are highly enjoyable considering the scale of the operations, and I particularly like the wines from their own estates – Riesling Les Murailles, Gewürztraminer Les Sorcières, Muscat Les Amandiers and Tokay Pinot Gris Les Maquisards. Their style is light and fresh, but they also make some Vendange Tardives and Sélection des Grains Nobles wines. Dopff et Irion were pioneers of the concept of Crémant d'Alsace. *Open: Mon–Sun 8am–6pm. By appointment in winter.*

Cave Vinicole d'Eguisheim

6 Grand Rue, 68420 Eguisheim. Vineyard owned: Grand
Cru and Alsace AC 967ha.
Produce: 9 million bottles. Coop (750 members).

The largest cooperative in Alsace, drawing its grapes from nine communes surrounding Eguisheim. In addition, it bottles wine for the cooperatives at Dambach-la-Ville and Cave Vinicole du Vieil Armand. Under the brand name Wolfberger, they make a full range of wines, from standard quality to special *cuvées*. Their Grand Cru wines come from Hengst, Eichberg, Steingrubler, Hatschbourg, Ollwiller, Spiegel and Pfirsberg vineyards. *Open: Appointment preferred.*

Jérôme Geschikt et Fils

1 Place de la Sinne, 68770 Ammerschwihr. Vineyards
owned: Alsace AC 8ha. *Produce: 70,000 bottles.* VP-R.

A small firm whose production includes Riesling and Gewürztraminer from the Kaefferkopf vineyard and a Crémant d'Alsace. Vendange Tardive wines from Gewürztraminer are also made. *Open: Mon–Fri 8am–noon; 2–6pm.*

Paul Ginglinger

8 Place Charles de Gaulle, 68420 Eguisheim. Vineyards
owned: Grand Cru and Alsace AC 9ha.
Produce: 80,000 bottles. VP-R.

Dryness and lightness are the characteristics of the wines from this small firm, which dates back to 1636. They use wood for much of the vinification and for maturing. Their largest production is of Riesling, but they also make the usual range of varietal wines. Also produced are a Crémant d'Alsace and Vendange Tardive wines. Grand Cru wines come from the Eichberg and Pfersigberg vineyards in Eguisheim. *Open: Mon–Sat morning and afternoon.*

Hugel et Fils

3 Rue de la Première Armée, 68340 Riquewihr. Vineyards
owned: Grand Cru 13.3ha; Alsace AC 2ha.
Produce: 1.3 million bottles. VP-R and N.

Certainly the most famous name in Alsace wine, the Hugel firm, founded in 1639, manages to live up to its reputation. Their style is for full, rich wines, but their standard range of varietals is always appealingly fresh and clean and of high quality. Their finest wines are matured in wood, but they also use stainless steel, and they use as few chemicals as possible in their winemaking. Hugel pioneered the idea of late-harvest wines – the Vendange Tardive and Sélection des Grains Nobles – and their examples are always superb and never too cloyingly sweet. Recently they have been producing quite the best red Pinot Noir wine in Alsace. Their range consists of three levels – standard varietals, Cuvée Tradition and Réserve Personelle – topped up by the late-harvest wines. *Open: Mon–Thur 9am–noon; 2–5pm. Fri 9am–noon. Shop open Mon–Sun.*

Cave Coopérative d'Ingersheim

1 Rue Georges Clémenceau, Ingersheim, 68000 Colmar. Vineyards owned: Grand Cru and Alsace AC 260ha. *Produce: 3 million bottles.* Coop (210 members).

A long-established cooperative which dates from 1925. Today, it makes the full range of varietals in a simple, attractive, very drinkable style. They also make a few more serious wines, including Gewürztraminer from the Letzenberg and Florimont vineyards, Riesling from the Steinweg vineyard and Riesling Grand Cru Sommerberg. *Open: Mon–Fri by appointment only; Sat–Sun no appointment necessary.*

Roger Jung

23 Rue de la Première Armée, 68340 Riquewihr. Vineyards owned: Grand Cru 1.2ha; Alsace AC 5ha. *Produce: 60,000 bottles.* VP-R.

Small family firm with vineyard holdings in the Schoenenbourg and Sporen vineyards, making a wide range of wines, using modern techniques. *Open: Appointment preferred.*

Cave Vinicole de Kientzheim-Kaysersberg

Kientzheim, 68240 Kaysersberg. Vineyards owned: Grand Cru and Alsace AC 140ha. *Produce: 2 million bottles.* Coop (150 members).

A 30-year-old cooperative making all the Alsace varietal wines, including some from the Grand Cru vineyards of Schlossberg, Kaefferkopf and Altenberg de Bergheim. They also produce a Crémant d'Alsace. *Open: Groups only, by appointment.*

Kuehn

3 Grande Rue, 68770 Ammerschwihr. Vineyards owned: Alsace AC 8.1ha. *Produce: 500,000 bottles.* VP-R and N.

A famous house, dating back to 1675, which makes good-quality wines from its own vineyards in Ammerschwihr (including some in the Kaefferkopf vineyard) and from grapes brought in from local growers. They use wood for most of their vinification, to make quite full, rich wines in a fine, old-fashioned style. Brand names include Charme d'Alsace (for an Edelzwicker), a Crémant d'Alsace called Baron de Schiele and a Gewürztraminer called Cuvée St-Hubert. A good way to try Kuehn wines is to visit the 3-star Michelin restaurant Aux Armes de France which occupies the same building as Kuehn. *Open: Appointment preferred.*

Kuentz-Bas

14 Route du Vin, Huesseren-les-Châteaux, 68420 Herrlisheim. Vineyards owned: Alsace AC 12ha. *Produce: 300,000 bottles.* VP-R and N.

A medium-sized firm producing excellent wines at all quality levels. They produce two ranges – Cuvée Tradition which is made from bought-in grapes, and Réserve Personelle from their own vineyards. Vendange Tardive wines are called Cuvée Caroline. In the past 10 years, they have increased the number of wines so as to make smaller quantities of each *cuvée*. I have particularly enjoyed their Muscat (blended from Muscat d'Alsace and Muscat Ottonel) and their Tokay Pinot Gris Réserve Personnelle, but all their wines are of high quality and elegantly restrained. *Open: Mon–Fri 8am–noon; 2–6pm.*

Gustave Lorentz

35 Grand Rue, 68750 Bergheim. Vineyards owned: Grand Cru 46ha; Alsace AC 105ha.
Produce: 3 million bottles. VP-R and N.

A large-scale firm which nevertheless manages to retain high quality in a wide range of wines, which includes Vendange Tardive and Sélection de Grains Nobles. They use some modern equipment in the cellars, with some temperature control of fermentation, and only use the natural yeast from the grapes because it "gives a natural quality to the wine". They have vineyards mainly in Bergheim, but also buy from growers in Ribeauvillé and Bergheim. Better wines are matured in wood, lesser ones in glass-lined tanks. Grand Cru wines come from the Altenberg de Bergheim and Kanzlerberg vineyards. *Open: Mon–Fri 8am–noon; 2–5pm.*

Jean Paul Mauler

3 Place des Cigognes, 68630 Mittelwihr. Vineyards owned: Alsace AC 4ha. *Produce: 25,000 bottles.* VP-R.

This long-established producer uses a mixture of wood for the top varietal wines and enamel-lined tanks for other wines in his small cellar in the centre of Mittelwihr. He makes a full range of varietal wines, of which I have most enjoyed the Riesling. *Open: Appointment preferred.*

Jos Meyer et Fils

76 Rue Clémenceau, Witzenheim, 68000 Colmar. Vineyards owned: Grand Cru and Alsace AC 14ha.
Produce: 400,000 bottles. VP-R and N.

Vineyards in Turckheim and Witzenheim (including some land in the Grand Cru Hengst) form the core of this grower-négociant business. While one of their specialities is Pinot Blanc, I have always been impressed by their Rieslings, especially Les Pierrets and by the Gewürztraminer Les Archenets. The Hengst vineyard produces fine Riesling and Gewürztraminer including some Vendange Tardive. Their style is often dry and elegant, but some of their top wines have considerable fullness. *Open: Mon–Fri 10am–noon; 2–5pm.*

Muré (Clos Saint-Landelin)

68250 Rouffach. Vineyards owned: Grand Cru 16ha.
Produce: 500,000 bottles. VP-R and N.

The land in the Clos Saint-Landelin Grand Cru Vorbourg vineyard is treated without chemicals, and vinified traditionally in wood. This vineyard produces about 140,000 bottles a year. Grand Cru varietals are Riesling, Tokay Pinot Gris, Muscat and Gewürztraminer. Standard Alsace AC wines include the full range of varietals. Since 1982, they have also made a

Crémant d'Alsace. All their wines tend to be full and soft, while the Grand Cru wines often age particularly well. *Open: Mon– Sat 8am–6pm.*

<hr>

Cave Vinicole de Pfaffenheim

5 Rue du Chai, 68250 Pfaffenheim. Vineyards owned: Grand Cru Goldert and Alsace AC 200ha.
Produce: 2.5 million bottles. Coop (200 members).

<hr>

A well-run modern cooperative, using stainless steel, and making wines which are attractive to drink young. They make a full range, but the largest production is of Sylvaner, Pinot Blanc and Gewürztraminer. The Grand Cru Goldert wine is Gewürztraminer. Company names used are Hartenberger, J. Hornstein and Ernest Wein, plus a whole range of different *cuvée* names. *Open: Mon–Sun 8am–noon; 1:30–6pm.*

<hr>

Preiss-Henny

68630 Mittelwihr. Vineyards owned: Alsace AC 20ha.
Produce: 250,000 bottles. VP-R and N.

<hr>

The Preiss family came to Mittelwihr in 1535 and the family firm is now the largest in the village. They supply over a half of their requirements from their own vineyards. In the cellars, they use few chemicals and like to bottle their wines *sur lie* direct from the fermentation vats to give extra flavour and to avoid any contact with the air by racking. Quality is high, and I have enjoyed all their wines. Cuvée Marcel Preiss and Camille Preiss are two of their brand names. *Open: No.*

<hr>

Preiss-Zimmer

42 Rue de Général de Gaulle, 68340 Riquewihr.
Vineyards owned: Alsace AC 8ha.
Produce: 200,000 bottles. VP-R and N.

<hr>

A small négociant house, whose reputation is higher than its production. They operate very traditionally in cellars beneath the main street of Riquewihr. All the vinification is in wood. Their best wines are Gewürztraminer, but they also make a good, peppery Tokay Pinot Gris. They produce Grand Cru Schoenenberg. *Open: By appointment only.*

<hr>

Cave Coopérative de Ribauvillé et Environs

2 Route de Colmar, 68150 Ribeauvillé.
Vineyards owned: Alsace AC 175ha.
Produce: 2 million bottles. Coop (90 members).

<hr>

Pinot Blanc, Riesling and Sylvaner are the biggest production from what is probably the oldest cooperative in France, founded in 1895. They have recently modernized and now have a range of equipment producing some very good middle-of-the-road wines. The small Clos de Zahnacker (planted with Riesling, Gewürztraminer and Tokay) produces their best wines. Brand names they use include Martin Zahn, Traber, Medaillon and Armoires. Their Crémant d'Alsace is called Giersberger. *Open: Mon–Sat 9am–noon; 2–5:30pm. Oct–Mar by appointment only.*

<hr>

Domaine Martin Schaetzel

68770 Ammerschwihr. Vineyards owned: Alsace AC 5.2ha.
Produce: 50,000 bottles. VP-R.

<hr>

M. Jean Schaetzel, who studied oenology in Dijon, uses small 30 hectolitre barrels for vinifying his wines, partly because he is handling small quantities of wine and partly because he believes this gives him better temperature control. He makes his wines – especially his Gewürztraminer and Tokay Pinot Gris – for ageing (up to 10 years, he says). His top Gewürztraminer is called Cuvée Isabelle. *Open: Mon–Sat 8am–7pm.*

Edgard Schaller et Fils

1 Rue du Château, 68630 Mittelwihr. Vineyards owned: Grand Cru 2ha. Alsace AC 5.5ha. *Produce: 75,000 bottles.* VP-R.

One of the many ancient family firms, founded in 1609. Much of their production is of Crémant, but they also make the full range of varietals. *Open: Mon–Fri 8am–noon; 2–7pm.*

André Scherer

Huesseren-les-Châteaux, 68420 Herrlisheim. Vineyards owned: Grand Cru and Alsace AC 8ha. *Produce: 120,000 bottles.* VP-R and N.

A wide range is produced by this firm. Half the wines come from their own vineyards, half from grapes which are bought locally. They make the usual range of varietals, including Grand Cru wine from the Eichberg vineyard and Cuvée Eguisheim. Brand names include Cuvée Jean-Baptiste and Cuvée Blanche. One of their best varietals is their Tokay Pinot Gris, and they are one of the rare Alsace producers whose red Pinot Noir is full-bodied and has good colour. *Open: By appointment only.*

Domaines Schlumberger

100 Rue Théodore Deck, 68500 Guebwiller. Vineyards owned: Grand Cru 60ha; Alsace AC 80ha. *Produce: 1 million bottles.* VP-R.

Schlumberger dominates the village of Guebwiller, controlling much of the vineyard area. Being the largest private vineyard owners in Alsace, they are able to develop new techniques of large-scale planting in horizontal rows on the steep slopes above Guebwiller, which contrasts with the normal Alsace method of vines growing up single stakes. They make Grand Cru wines from Kitterlé, Kessler, Spiegel and Saering vineyards. Their wines can be variable, but their Riesling Kitterlé and the Gewürztraminer Cuvée Christine Schlumberger are good. *Open: By appointment only.*

Domaine Sick-Dreyer

9 Route de Kientzheim, 68770 Ammerschwihr. Vineyards owned: Alsace AC 12ha. *Produce: 90,000 bottles.* VP-R.

The finest wine from this small estate is its Gewürztraminer from their holding on the Kaefferkopf vineyard. They make the full range of varietals to a good quality level, using a mix of traditional and modern techniques and vinifying 90% of the wine in wood. While most of their vineyards are in Ammerschwihr, they also own land in Eguisheim, Katzenthal and Sigolsheim. *Open: Appointment preferred.*

Société Coopérative Vinicole de Sigolsheim et Environs

12 Rue Saint-Jacques, Sigolsheim, 68240 Kaysersberg. Vineyards owned: Grand Cru 31.5ha; Alsace AC 248ha. *Produce: 3 million bottles.* Coop (230 members).

One of the largest cooperatives in Alsace, with modern

equipment producing a wide range of good quality wines. They produce wines from the Grand Cru Mambourg vineyard and from the Vogelgarten vineyard, plus Vendange Tardive and Sélection des Grains Nobles – all from Gewürztraminer. Brand names include Comte de Sigold for Crémant d'Alsace. *Open: Mon–Fri 8–10:30am; 2–4:30pm. Sun in summer. Appointments preferred for groups.*

Pierre Sparr et ses Fils

2 Rue de la Première Armée Française, 68240 Sigolsheim.
Vineyards owned: Grand Cru 4.2ha; Alsace AC 23.8ha.
Produce: 1.6 million bottles. VP-R and N.

This firm of négociants buys in three quarters of its requirements from other growers in the Sigolsheim and Kaysersberg area. Their own vineyards are in Sigolsheim (including Grand Cru Mambourg), Kientzheim and Turckheim (including Grand Cru Brand). Brand names they use include Edelzwicker Alsaflor, Edelzwicker Rayon d'Alsace, Diamant d'Alsace (for Pinot Blanc), Crustalsa and Sparr Prestige (for their best wines). They make Vendange Tardive from Tokay Pinot Gris and Sélection des Grains Nobles from Gewürztraminer. *Open: Sun–Fri 8am–noon.*

Jean-Paul et Denis Specht

2 Rue des Eglises, 68630 Mittelwihr. Vineyards owned:
Grand Cru and Alsace AC 6.5ha.
Produce: 70,000 bottles. VP-R.

Traditional techniques are practised at this small firm. They have a holding in the Grand Cru Mandelberg vineyard of Riesling and Gewürztraminer and in addition make a range of varietal wines and Crémant d'Alsace. *Open: appointment preferred.*

F.E. Trimbach

68150 Ribeauvillé. Vineyards owned: Alsace Grand Cru and
Alsace 28ha. *Produce: 750,000 bottles.* VP-R and N.

One of the oldest (1626) firms in Alsace, with a long tradition of making fine wines both as a merchant house and vineyard owner. They make three quality levels: standard, Réserve and Réserve Personelle. Their own vineyards include land in Ribeauvillé, Hunawihr (Clos Ste-Hune), Bergheim, Riquewhir and Mittelwihr. Top *cuvées* are of Clos Ste-Hune, Frederic Emile and Seigneurs de Ribeaupierre. *Open: No.*

Cave Coopérative de Turckheim

68230 Turckheim. Vineyards owned: Alsace Grand Cru and
Alsace 200ha. Coop (260 members).

This medium-sized cooperative covers seven communes around Turckheim. They specialize in Gewürztraminer and Pinot Blanc, although a complete range is produced. *Open: Mon–Sat 8am–noon; 2–6pm.*

Domaine Weinbach

68240 Kaysersberg. Vineyards owned: Alsace AC 22ha.
Produce: 180,000 bottles. VP-R.

Mme Théo Faller and her children, who run the Domaine Weinbach estate (also known as the Clos des Capucins), have established an enviable reputation for top-quality Alsace wines.

They have stayed faithful to traditional methods, vinifying in wood, avoiding the centrifugation which so many Alsace producers seem to insist on, and producing full-bodied yet perfectly characteristic wines. The grapes are harvested late to give the wines considerable ageing potential. Cuvée Théo is the best Riesling from this estate. *Open: By appointment only.*

Coopérative Vinicole de Westhalten

52 Rue de Soultzmatt, 68250 Westhalten. Vineyards owned: Grand Cru and Alsace AC 270ha. *Produce: 3 million bottles.* Coop (220 members).

This cooperative now controls the négociant firm of Alfred Heim, also based in Westhalten. They make a wide range of wines at different levels of quality, including Grand Cru wine from the Vorbourg and Zinnkoepfle vineyards. The quality of some of the more basic wines is disappointing, but in the top ranges they make some good wines, especially Muscat d'Alsace (Westhalten is in a sheltered side valley which is advantageous for the ripening of Muscat) and Gewürztraminer. The Heim wines are still sold under separate labels. *Open: Mon–Sat 8am–noon; 2–6pm.*

Widerhirn

68340 Riquewihr. Vineyards owned: Grand Cru and Alsace AC 5.3ha. *Produce: 40,000 bottles.* VP-R.

High quality, but small scale producer who has a small holding in the Schoenenbourg and Sporen vineyards. His methods are traditional, with much wood in evidence in his small cellar. M. Widerhirn's wines age well – especially his Riesling and Tokay Pinot Gris. He makes small quantities of Gewürztraminer Vendange Tardive, but normally his style is dry. *Open: By appointment only.*

Domaine Zind-Humbrecht

34 Rue du Maréchal Joffre, Witzenheim, 68000 Colmar. Vineyards owned: Grand Cru and Alsace AC 30.5ha. *Produce: 200,000 bottles.* VP-R.

For Alsace, this is a large vineyard holding. The majority of it consists of 30% Riesling and 34% Gewürztraminer, but they have the full range of varietals. They bottle their wines *sur lie* without filtration, which gives them extra body and considerable depth of flavour. Their Grand Cru wines come from Brand in Turckheim, Goldert in Gueberschwihr, Hengst in Witzenheim and Rangen in Thann – the southernmost vineyard in Alsace, which Zind-Humbrecht has effectively resurrected in recent years. *Open: Mon–Fri 8am–noon; 2–6pm.*

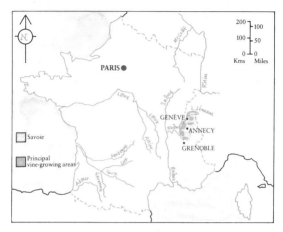

The Alpine vineyards of Savoie lie south of Lake Geneva. Most are set along the upper valley of the Rhône as it flows towards Lyons, in its tributary valley with the Lac du Bourget, and along the valley of the Isère as it flows southwest to Grenoble. Slopes above the lakes or the Rhône at around 300 metres are the favoured sites. Major towns in the area include Annecy and Aix-les-Bains as well as Chambéry, the home of France's best vermouths. It is almost as if the wines of Savoie were designed for the après-ski parties during which they are consumed in quantity. Both the reds and the whites are best drunk in the year of the harvest – light, refreshing and enjoyably unmemorable. The sparkling wines are the only ones that tend to leave the region. Because the vineyards of Savoie are so scattered, microclimates play an important part in the quality of the wines. The two lakes, of Geneva and of Bourget near Aix-les-Bains, influence and moderate the Alpine weather extremes, as do the fast-moving rivers.

There's a hint of Switzerland in the wines made from the Chasselas grape on the southern shores of Lake Geneva at Crépy, and an influence from Beaujolais in the Gamay which is used to make light red wines. But there are also local grape varieties in the 1,500 hectares of vineyard. The Mondeuse makes a simple full-bodied red. The Jacquère is a widely-planted white grape which makes crisp wines to be drunk young. The Altesse (or Roussette) makes soft wines, while the Bergeron (akin to the Roussanne of the southern Rhône) makes finer whites around Chambéry. The sparkling wines, made in the region of Seyssel, are a blend of Chasselas with Altesse and Molette.

The Appellations

The AC system is probably more complex than the styles of

wine warrant – a product of the fragmented vineyards.

Crépy: Dry, slightly sparkling whites from the southern shore of Lake Geneva. The grape is the Chasselas (Swiss Fendant). Some claim they age, but the chance to prove this is rare since most is drunk young and locally.

Roussette de Savoie: Dry white wines made mainly around Frangy north of Lac du Bourget and around Cruet in the Isère valley. The wine is normally a blend of Roussette (or Altesse) and Chardonnay (called locally Petite Sainte-Marie) with Mondeuse.

Roussette de Savoie cru: Four communes have the right to add their name to the generic Roussette de Savoie AC – Frangy, Marestel, Monterminod and Monthoux.

Seyssel: Dry white wines from the commune of Seyssel on the Rhône. Only the Altesse is permitted.

Seyssel Mousseux: Sparkling *méthode champenoise* wines made from the Altesse and Chasselas.

Vin de Savoie: Widespread AC taking in reds, dry whites and rosés. Reds and rosés come from Mondeuse, Gamay and Pinot Noir; whites from Jacquère and Altesse with smaller amounts of Chardonnay, Aligoté and Chasselas.

Vin de Savoie cru: 15 communes are allowed to add their name to generic Vin de Savoie – Marignan and Ripaille (on Lake Geneva); Ayse, Charpignat and Chautagne (on Lac du Bourget); les Abîmes, Apremont, Arbin, Chignin, Chignin-Bergeron, Cruet, Montmélian, St Jean-de-la-Porte and Ste Jeoire-Prieuré (south of Chambéry) and Ste Marie d'Alloix (towards Grenoble).

Vin de Savoie Ayse Mousseux: Sparkling *méthode champenoise* wine made in the commune of Ayse.

Vin de Savoie Mousseux: Mainly white (with a little rosé) sparkling *méthode champenoise* wine made in other vin de Savoie cru villages.

Vintages: Most Savoie wines need to be drunk young. Occasional wines made from the Mondeuse grape repay keeping for a couple of years. 1983, '85 and '86 were good recent vintages.

Canelli-Suchet

Caves de la Tour de Marignan, 74140 Sciez. Vineyards owned: Vin de Savoie 5ha. *Produce: 25,000 bottles.* VP-R.

M. Canelli-Suchet's family has been in Savoie for more than three centuries and his name recalls that the area used to be part of an Italian kingdom. He makes wine traditionally, from Chasselas grapes. His range includes still wine aged in cask under the Marignan name and a small amount of *méthode champenoise* dry and medium-dry sparkling wine, called La Perle. *Open: By appointment only.*

Cave Coopérative de Chautagne

73310 Ruffieux. Vineyards owned: Chautagnes 150ha. *Produce: 400,000 bottles.* Coop (200 members).

The grapes for this cooperative come from the area north of Lac du Bourget. Unusally for Savoie, over half the production here is of red and rosé wine, mainly from the Gamay, with some Pinot Noir and Mondeuse. Some reds are aged in wood after stainless steel vinification. The Pinot Noir wines age well for a couple of years. *Open: By appointment only.*

Caveau du Lac St-André (J-C Perret)

St André-les-Marches, 73800 Montmelian. Vineyards owned:
10ha (including some in the cru of Apremont).
Produce: 100,000 bottles. VP-R.

The main production in this modern winery is of an attractively
perfumed white Vin de Savoie Apremont, made in stainless steel
with a long cool fermentation to bring out the fruit. Red and
rosé are made from Gamay using carbonic maceration. *Open:
By appointment only.*

Cave Cooperative des Vins Fins Cruet

73800 Cruet. Vineyards owned: 83ha.
Produce: 400,000 bottles. Coop.

The best wine from this cooperative is the Vin de Savoie Arbin,
made from Mondeuse, more sophisticated than the usual red
from this grape. They also make a varietal Mondeuse and a
white from Chignin. *Open: Mon–Sat 8am–noon; 2–6pm.*

L. Mercier et Fils

Grande Cave de Crépy, 74140 Douvaine. Vineyards owned:
Crépy (Vin de Savoie AC) 30ha.
Produce: 350,000 bottles. VP-R and N.

The principal wine made by this large firm is a white, slightly
sparkling Chasselas Vin de Savoie Goutte d'Or, which is
vinified traditionally in wood. They also act as négociants.
Open: Mon–Fri 5–6pm. By appointment only.

Château de Monterminod

73230 St-Alban Lyesse. Vineyards owned: 5ha.
Produce: 25,000 bottles. VP-R.

A Vin de Savoie producer who makes Mondeuse rosé and red.
Both of the wines are full-bodied and easy-to-drink styles, and
the red can also age. *Open: By appointment only.*

Michel Million Rousseau

Monthoux, 73170 St-Jean de Chevelu. Vineyards owned:
Vin de Savoie 4ha; Roussette de Savoie Monthoux 1ha.
Produce: 40,000 bottles. VP-R.

The range of Vin de Savoie AC from this small family firm
includes Gamay, Mondeuse, Pinot Noir and Jacquère, all of
which are vinified and sold separately. M. Million Rousseau
also makes small quantities of an attractive fresh Roussette de
Monthoux. The reds need around three to seven years, but the
whites need to be drunk young. *Open: Mon–Sat 8am–noon;
2–7pm.*

Michel et Jean-Paul Neyroud

Les Aricoques, Designy, 74270 Frangy. Vineyards owned:
Les Aricoques (Frangy) 3ha; Planaz (Designy) 3.5ha.
Produce: 35,000 bottles. VP-R.

While most of this firm's production is a nutty white Roussette
de Savoie from Frangy, made in a modern style using stainless
steel, there is also some more traditional red Vin de Savoie made
from the Mondeuse grape, which can age well for two or three
years. The other wine made is a Gamay, Vin de Savoie Rouge.
*Open: During working hours. Appointments necessary for
groups.*

J. Perrier et Fils

St André-les-Marches, 73800 Montmélian. Vineyards owned: Apremont 8ha; les Abîmes 2ha. *Produce: 1,500,000 bottles.* VP-R and N.

Apart from their own vineyards at Apremont and les Abîmes which produce 100% Jacquère Vin de Savoie AC wines, the firm also makes a large range of wines: a white Chignin and Roussette de Savoie, and Gamay de Savoie and Gamay de Chantagne. Pinot Noir is also bought in to make a Pinot de Savoie, while Mondeuse is bought from Arbin. Recent launches include a sparkling *méthode champenoise* and a *pétillant* wine. The quality from one of the largest firms in the area is generally good, if not exciting. *Open: Mon–Fri 8am–noon; 2–6pm. By appointment only.*

André Quenard et Fils

Tormery, 73800 Chignin. Vineyards owned: Chignin and Chignin-Bergeron 14ha. *Produce: 100,000 bottles.* VP-R.

All the wines made in this modern winery are 100% varietals. Chignin Blanc is Jacquère; Chignin-Bergeron is Roussanne; Vin de Savoie rouge is Mondeuse, with some ageing potential; Vin de Savoie rosé is Gamay. The brand-name is Coteaux de Tormery. The top wine made is a rich, intense Chignin-Bergeron. *Open: By appointment only.*

Le Vigneron Savoyard

73190 Apremont. Vineyards owned: Apremont AC 25ha; les Abîmes AC 8ha; Vin de Savoie AC 3ha. *Produce: 40,000 bottles.* Coop (10 members).

White Vin de Savoie from the two cru villages of Apremont and les Abîmes is the main production of this cooperative. Small quantities of red Vin de Savoie are also made. Modern equipment produces straightforward attractive clean wines. The cellars are in the farm of the château at Apremont. *Open: No.*

Marcel Tardy et Fils

La Plantée, Apremont 73190 Challes-les-Eaux. Vineyards owned: 5ha. *Produce: 40,000 bottles.* VP-R.

Small producer making a very attractive white Vin de Savoie Apremont, adding a touch of Sauvignon to give it extra crispness and freshness. *Open: By appointment only.*

Varichon et Clerc

Les Séchallets, 01420 Seyssel. Vineyards owned: Seyssel 100ha. *Produce: 600,000 bottles.* VP-R and N.

Good quality sparkling wines are the speciality of this firm. Some, such as the Royal Seyssel, are made from local grapes, but their Mousseux Méthode Champenoise is made from grapes brought in from other areas. They also make a Pétillant de Savoie and still wines from the AC Savoie. *Open: Appointments preferred.*

Bugey

Bugey lies immediately to the west of the Savoie vineyards. This small VDQS area has recently returned to life after a long period when it was almost moribund. In style the white wines are directly related to Savoie, while the reds (made principally from the Gamay) are closer to the Jura. The various appellation names are extraordinarily complex for such a minor area.

VDQS Bugey

Vin de Bugey: Red, dry white and rosé from Gamay, Pinot Noir, Poulsard, Mondeuse (for red and rosé) and Altesse, Jacquère, Mondeuse Blanche, Chardonnay, Aligoté and Pinot Gris (for white).

Vin de Bugey Crus: As above. Five communes can use their names: Cerdon, Machuraz, Machuraz, Manicle, Vineu-le-Grand.

Roussette de Bugey: A white made from Roussette (Altesse) and Chardonnay.

Roussette de Bugey Cru: A 100% Roussette from six communes: Anglefort, Arbignieu, Chanay, Lagnieu, Montagnieu, Vineu-le-Grand.

Mousseux de Bugey/Pétillant de Bugey: Sparkling *méthode champenoise* and naturally semi-sparkling white made with the white grapes used in Vin de Bugey. The commune of Cerdon can attach its name to the wine.

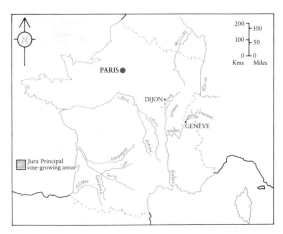

The Jura vineyard is a shadow of its former self. As with so many out-of-the-way areas, phylloxera during the last century is the culprit in the decline. But traditions have survived in this remote corner of France and at least two remarkable wines are still made here. And today new ideas are reviving old fortunes. The vineyard area of 1,400 hectares is on the eastern slopes of the Sâone valley, facing across to the Burgundian Côte d'Or. The vines grow at heights of between 250 and 500 metres in wooded valleys and between half-timbered towns. The Burgundian influence is here in some of the grape varieties – Chardonnay and Pinot Noir – but there is also a flourishing set of local grape varieties which are still commonly planted.

Red, white, rosé and sparkling wines are all made in the Jura. Some rosé is sometimes known as *vin gris*, on account of its pale pink colour achieved before fermentation. Little Jura wine – apart from *vin jaune* (see below) – is seen outside the area. Methods tend to be old-fashioned, although the main producer of the region (Henri Maire) has an ultra-modern plant. Traditionally, the wines are aged for considerable periods, which can make them over-oxidized for modern tastes. Sparkling wine is a growing speciality.

Red grapes include the Poulsard (or Plousard) a light-coloured grape which is used to make rosé wines. Because of its paleness, the Poulsard can be left in contact with the must for several days, so Jura rosés tend to have great weight – akin to the Tavel of the southern Rhône. The Trousseau is used to give bite in red wines and is also used to make a sparkling *blanc de noirs*.

While Chardonnay is used to make many of the white Jura wines, it is the local grape, the Savagnin (a type of Traminer) which is used in the most unusual wines of the region. *Vin Jaune* – yellow wine – is a sherry-type wine, made by ageing Savagnin in small barrels for a minimum of six years. A type of yeast – a flor as in Jerez – grows on the surface of the wine, producing a characteristic dry, oxidized taste. The barrels are not topped up, thus allowing the flor to develop in the air. It is bottled in the traditional *clavelin* bottle of Jura, with its long neck and sloping shoulders and containing 64cl (the amount left from a litre after evaporation).

The other rare wine of the region – rarer now than *vin jaune* – is called *vin de paille*. This is a sweet wine made from grapes dried on straw (*paille*) mats until they are like raisins. The nearest equivalent is the Italian Vin Santo.

Vintages: reds 1976, '78, '79, '82, '83. *Vin Jaune*: 1967, '71, '73, '76, '78, '79, '82. Standard whites and rosés should be drunk in two years.

The Appellations

Arbois: Red, dry white, rosé, *gris* and *vin jaune*.
Arbois Mousseux: Sparkling wines fermented in the same bottle.
Arbois-Pupillin: Red, dry white and rosé from the commune of Pupillin. Slightly richer than straight Arbois.
Château Chalon: Tiny appellation making only 70,000 bottles a year, but producing the best *vin jaune*.
Côtes du Jura: Catch-all AC, making red, dry white, rosé, *gris* and *vin jaune*.
Côtes du Jura Mousseux: Sparkling wines.
L'Etoile: White wines made from Chardonnay, Savagnin and Poulsard (vinified as white). Also *vin jaune* and *vin de paille*. Small production, but good quality.
L'Etoile Mousseux: Sparkling version of above, blending Chardonnay and Savagnin.

Château d'Arlay
Arlay, 39140 Bletterans. Vineyards owned: Château d'Arlay (Arlay) 27ha. *Produce: 60,000 bottles.* VP-R and N.

The English King William III was, among other things, Baron d'Arlay, a title still held by the Dutch Royal family. The estate has a history stretching back to the Middle Ages and vines cover the slopes beneath the medieval castle. A 19th century château is home to the present owner, Comte de Laguiche.

Quality is important at the estate and only the free-run juice is used for the top Château d'Arlay range of red, rosé and white. Modern vinification is followed by wood ageing (seven years for *vin jaune*). A small quantity of top quality *vin jaune* is made, and in 1985, for the first time, some *vin de paille*. Négociant marques include Comte de Guichebourg, Baron de Proby and Cuvée de l'Épinette. *Open: Mon–Sat 9am–noon; 2–5:30pm.*

Caves Jean Bourdy
Arlay, 39140 Bletterans. Vineyards owned: Côtes du Jura 4.5ha; Château-Chalon 0.5ha. *Produce: 20,000 bottles.* VP-R and N.

Vin Jaune and Château-Chalon are the star wines from this old-established (1781) firm. They buy in finished wine as well as making Côtes du Jura white and red from their own vineyards. They also make a Marc de Franche-Comté. A highly reliable producer. *Open: Mon–Fri 9am–noon; 2–7pm. Appointments necessary for groups.*

Hubert Clavelin et Fils

Le Vernois, 39210 Voiteur. Vineyards owned: Côtes du Jura
24ha. *Produce: 100,000 bottles.* VP-R.

The bulk of production here is of a good *méthode champenoise*
made from Chardonnay, but M. Clavelin also makes Côtes du
Jura white and red and Vin Jaune (from Savagnin). Methods
are traditional and vinification takes place in wood. *Open: By
appointment only.*

Cave Cooperative de Château Chalon et Côtes de Jura

39120 Voiteur. Vineyards owned: 66ha.
Produce: 240,000 bottles. Coop (68 members).

The importance of this small cooperative is that it is one of the
few sources for the Vin Jaune of Château Chalon AC. But they
also make Côtes du Jura white and rosé, and Vin Jaune from the
Côtes du Jura AC. *Open: By appointment only.*

Château Gréa

Rotalier, 39190 Beaufort. Vineyards owned: Le Clos
(Rotalier) 3.3ha; Sur Laroche (Rotalier) 0.7ha; Le Chanet
(Rotalier) 1.5ha; En Cury (Rotalier) 1ha.
Produce: 30,000 bottles. VP-R.

A small domaine in the same family since 1679. The existing
château dates from the 1770s, when the cellars were also built.
The vineyards are all in the Côtes du Jura general AC. Despite
the history, modern methods are used to make a clean rosé, and
a champagne-method Brut from Chardonnay and Pinot Noir. A
fine, richer white, Le Chanet, is made from a blend of
Chardonnay and Savagnin which is given three years in wood.
Around 2,000 bottles of *vin jaune*, called En Cury, are made in
good years. Fine eaux-de-vie wines are also made here.
*Open: Mon–Fri 10am–12:30pm; 2–7pm. Appointments pre-
ferred.*

Henri Maire (Château Montfort)

39600 Arbois. Vineyards owned: 321ha.
Produce: 4.8 million bottles. VP-R and N.

Henri Maire dominates Jura in a way that few producers can
ever dominate larger wine producing areas. The firm has
revitalized the region, and its offices at Château Montfort
house a fine collection of 19th century glasses as well as the
largest stocks of Vin Jaune anywhere. The estate is centred
mainly around Montfort, Grange Grillard, Sorbief and La
Croix d'Argis. All the Jura AC wines are made, plus a number
of brands (sparkling Vin Fou is the best known). Despite the
size, they can also produce small quantities of one of the best
Vin Jaune. *Open: By appointment only.*

Désiré Petit

Pupillin, 39600 Arbois. Vineyards owned: Pupillin 8ha;
Arbois 0.8ha; Côtes du Jura 3.3ha.
Produce: 75,000 bottles. VP-R.

Modern vinification in stainless steel produces whites, rosés
and reds which need little ageing. A *vin jaune* is also made and
this is aged in wood. The firm is one of the major land owners in
the Arbois-Pupillin AC having in total 12.1 hectares. *Open:
Mon–Sun.*

André Tissot

Quartier Bernard, Montigny-les-Arsures, 39600 Arbois.
Vineyards owned: Montigny-les-Arsures (Arbois) 11ha.
Produce: 80,000 bottles. VP-R.

A relatively new firm (founded 1959) which produces traditional wines in the vineyards where Pasteur made his studies of vine disease. Red and rosé are made from a blend of Trousseau, Poulsard and Pinot Noir, giving the red considerable depth of colour for the region. The white is 100% Chardonnay. All these wines are aged in wood for at least 18 months, and treatments are minimal. Small quantities of *vin jaune* and *vin de paille* are also made. *Open: Mon–Sun.*

Fruitière Vinicole d'Arbois

39600 Arbois. Vineyards owned: Arbois 195ha.
Produce: 700,000 bottles. Coop (152 members).

As the name suggests, this cooperative is also involved in other fruit crops and is certainly one of the oldest cooperatives in France (founded 1906). A new stainless steel vinification plant has been installed to produce the two principal wines: a champagne-method sparkler and a simple dry white. Smaller quantities of red and rosé are also made. *Open: Mon–Fri (summer only) 9am–noon; 2–6pm. Appointments necessary for groups.*

Fruitière Vinicole de Pupillin

Pupillin, 39600 Arbois, Vineyards owned: Arbois-Pupillin 40ha. *Produce: 200,000 bottles.* Coop (25 members).

The cooperative keeps this tiny village alive. The bulk of production is a rosé, made from Poulsard. Red is made from Pinot Noir, white from Chardonnay. Champagne-method sparkling Brut and rosé are also made under the brand name Papillette. There are also small quantities of *vin jaune. Open: Mon–Sun (May to Sept) 8am–noon; 2–6pm. By appointment only.*

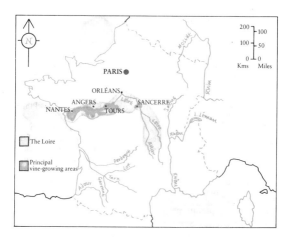

In its unhurried 635-mile meander through France, the Loire passes through some of the most quintessentially French countryside. Leaving the mountainous Ardèche, it passes woods and open fields, great châteaux and historic towns: gentle countryside devoted to agriculture. The light is filtered through the trees that line the river, the waters of the river reflecting its rays and tinging the air with softness.

For the first part of its course, the river runs north, parallel to the Saône and the Burgundy vineyards – which are only a few miles west. Almost halfway along its journey, in a huge arc, it turns west towards the Atlantic.

The largest Loire vineyards are almost entirely in the second half of the river's course. Well to the south – on a level with the Beaujolais – are the small VDQS areas of Côte Roannaise, Côtes du Forez and Côtes d'Auvergne and, a few miles north, St-Pourçain-sur-Sioule. But the first major wine areas appear just before the river turns to the west, at Sancerre and Pouilly-sur-Loire. Nearby but away from the river are the wine districts of Reuilly, Quincy and Ménétou-Salon. A little further north of Pouilly there is a small vineyard area at Gien.

At the top of the river's arc, to the west, the historic cathedral city of Orléans is the centre of a minor area of light red, white and rosé wine production. From here the river runs on westward, passing the châteaux of Touraine. At Blois, the vineyards of Cheverny produce white wines. This district is on the edge of the main Touraine wine-producing area, which has a number of smaller appellations: Vouvray and Montlouis, Chinon and Bourgueil, and towns – like Amboise and Mesland – which are crus within the general Touraine area.

Away to the north are the outlying vineyards of Vendôme,

Coteaux du Loir and Jasnières, while to the south are the vineyards of Valençay and Haut-Poitou.

Touraine – centred around the cathedral city of Tours – is at the transitional point of the Loire vineyards. Here the Sauvignon Blanc of Sancerre and Pouilly-Fumé meets the Chenin Blanc of Anjou; the Pinot Noir and Gamay of Burgundy meet the Cabernets of Bordeaux. It is the Chenin Blanc and the Cabernets which take over in the neighbouring province of Anjou. The Chenin makes a whole range of whites, from piercingly acid and dry, still and sparkling, to lusciously sweet. The Cabernet Franc is joined by the Groslot to produce rosés: on its own it makes reds. Then, as the river continues westward, nearing its mouth, there is an abrupt change. The Chenin Blanc is replaced by the Melon de Bourgogne and the vineyards of Muscadet stretch out to the Atlantic horizon. Small pockets of Malvoisie produce a sweet white at Ancenis and the Gros Plant makes a white that can make lemon juice seem soft.

While there is a great variety in the wines of the Loire, there is also a common thread. These are northern vineyards. The growing season is long and comparatively cool. This gives Loire wines their general character of intense fruit flavours and often piercing acidity. They are cool wines in climate and also in taste.

There was a time, a few years ago, when Loire wines were relative unknowns. In recent years some have been discovered – while others still await their Prince Charming. The wines of Sancerre and Pouilly-Fumé and those of Muscadet are the classic discoveries. Suddenly fashionable, their price has shot up. Often the price rises have been unreasonable: these are, after all, still country wines, never reaching the peaks of Bordeaux and Burgundy.

While some wines have become fashionable, others – potentially greater – have languished. Anjou makes some of the world's great sweet wines in the small areas of Quarts de Chaume and Bonnezeaux and few people bother to know more about them. They are the equal of Sauternes, German Trockenbeerenauslese or Late Harvest wines and their prices are crazily cheap.

The reds of Chinon and Bourgueil also deserve more attention than normally received. While always suffering from their northerly situation, in good years these vineyards can produce smooth, rich wines, much more generous and rewarding than the tart reds of Sancerre which command such absurd prices.

And finally there are the tiny VDQS areas, hanging like forgotten fruit from the branches and tributaries of the Loire. Many were decimated by phylloxera and only a few dedicated growers keep them alive. Others – like Haut-Poitou – have been discovered because they have learnt how to compete in the big wine world.

The Appellations

There are currently 60 names or permutations on the full list of Loire ACs and VDQS areas. The list is arranged here as it is in the producers' directory which follows.

Upper Loire: AC

Blanc Fumé de Pouilly: See Pouilly-Fumé.

Ménétou-Salon: White, red and rosé wines, made on 100 hectares of chalky soil to the west of Sancerre. Whites from Sauvignon, rosés and reds from Pinot Noir. The whites can match the average Sancerre, reds and rosés can often be fuller.

Pouilly-sur-Loire: White wine made in the same area as Pouilly-Fumé, but from the Chasselas grape.

Pouilly-Fumé: White wines made from Sauvignon around the village of Pouilly-sur-Loire. 606 hectares of calciferous (*marne argileuse*) and flint (*silex*) soils. There are no reds or rosés produced under this appellation. The wines tend to be fuller, higher in alcohol and richer and more long-lasting than Sancerre, but sometimes lack the initial crisp fruit.

Quincy: White wine from the Sauvignon grape. 108 hectares of gravelly soil along what was once the bed of the River Cher. The wine can be attractively soft and round while retaining the gooseberry acidity of the Sauvignon grape.

Reuilly: White from Sauvignon and rosé from Pinot Gris and Pinot Noir. 60 hectares of chalk soil. The white wine is light and fresh, the rosé (especially from the Pinot Gris) is very attractive.

Sancerre: White, rosé and red wines. White from Sauvignon, red and rosé from Pinot Noir. About 1,620 hectares. This is the most important appellation in terms of production in the upper Loire. The soil – a mixture of *caillottes* (calciferous and gravel), flint and the heavier *marne argileuse* – produces three distinct styles of wine. While many are blended, wines from Chavignol and Bué reflect the qualities of the *caillottes* soil, while those from Verdigny have more of the character of the heavier *marne argileuse*. Around the town of Sancerre, *silex* (flint) soil predominates. The whites have the classic Sauvignon taste of gooseberries and grapefruits and are immediately attractive. Some fine barrel-aged reds are made, but on the whole these and the rosés tend to be over-rated.

Upper Loire: VDQS

Châteaumeillant: Red and rosé from Gamay, due south of Sancerre.

Côtes d'Auvergne: Gamay red from near Clermont-Ferrand in the Puy de Dôme.

Côtes du Forez: Gamay red from near St-Etienne, almost at the source of the Loire.

Vin des Coteaux du Giennois or Côtes de Gien: Area centred around Cosne, north of Sancerre and Pouilly-sur-Loire. Red from Pinot Noir and Gamay, white from Sauvignon.

Côte Roannaise: Attractive Gamay red, further down river from Côtes du Forez. Due west of Beaujolais.

Saint-Pourçain: On the Allier river, north of the Côtes d'Auvergne. Whites from Tressalier and Chardonnay, reds and rosés from Gamay and Pinot Noir.

Vin de l'Orléanais: Vineyards around the city of Orleans, make this the most northerly Loire vineyard. Red, white and rosé wines are made. Largest production is rosé from Pinot Meunier.

Touraine: AC

Bourgueil: Red and rosé wines made from the Cabernet Franc and Cabernet Sauvignon, in a district at the western end of Touraine on the north bank of the Loire. There are about 890 hectares under vine on three different soil types running in bands parallel to the Loire: gravelly soil near the Loire (the least important); a higher level called *la terrasse* made of sand and gravel soil (the most important); and *les coteaux* at a higher level. Bourgueil is one of the few Loire reds that needs time to develop. Five or six years is a minimum. Vintages: 1976, '78, '82, '83, '85.

Chinon: This district lies due south of Bourgueil, between the Loire and Vienne rivers. There are nearly 1,212 hectares and, like Bourgueil, there are three soil types moving away from the Vienne river: the gravel nearest to the river; clay and gravel on *les plateaux*; and clay and lime from *les coteaux* which produces the best wines. More immediately attractive than Bourgueil, Chinon wines tend to mature more quickly, although given careful ageing in old barrels, they can last for some years. Vintages: 1976, '78, '82, '83, '85.

Coteaux du Loir: Le Loir is a tributary of the main river La Loire, running northwest from Angers past Vendôme. The Coteaux du Loir vineyards are tiny – only 74 hectares – lying 40 kilometres north of Tours. Red wines are made from Cabernet Franc, Pineau d'Aunis, Gamay and Cot; rosés from Groslot; whites from Pineau de la Loire.

Crémant de Loire: A general Loire-wide AC for white and rosé wines made in small quantities in Touraine and Anjou (including Saumur). A *crémant* has lower pressure than a normal *méthode champenoise* sparkler, but it is otherwise made with the same second fermentation in the bottle. This method can give good flavour and the wine ages well in bottle.

Jasnières: White wine made from Pineau de la Loire in two communes – L'Homme and Ruille-sur-Loir in the Coteaux du Loir AC. 19 hectares make this rare dry wine.

Montlouis: The twin vineyard of Vouvray (q.v.) on the southern bank of the Loire east of Tours on the tongue of land between the Loire and the Cher. The wines come from the three communes of Montlouis-sur-Loire, Lussault and St-Martin-le-Beau. Chalk underlies a sandy top soil. Only white wines are produced from the Chenin Blanc. Most of the still wines are dry, less full-bodied but softer than Vouvray and more attractive when young. In very good years, demi-sec and *moelleux* (sweet) wines can be made. Vineyard area is around 300 hectares.

Montlouis Pétillant and Mousseux: Slightly sparkling (*pétillant*) and *méthode champenoise* sparkling wines (*mousseux*) are made from the same vineyards as still Montlouis. Generally made in cooler years.

Rosé de Loire: Dry rosé which can be made in Touraine, Anjou and Saumur – but mainly comes from Touraine. Groslot and the two Cabernets (minimum of 30% Cabernet – higher than for Rosé d'Anjou).

Saint-Nicholas-de-Bourgueil: A commune just west of the main Bourgueil vineyard makes a lighter red from Cabernet Franc that ages more quickly. Some regard the wine as nearer to a Chinon than a Bourgueil in style. 498 hectares. Vintages: 1983 '85.

Touraine: A catch-all AC for the whole Touraine region. It covers 2,990 hectares – about one third of the vineyard area in the province (the other two thirds are in smaller, more precise ACs). Red, rosé and white, still and sparkling wines are made from a variety of grapes. The reds are made from Cabernet Franc, Cabernet Sauvignon, Gamay and Malbec, or from Pinot Gris, Pinot Meunier and Pinot Noir. Rosés from the red grapes or from Groslot or Pineau d'Aunis. Whites from Chardonnay, Chenin Blanc, Pineau Menu and Sauvignon. Gamay and Sauvignon are the most widely planted grapes.

Touraine Villages: Three smaller districts have the right to add their name to the general Touraine AC. Touraine-Amboise is on the Loire due east of Tours and makes reds from Gamay,

Malbec and both Cabernets, rosé from Gamay and Cabernet Franc and a little dry white from the Chenin Blanc (149 hectares). Touraine Azay-le-Rideau, to the southwest of Blois, makes dry and semi-sweet white from the Chenin Blanc and rosé from Groslot and red grapes (98 hectares). Touraine-Mesland produces red from Gamay, the Cabernets and Cot (Malbec), smaller amounts of white from Chenin Blanc (250 hectares). On the whole, the reds are better than the whites in Mesland and Amboise: Mesland especially makes some fine long-lasting wines from Cabernet Franc. Azay-le-Rideau is better at whites (especially the sweeter wines) than rosés.

Touraine Pétillant and Mousseux: Slightly sparkling (*pétillant*) and *méthode champenoise* sparkling (*mousseux*) wines made all over the Touraine AC area. Little *mousseux* under this AC is made, most coming, confusingly, as Crémant de Touraine under the ordinary Touraine AC.

Vouvray: White wine made on the north bank of the Loire, just east of Tours. The vineyards are on the plateau above the river on chalk soil. The cliff facing the river and the small side valleys are riddled with caves and cellars – some people still live in troglodyte houses half built into the cliff. There are three styles of still Vouvray – dry, semi-dry and sweet (*moelleux*). The only grape variety is the Chenin Blanc (Pineau de la Loire). The sweeter – and even some of the better dry – wines can age seemingly for ever. They can be luscious but also with the hard edge of acidity which the Pineau provides and which gives them long life. At its best, one of the finest Loire wines – but much inferior Vouvray is bottled elsewhere by négociants; much better are the local bottled wines from the top estates. Vintages (for sweet): 1969, '71, '76, '82, '83, '85.

Vouvray Mousseux: The *méthode champenoise* sparkling Vouvray, normally dry but sometimes semi-sweet or even sweet. Must be white. Vintages (for dry): 1984.

Coteaux du Vendômois: Just to the east of Coteaux du Loir AC is this larger (40 hectare) area, based around the town of Vendôme on the Loir. Red (from Cabernet Franc, Gamay and Pinot Noir), rosé (from Pineau d'Aunis and Gamay), white (from Chenin Blanc and Chardonnay).

Cheverny: White, red and rosé wines from 500 hectares, from a district southwest of Blois. The major production is of a very dry white, from the local Romorantin grape. Other whites come from Chenin Blanc, Sauvignon, Chardonnay and Pineau Menu (Arbois). Red comes mainly from Gamay, as does the rosé. Some sparkling wine is also made.

Valençay: Mainly red Gamay-based wine from a small area to the south of the Cher in southeast Touraine. Some rosé is also made from the Gamay, while white comes from Pineau Menu, Chardonnay or Sauvignon. A little Romorantin is also planted.

Anjou: The general AC for the vineyards of the whole region not covered by more precise appellations. White, red and rosé are made under this name. There are around 17,000 hectares making wine – 15% red, 55% rosé, 30% white. Reds are from Gamay (wine called Anjou Gamay) and the two Cabernets (wine called Anjou). Rosé (which is semi-sweet) is mainly made from Groslot (Grolleau), with some Cabernet Franc, Cabernet Sauvignon, Gamay, Pineau d'Aunis and Malbec. White mainly from Chenin Blanc (Pineau de la Loire) with some Chardonnay or Sauvignon; the style of white ranges from dry to sweet.

Anjou Coteaux de la Loire: White wines from the area just south of Angers. Can be dry or semi-sweet. Grape is the Chenin Blanc (Pineau de la Loire).

Anjou Gamay: Red wines from the general Anjou AC made from the Gamay grape.

Anjou Pétillant and Mousseux: Semi-sparkling (*pétillant*) and *méthode champenoise* sparkling wines made in the general Anjou AC area. Can be from Chenin Blanc or from red grapes (pressed to make white wine). Tiny production.

Bonnezeaux: One of the two great sweet white wine ACs (*see also* Quarts de Chaume). The small vineyard area is in the commune of Thouarcé, part of the larger Coteaux du Layon AC (q.v.). 121 hectares of clay and limestone soil. The grapes should ideally be left to develop noble rot – certainly they need to be late-harvested to give the required sweetness and intensity, and the wine can only be made in good years (the better producers sell it as Coteaux du Layon in bad years). Vintages: 1975, '76, '79, '82, '83, '85.

Cabernet d'Anjou: A rosé wine made throughout the Anjou AC area from Cabernet grapes. It can be sweet or dry. The wine can be attractive when properly made (without too much sulphur) but sweet varieties tend to become cloying quite easily; the dry style often suffers from poor vinification.

Cabernet de Saumur: Rosés from the Saumur AC area, normally semi-sweet and made from the two Cabernet grapes. Small production of wines which tend to be better than ordinary Cabernet d'Anjou.

Coteaux de l'Aubance: Small-production white wine area to the east of Coteaux du Layon, due south of Angers on the Aubance river. The delimited area is large but only about 80 hectares make the wine. Normally a medium dry white wine made from ripe Chenin Blanc grapes which have been fermented slowly. Good examples can age well, although they are not too harsh when young.

Coteaux du Layon: The modest river Layon runs southwest to northeast towards the Loire, making a wide valley. On the southwest facing slopes are around 1,616 hectares of Chenin Blanc making sweet white wines from very ripe grapes, some with noble rot. Coteaux du Layon is the general AC and there are smaller ACs with an even higher quality as enclaves in the area (Quarts de Chaume, Bonnezeaux). The wines represent remarkable value.

Coteaux du Layon Villages: Seven communes are allowed to add their name to the main Coteaux du Layon AC. Their wines are generally better with a higher alcoholic level and there are lower yields in one commune (Chaume) as well. The seven are: Beaulieu-sur-Layon, Faye d'Anjou, Rablay-sur-Layon, Saint Aubin de Luigné, Rochefort-sur-Loire, Saint-Lambert-du-Lattay, Chaume.

Coteaux de Saumur: Semi-sweet wine from Chenin Blanc made in tiny quantities in the Saumur AC area. It has similar qualities to some Vouvray or Montlouis with a rich, full-bodied, slightly honeyed flavour balanced by a touch of bitter acidity.

Crémant de Loire: *See under* Touraine.

Quarts-de-Chaume: Along with Bonnezeaux (q.v.) the other great sweet wine area of Anjou. The vineyard area covers 48 hectares on four fingers of hilly land which stretch out towards the Layon valley in the centre of the Coteaux du Layon AC area. The higher plateau behind protects the vineyards from winds. The wine is sweet, made from late-harvested grapes, in good years infected with noble rot but always picked to be as ripe as possible. The wine tastes surprisingly fresh in its youth (rather like young Sauternes) but between three and 10 years becomes quiescent. It is at its greatest between 10 and 20 years – but fine wines will last for longer. Good Quarts de Chaume ranks equally with Sauternes and German Trockenbeerenauslesen as one of the world's great sweet wines. Vintages: 1975, '76, '79, '81, '82, '83, '85; older vintages if you can find them.

Rosé d'Anjou: Medium sweet rosé wine made anywhere in the general Anjou region (see under general Anjou AC).

Rosé d'Anjou Pétillant: Rarely found semi-sparkling medium sweet Rosé d'Anjou.

Savennières: From a small area on the north bank of Loire west of Angers, opposite Rochefort-sur-Loire and the Coteaux du Layon vineyards. Made from Chenin Blanc, the wine can be sweet or dry, but is now normally dry. Only about 60 hectares in production. Grapes are picked very ripe and fermented dry, giving high alcohol. In the rare good years, the wine is superb, combining a dry palate with a peaches and cream bouquet. Like many great Chenin Blanc wines, they age well. Vintages: 1976, '78, '82, '83, '85.

Savennières-Coulée-de-Serrant: The Coulée-de-Serrant vineyard is the heart of Savennières with six hectares making fine dry white wines with an immensely long life. Vintages: 1976, '78, '82, '83, '85, but older wines will survive better.

Savennières-Roches-aux-Moines: Second great Savennières vineyard. Six hectares under production. Wines tend to be lighter than Coulée-de-Serrant. Vintages: 1976, '78, '82, '83, '85.

Saumur: White and red still wines from 38 communes around Saumur. The bone-dry white is made from Chenin Blanc with up to 20% Chardonnay or Sauvignon and is normally rather tart and acid. The red comes mainly from Cabernet Franc with Cabernet Sauvignon and Pineau d'Aunis.

Saumur-Champigny: A red wine, also from Saumur, but from seven communes in the best part of the area for reds on a plateau above St-Cyr-en-Bourg. A finer wine than ordinary red Saumur, it is in great demand and prices are rather too high. Like Chinon and Bourgueil it has characteristic bitter cherries and vanilla flavours. Vintages: 1978, '82, '83, '85, '86.

Saumur Pétillant and Mousseux: While only small quantities of *pétillant* are made, Saumur Mousseux is the second AC sparkling wine to Champagne in France, producing around 12 million bottles a year. Made in the same way as champagne, much of the production is now linked to Champagne companies. Chenin Blanc, Chardonnay, Sauvignon are white grapes used; the two Cabernets, Gamay, Groslot, Malbec, Pineau d'Aunis and Pinot Noir are the red (which are pressed as white). The soil is generally chalk. Most Saumur is made by big négociant houses and, like champagne, blending ensures continuity of house style. While not an exciting wine, Saumur is reliable and easy-to-drink and is much cheaper than champagne. There is also rosé *mousseux* made from any of the combination of red grapes. The wine is now known in publicity as Saumur d'Origine.

Anjou: VDQS

Vin de Haut-Poitou: While this area is not in Anjou, it is normally linked in for convenience. It is an isolated pocket of winemaking away from the main area, near Vienne in the province of Poitou to the south. Nothing would be known about Haut-Poitou were it not for the cooperative, which is making delightful varietal wines from Chardonnay and Sauvignon – Sauvignon the more successful. But Chenin Blanc is also permitted for whites. Reds and rosés are made from Gamay, Pinot Noir, Cabernet Sauvignon and Grolleau (Groslot). The wines are fresh and fruity and should be drunk young.

Vins de Thouarsais: Red, rosé and dry white wines from the Deux-Sevres département, south of Angers and west of Poitiers. The red and rosé come from Cabernet Franc and Cabernet Sauvignon; the white, which is normally medium dry, from Chenin Blanc. The wines should be drunk young.

Western Loire: AC

Muscadet: This is the basic AC for the white wines of what is called the Pays Nantais — the region south of the city of Nantes, almost at the mouth of the Loire. Simple Muscadet made from the Muscadet grape (also called Melon de Bourgogne) comes mainly from the area around the Lac du Grand Lieu on about 808 hectares of vineyard. The area used to be larger than it was, but the Muscadet de Sèvre et Maine (q.v.) area has been enlarged to take in some of the simple Muscadet country. The straight Muscadet very rarely reaches the character or the freshness and fruit of a Muscadet de Sèvre et Maine – and it's normally worth paying the extra to buy the superior wine.

Muscadet des Coteaux de la Loire: A small area of 400 hectares of vineyards on chalky soil along the banks of the Loire east of Nantes in the same area as the Coteaux d'Ancenis. The different soil produces a fuller, somewhat coarse wine, which rarely leaves its native area.

Muscadet de Sèvre et Maine: This is the biggest Muscadet area by far, covering 8,100 hectares south of Nantes. The best vineyards are generally agreed to be in Saint-Fiacre and Vallet, but much of the production is bought by négociants – either local or from Saumur and points west. The area has been vastly expanded to take in what was simple Muscadet vineyard – a classic French sleight of hand when they saw the difference in price the two wines could command.

Superior Muscadet de Sèvre et Maine is described as being bottled *sur lie* – i.e. straight from the unracked, unfiltered cask or tank, giving a slight prickle and extra freshness to the taste. This should be done on the spot in the place where the wine was made (*mis en bouteilles au château* will tell you this has happened). But increasingly the wine is taken off the lees and then transferred elsewhere for bottling – and a little CO_2 added to give the prickle. Muscadet has been an immense success story. From humble origins as the local wine for Breton seafood, it has conquered the world as an easy-to-drink dry white that is sufficiently anonymous to suit most occasions. No Muscadet can, or should, be pretentious: the character of the Melon de Bourgogne grape can't take it.

Western Loire: VDQS

Coteaux d'Ancenis: White, rosé and red wines made in the same area as Muscadet Coteaux de la Loire AC. Only a little white is made from the Chenin Blanc (Pineau de la Loire) and Malvoisie (Pineau Beurot) which makes both dry and sweet wines. Gamay and Cabernet Franc produce the red and rosé. Small production from 214 hectares. All Coteaux d'Ancenis wines have to carry the name of the grape variety on the label: Pineau de la Loire, Chenin Blanc, Malvoisie, Pinot-Beurot, Gamay, Cabernet.

Gros Plant or Gros Plant du Pays Nantais: This is an extremely dry white wine from the lesser grape of the Muscadet area. The Gros Plant (or Folle Blanche) grape covers 2,430 hectares mostly in the same area as the simple Muscadet. It's more acid than Muscadet and not a wine to drink by itself – but it goes well with shellfish. It can be bottled *sur lie*. A little sparkling wine is also made.

Fiefs Vendéens: Red, dry white and rosé wines from the Vendée, south of the Pays Nantais. Red and rosé from Cabernet Franc, Cabernet Sauvignon, Gamay, Pinot Noir, Pineau d'Aunis. Whites from Chenin Blanc, Chardonnay, Gros Plant and Sauvignon. Only a little white is made. The wine is simple and should be drunk young.

Upper Loire: Ménétou-Salon

Bernard Clement et Fils (Domaine de Châteney)

18510 Ménétou-Salon. Vineyards owned: Ménétou-Salon
Sauvignon 12ha; Pinot Noir 8ha.
Produce: 100,000 bottles. VP-R.

Family firm dating back to 1560. The estate at the Domaine de Châtenay is much larger than the present vineyard planting and expansion is going on. The white tends to a full style, pleasantly perfumed but a little heavy to my taste. The red is much more interesting – vinified traditionally and aged for up to a year in new barrels, giving a wine which needs time to mature and has life of anything up to 10–12 years. *Open: Appointments preferred.*

Georges Chavet et Fils

GAEC des Brangers, 18510 Ménétou-Salon. Vineyards
owned: Ménétou-Salon: Sauvignon 5.5ha; Pinot Noir 5.5ha.
Produce: 70,000 bottles. VP-R.

For those who want large bottles of Ménétou-Salon – especially reds – this is where to come. The red wine inside is a well-balanced product, made half from grapes which have been pressed and half from maceration, with some ageing in wood. The whites are very fresh and full of grape fruit. A small amount of attractive, lively rosé is also made. The firm goes back to the 18th century and has only slowly begun the change to modern vinification techniques for white wines. *Open: Mon–Sun 8am–8pm. Appointments necessary for groups.*

Domaine Henri Pelle et Fils

Morogues, 18220 Les Aix-d'Auguillon. Vineyards owned:
Sauvignon 13ha; Pinot Noir 2ha.
Produce: 50,000 bottles. VP-R.

The mayor of Morogues, Henri Pelle is also one of the best producers of Ménétou-Salon. Most of his production is of a very fine white, but he also makes red and rosé. The red is sometimes aged for a year in wood. He uses the village name of Morogues as a brand name. *Open: By appointment only.*

Upper Loire: Pouilly-Fumé and Pouilly-sur-Loire

Michel Bailly

Les Berthiers, Les Loges, 58150 Pouilly-sur-Loire. Vineyards owned: 7ha. VP-R.

This small estate is the result of a division of land between the sons of Maurice Bailly. Jean-Louis took one portion, while Michel took the other. He makes very good wine from land in the Champ de Gris, Les Griottes and Les Perriers. *Open: Appointments preferred.*

Caves de Pouilly-sur-Loire

Les Moulins à Vent, 58150 Pouilly-sur-Loire. Vineyards owned: 100ha. *Produce: 800,000 bottles.* Coop (130 members).

This cooperative was the first cellar in Pouilly to go over to stainless steel, and now produces a reliable Pouilly-Fumé, a simple Pouilly-sur-Loire from the Chasselas and also red and rosé wines from the Coteaux du Giennois to the north. Their best wine is the Pouilly-Fumé Vieilles Vignes. There is a tasting cellar here. *Open: By appointment only.*

Didier Dagueneau

Les Berthiers, 58150 Pouilly-sur-Loire. Vineyards owned: Les Berthiers 6ha. *Produce: 40,000 bottles.* VP-R.

One of the most original and innovative producers of Pouilly-Fumé, influenced by developments among the younger generation of Burgundy winemakers. Fermentation now takes place in small new oak barrels, using specially selected yeasts. Some of this wine is later blended with wine fermented in stainless steel. Much of the land is on high quality flinty *silex* soil, and this name is used on his finest wine. All his wines age well and should not be drunk too young. *Open: By appointment only.*

Domaine Masson-Blondelet

1 Rue de Paris, 58150 Pouilly-sur-Loire. Vineyards owned: Pouilly 9ha; Sancerre 3ha. *Produce: 70,000 bottles.* VP-R.

Modern cellars and vinification produce some very reliable wines and one or two fine ones. The best wines from Masson-Blondelet (the name comes from the union of the husband and wife) are from Les Bascoins vineyard in Pouilly, and there is a top *cuvée* from old vines called Tradition Cullus. A small amount of red and white Sancerre is also made here. *Open: By appointment if possible.*

Château de Nozet

58150 Pouilly-sur-Loire. Vineyards owned: 52ha. *Produce: 1.5 million bottles.* VP-R and N.

By far the largest producer in Pouilly-sur-Loire, Patrick de Ladoucette owns a magnificent 19th century château in the centre of his vineyard on high ground above the village of Pouilly-sur-Loire. He buys in much of his needs, reserving his own estate for top wines like Baron de L (made only in good years). He also owns the Sancerre firm of Comte Lafond, apart from other interests elsewhere on the Loire and in Chablis. The quality is good, even if the wines from this estate are not the most exciting Pouilly-Fumé around. *Open: By appointment only.*

Didier Pabiot

Les Loges, 58150 Pouilly-sur-Loire. Vineyards owned: Les
Loges Sauvignon 4ha; Chasselas 0.5ha.
Produce: 30,000 bottles. VP-R.

A small production from a young vigneron, who prefers
traditional techniques. The wines are becoming better each
year and the Pouilly-Fumé (some sold under the brand Les
Champs de Cri) is in a full, rich style. *Open: By appointment
only.*

Michel Redde et Fils

La Moynerie, 58150 Pouilly-sur-Loire. Vineyards owned:
Pouilly 27ha. *Produce: 250,000 bottles.* VP-R.

One of the larger estates in Pouilly run by the sixth generation of
the Redde family. They only make Pouilly-Fumé, mainly from
flinty soil which gives the wine a potential for ageing. Their
finest wine is called Cuvée Majorum, only made in better years
(the last four were 1982, '83, '85 and '86). All their wine is made
in stainless steel and bottled as quickly as possible. *Open: By
appointment if possible.*

Guy Saget

58150 Pouilly-sur-Loire. Vineyards owned: Pouilly 18ha;
Sancerre 1ha. *Produce: 2.5 million bottles.* VP-R and N.

An old-established family firm which has expanded into a
négociant business from vineyard holdings. The wines are
made by low-temperature, controlled vinification which gives
them good fruit but not too high acidity. Their vineyard
holdings are in Chantalouettes, Les Loges, Les Bascoins,
Château de la Roche for Pouilly; Clos du Roy for Sancerre.
Their wines are generally soft and very accessible. *Open: By
appointment only.*

Château de Tracy

Tracy-sur-Loire, 58150 Pouilly-sur-Loire. Vineyards owned:
Tracy and Les Loges 24ha. *Produce: 80,000 bottles.*

Traditional family firm, owned by the Comte d'Estutt d'Assay
and run by his two sons. The estate has been in the family since
the 16th century. The wines are full of character, tending
towards a considerable heaviness and richness and can age well
in good years. Poor years are to be avoided, since their old-
fashioned techniques cannot cope with poor fruit. *Open: By
appointment only.*

Upper Loire: Quincy

Raymond Pipet

Quincy, 18120 Lury-sur-Arnon. Vineyards owned: Quincy
14ha. *Produce: 86,000 bottles.* VP-R.

As little treatment as possible is meted out to the white Quincy
wines of M. Pipet. He only filters after a brief period in glass-
lined tanks. The result is a wine with full flavour and only
moderate acidity which is one of the best from Quincy. He also
makes a little rosé Vin de Pays des Coteaux Cher et Arnon from
a small holding of Pinot Gris. Both the white and the red should
be drunk as young as possible. *Open: Mon–Fri 9am–noon;
2–6pm. Appointments preferred.*

Upper Loire: Reuilly

Olivier Cromwell

Reuilly, 18120 Lury-sur-Arnon. Vineyards owned: Reuilly: Sauvignon 2.85ha; Pinot Gris 1.2ha. *Produce: 30,000 bottles.*

For English readers the name reeks of history and derives, so M. Cromwell believes, from one of the Scots guards at the French court during the Middle Ages. Today, his tiny holding makes excellent clean, sharp white Reuilly and an attractive quite full-bodied rosé. *Open: By appointment only.*

Claude Lafond

Le Bois-St-Denis, 36260 Reuilly. Vineyards owned: Reuilly: Sauvignon 3.5ha; Pinot Gris 1ha; Pinot Noir 1.6ha. *Produce: 40,000 bottles.* VP-R.

This young grower makes a very dry white Reuilly from the vineyard of La Raie; a slightly sweet rosé from Pinot Gris grown in La Grande Piece vineyard; and a light, fresh red from Pinot Noir in Les Grands Vignes. A certain amount of the wine for the rosé and red is matured in wood. Claude Lafond is one of the more dynamic producers in the Reuilly area and he is vice-chairman of the local Syndicat Vinicole. *Open: By appointment only.*

Guy Malbête

Le Bois-St-Denis, 36260 Reuilly. Vineyards owned: Reuilly: 5.5ha of Sauvignon, Pinot Gris, Pinot Noir. *Produce: 25,000 bottles.*

A small-scale producer making some quality wines using traditional techniques. The red is aged in wood to give it some structure, while retaining the wild strawberry bouquet and taste. The rosé is a crisp wine with an attractive salmon-pink colour. The white is quite rounded for a Reuilly, with a lingering fragrance. *Open: By appointment only.*

Didier Martin

30 Route d'Issoudun, 36260 Reuilly. Vineyards owned: Reuilly 4ha. *Produce: 13,000 bottles.* VP-R.

Sauvignon Blanc makes the white wines on this small holding, while Pinot Gris is used to make an attractive rosé and Pinot Noir a light red. M. Martin vinifies in wood. *Open: By appointment only.*

Upper Loire: Sancerre

Pierre Archambault

Caves du Clos la Perrière, Verdigny, 18300 Sancerre. Vineyards owned: Verdigny (Sancerre): Sauvignon 27ha; Pinot Noir 3ha. *Produce: 600,000 bottles.* VP-R and N.

This vigneron and négociant produces a wide range of single vineyard Sancerre, producing red, rosé and white wines from their own vineyard and from bought-in grapes. Their finest wine is the very dry white Carte d'Or la Perrière. White wines are made in stainless steel, but wood is used to age the reds. A small amount of Pouilly-Fumé La Toge aux Moines is also made from bought-in grapes. *Open: Mon–Fri 2:30–6pm; Holidays (April–Sept) 2:30–7pm. Appointments necessary for groups.*

Bernard Bailly-Reverdy et Fils

Bué, 18300 Sancerre. Vineyards owned: Sancerre: Sauvignon 10ha; Pinot Noir 7ha. *Produce: 75,000 bottles.* VP-R.

Red wines are a speciality with this firm, aged partly in new wood, giving a surprisingly spicy, rich result, which is sold two years after the vintage. The white wine, Clos du Chêne Marchand, is fermented slowly at a controlled temperature, giving considerable flavour and fruit. Other wines sold under Domaine de la Mercy-Dieu. *Open: By appointment only.*

Bernard Balland et Fils

Bué, 18300 Sancerre. Vineyards owned: Sancerre: Sauvignon 13ha; Pinot Noir 4ha. *Produce: 100,000 bottles.* VP-R.

An old-established firm (1730) with new ideas. Treatment of the wine is kept to a minimum with modern equipment. Two whites – Le Grand Chemarin and Le Clos d'Ervocs are bottled separately; a red, Les Marnes, is in a modern style. The whites are fresh and very fragrant, the red less interesting. *Open: By appointment only.*

Roger Champault (Domaine de Colombier)

Crézancy en Sancerre, 18300 Sancerre. Vineyards owned: Sauvignon 6.8ha; Pinot Noir 3.8ha. *Produce: 80,000 bottles.* VP-R.

An old-established vineyard which has been in the Champault family for generations. They produce traditional wines, which see some wood before bottling. Domaine de Colombier is the main vineyard, but the family also owns land in Clos du Roy, Moulin à Vent and Côte de Champtus (all in Crézancy). *Open: By appointment only.*

Lucien Crochet

Place de l'Eglise, Bué, 18300 Sancerre. Vineyard owned: Bué, Crézancy, Sancerre: Sauvignon 15ha; Pinot Noir 5ha. *Produce: 250,000 bottles.* VP-R and N.

A family firm with holdings in some of the best Sancerre vineyards: Chêne Marchand and Grand Chemarin for white; Clos du Roy for red. About 40% of production is from bought-in grapes and must, 60% from their own vineyards. The quality of the wines is sound rather than exciting, but the single-vineyard Chêne Marchand has great character. *Open: No.*

Vincent Delaporte

Chavignol, 18300 Sancerre. Vineyards owned: Chavignol and Sancerre: Sauvignon 10ha; Pinot Noir 3ha. *Produce: 80,000 bottles.* VP-R.

A top quality producer, especially for his whites from Chavignol, which age unusually well for Sancerre. One of his best wines comes from the Clos Beaujeu. The reds tend to be quite tannic when young, and benefit from some ageing. White wines are produced in modern stainless steel, reds are aged in wood. *Open: By appointment only.*

Fournier Père et Fils

Verdigny, 18300 Sancerre. Vineyards owned: Sauvignon 12ha; Pinot Noir 3ha. *Produce: 480,000 bottles.* VP-R and N.

Cave des Chaumières is the brand name for the estate white, red and rosé Sancerre made by this firm of growers and négociants. They use only stainless steel and their wines are light, fruity and immediately attractive. The négociant wines go under a whole range of marques: Léon Vatan, Célestin Blondeau, Patient Cottat, Henry de Chanvre, Charles Dupuy. They also use Sauvignon grapes to make a Vin de Pays de Jardin de la France. *Open: Appointments preferred.*

Michel Girard

18300 Verdigny en Sancerre. Vineyards owned: Sancerre 6ha. *Produce: 60,000 bottles.* VP-R.

A traditional producer, whose best white, Clos les Perriere, is very lively when young. A quarter of the production is of red and rosé wines. The red is aged in wood, giving it some roundness. A son is in the process of joining the business, assuring continuity. *Open: By appointment only.*

Gitton Père et Fils

Chemin de Lavaud, Ménétréol, 18300 Sancerre. Vineyards owned: Sancerre: Sauvignon 18.7ha; Pinot Noir 1.6ha. Pouilly-sur-Loire: Sauvignon 9ha. *Produce: 280,000 bottles.* VP-R.

One of the larger landowners in the area, from holdings built up since World War II. The firm specializes in separate bottlings for different holdings. Fruit from young vines is vinified in stainless steel, that from old vines in wood. There are 10 different Sancerre (including two reds) and five different Pouilly-Fumé. The wines retain the characteristics of the different vineyards to a considerable degree. *Open: Mon–Fri 8am–noon; 2–6pm. Sat 9am–noon.*

Château de Maimbray

Sury-en-Vaux, 18300 Sancerre. Vineyards owned: Sancerre: Sauvignon 8.4ha; Pinot Noir 3.6ha. *Produce: 70,000 bottles.* VP-R.

The château is owned by the Roblin family, who produce an absolutely true-to-type white, clean, racy and full of flavour. Vinification takes place in stainless steel, with some wood ageing for the small production of reds. Some impressive winemaking. *Open: By appointment only.*

Paul Millérioux

Champtin, 18300 Crézancy-en-Sancerre. Vineyards owned: Sauvignon 10ha; Pinot Noire 3ha. *Produce: 100,000 bottles.* VP-R.

A top class producer whose Clos du Roy white has a surprising ability (for a Sancerre) to age. M. Millerioux' vineyards are ideally situated in the northern slopes of Sancerre facing south and southwest. His red Sancerre, Côte de Champtin, also has good ageing ability. Both red and white mature for a while in wood. *Open: Mon–Sat 8am–noon; 2–8pm.*

Roger Neveu (Domaine du Colombier)

18300 Verdigny-en-Sancerre. Vineyards owned: Sancerre: Sauvignon 8ha; Pinot Noir 2ha. *Produce: 55,000 bottles.* VP-R.

Established in the 18th century, a family firm run by father and two sons. The white is Clos des Bouffants, the red Domaine du

Colombier. The white tends to be quite delicate in style. As with many other producers in Sancerre, old and new techniques are combined in the winery. *Open: Mon–Fri, during working hours.*

Paul Prieur et Fils

Verdigny, 18300 Sancerre. Vineyards owned: Sancerre: Sauvignon 6ha; Pinot Noir 4ha.
Produce: 80,000 bottles. VP-R.

Family firm which owns one part of the best Sancerre vineyards, les Monts Damnés, giving a particularly elegant wine from chalky soil. The red and rosé come from the gravelly Pichon vineyard in Verdigny and they place great emphasis on the red, which they exported to England in the last century. I prefer the white. *Open: By appointment only.*

Jean Reverdy et Fils (Domaine des Villots)

Verdigny, 18300 Sancerre. Vineyards owned: Sancerre: Sauvignon 5.5ha; Pinot Noir 2ha.
Produce: 60,000 bottles. VP-R.

This family firm was established in 1646. Today, it owns the whole of the Clos de la Reine Blanche vineyard at Verdigny. The white wines age attractively and their smooth fruit can certainly sustain four or five years' cellaring. The red also gives plenty of fruit and a surprising depth of colour. *Open: By appointment only.*

Pierre and Etienne Riffault

Chaudoux, Verdigny, 18300 Sancerre. Vineyards owned: Verdigny: Sauvignon 9ha; Pinot Noir 1ha.
Produce: 90,000 bottles. VP-R.

Soft fruit characterizes the wines from this small family firm. The wines are attractive if unexciting; the red, with a touch of new wood on the palate, has more character than the white. Modern, low-temperature fermentation is used for the white wine, while the red is partly aged in stainless steel, partly in wood. *Open: By appointment only.*

Domaine Jean-Max Roger

Bué, 18300 Sancerre. Vineyards owned: Sancerre: Sauvignon 10.4ha; Pinot Noir 2.6ha. Ménetou-Salon: Sauvignon 4ha.
Produce: 200,000 bottles. VP-R and N.

40% of the production from this firm is from grapes and wines which are bought in. Principal holdings in Sancerre are in Le Grand Chemarin and Le Chêne Marchand. In Ménetou-Salon, the small holding is at Morogues in Le Petit Clos. Quality is average, with Le Grand Chemarin the best Sancerre. But the Ménetou-Salon is probably the most attractive white wine. *Open: By appointment only.*

Château de Sancerre

18300 Sancerre. Vineyards owned: Sauvignon 19ha.
Produce: 150,000 bottles. VP-R.

The old château at Sancerre is now owned by the company which produces the Grand Marnier liqueur. Here, though, they make a white Sancerre, using mainly stainless steel, with 20% of the wine matured briefly in wood. The style is modern with few pretensions. *Open: No.*

Domaine Thomas et Fils

Chaudoux, Verdigny, 18300 Sancerre. Vineyards owned:
Verdigny: Sauvignon 6.8ha; Pinot Noir 1.2ha.
Produce: 60,000 bottles. VP-R.

The best wine from this house is the white Clos de la Crele,
while the Clos Terres Blanches is flintier and more austere. The
1983 red, aged in wood, was mellow and soft and had good
colour. White wines, made in stainless steel at a low temperature, are bottled immediately. *Open: By appointment only.*

Domaine Vacheron

1 Rue du Puits Poulton, 18300 Sancerre. Vineyards owned:
Sancerre 20ha. *Produce: 130,000 bottles.* VP-R.

Top quality wines come out of the Vacheron cellars in the
centre of Sancerre, one of the most popular visits for tourists.
Wines can be tasted at le Grenier à Sel in the town during the
summer months. The reds are the stars with this firm – although
the whites are of high quality as well. The reds can age
remarkably – a 1975 was still tasting too young at 11 years old.
Some red is aged in new wood and all red is kept in small barrels
for a year. *Open: Mon–Fri 9am–noon; 3–7pm. Appointments
necessary for groups.*

André Vatan

Chaudoux, Verdigny, 18300 Sancerre. Vineyards owned:
St-Satur 2ha; Verdigny 2ha. *Produce: 20,000 bottles.* VP-R.

Unusually among Sancerrois, M. Vatan only makes white wine,
using modern stainless steel equipment. His wines are full of life
and fruit and he has obviously learnt much from his father, Jean
Vatan, with whom he has also worked. *Open: By appointment
only.*

Upper Loire: Côtes du Forez

Les Vignerons Foreziens

Trelins, 42130 Boen-sur-Lignon. Vineyards owned: Côtes du
Forez 200ha; Vin de Pays d'Urfé 100ha.
Produce: 800,000 bottles. Coop (250 members).

The cooperative dominates the tiny Côtes du Forez VDQS
region. The red, mainly from Gamay, is made with some
carbonic maceration in a sub-Beaujolais style, to be drunk
young and chilled. The two top wines are a Cuvée de Prestige
and the explosively named Cuvée Volcanique. A small amount
of rosé is made from Pinot Noir, some of it medium-dry. *Open:
By appointment only.*

Upper Loire: Coteaux du Giennois

Alain Paulat

Villemoison, Saint-Père, 58200 Cosne-sur-Loire. Vineyards
owned: Villemoison 5.5ha. *Produce: 45,000 bottles.* VP-R.

M. Paulat practices organic farming and winemaking in his
small holding, while using modern equipment in his cellars. He
makes a light, fresh white from Sauvignon and a rosé from Pinot
Noir and Gamay (80%). The red Réserve Traditionnelle is a
more serious affair, made from Pinot Noir and aged for up to 18
months in large barrels, it needs at least four to five years for

maturity. If any wines will ensure the survival of this small appellation, here they are. *Open: Mon–Fri 8am–9pm. Appointments necessary for groups.*

Jean Poupat et Fils

47 Rue Georges Clemenceau, 45500 Gien. Vineyards owned: Gien 7ha. *Produce: 35,000 bottles.* VP-R.

A Gamay-based red is the main production here, with small amounts of rosé and white. The white, from Sauvignon, is the best of the three and has something of the character of Sancerre in its crispness and liveliness. *Open: By appointment only.*

Upper Loire: Côtes Roannaises

Pierre Gaume

Les Gillets, 42155 Lentigny. Vineyards owned: Lentigny 1.5ha. *Produce: 10,000 bottles.* VP-R.

Simple Gamay wines are made using both stainless steel and wood. M. Gaume makes a red and rosé from the VDQS Côtes Roannaises and also a Gamay rosé Vin de Pays d'Urfe. All his wines are lively, with plenty of cherried fruit. *Open: By appointment only.*

Maurice Lutz (Domaine de Pavillon)

42820 Ambierle. Vineyards owned: Côtes Roannaises 5ha. *Produce: 24,000 bottles.* VP-R.

A Gamay wine, made using semi-carbonic maceration techniques to give plenty of strawberry fruit and colour, is the bulk of M. Lutz's production. He also makes a little soft, fruity rosé, also from Gamay. *Open: Mon–Sun.*

Upper Loire: St-Pourçain

Union des Vignerons

Quai de la Ronde, 03500 Saint-Pourçain-sur-Sioule. Vineyards owned: 300ha of Gamay, Pinot Noir, Chardonnay, Sauvignon, Tressalier. *Produce: 1.5 million bottles.* Coop (200 members).

This is by far the biggest production unit in St-Pourçain and, luckily, methods are good and the wines are reliable examples. The bulk of production is of red, made from Gamay and a little Pinot Noir. Rosés include a *vin gris* from Gamay. Standard whites are made using the local Tressalier grape, but the top quality wine is made from Sauvignon and Chardonnay (50/50). There is also a *méthode champenoise* sparkling, Anne de Bourbon. *Open: Mon–Fri 8am–noon; 2–4pm. Appointments preferred.*

Ray Père et Fils

Saulcet, 08600 St-Pourçain-sur-Sioule. Vineyards owned: Saulcet 8ha in red and white. *Produce: 65,000 bottles.* VP-R.

One of the best St-Pourçain producers, concentrating on a Gamay/Pinot Noir red which takes two or three years' ageing. The white is soft with a high Chardonnay content (50%) and a touch of Sauvignon to balance the rather bland Tressalier. The rosé, from Gamay, is a very fresh style, which needs to be drunk young. Modern techniques are used in the cellars. *Open: By appointment only.*

Touraine

Jacques Bonnigal

17 Rue d'Enfer, Limeray, 37530 Amboise. Vineyards owned: Limeray 10ha. *Produce: 40,000 bottles.* VP-R.

M. Bonnigal's traditional techniques produce an excellent red Touraine-Amboise, Cuvée François I, a blend of Gamay, Cot (Malbec) and Cabernet Franc, which needs three or four years for maturity. He also makes an average Sauvignon and a honeyed medium sweet still white from the Chenin Blanc. A small proportion of this production is of a *méthode champenoise* wine from Chenin: he's planting Chardonnay for future blending in this wine, so it should improve. *Open: Mon–Fri 8am–7pm. Appointments necessary for groups.*

Philippe Brossillon

Domaine de Lusqueneau, Mesland, 41150 Onzain. Vineyards owned: Mesland 18ha; Mouteaux 10ha; Onzain 2ha. *Produce: 150,000 bottles.* VP-R.

A 200-year-old family firm which still relies on traditional practices, apart from mechanical harvesting. All the Domaine de Lusqueneau lies in the Touraine-Mesland AC area and most of the production is of red, with small amounts of rosé and white, and two sparklers – a rosé and a white. Some of the reds (90% Gamay, 10% Cot and Cabernet) are now aged in wood, giving extra longevity. *Open: Appointments preferred.*

Pierre Chainier (Château de la Roche)

Chargé, 37530 Amboise. Vineyards owned: Chargé 30ha; Pocé 35ha. *Produce: 8 million bottles.* VP–R and N.

Besides owning two estates in the Amboise district, this firm runs a big négociant business, buying in 80% of its requirements. A full range of Touraine wines is made, of which the Touraine-Amboise from the Château de Pocé is the best. Also made is Vin de Pays du Jardin de la France, the general Loire vin de pays. Another name used is Philippe de Guerois. *Open: No.*

Confrèrie des Vignerons de Oisly et Thésée

Oisly, 41700 Contres. Vineyards owned: 275ha. *Produce: 1.8 million bottles.* Coop (50 members).

This is generally regarded as the best cooperative on the Loire, and one of the best in France. It was started in 1961 in an attempt to improve the quality of the Touraine wines and strict quality control is practised, with below standard grapes being sold off. The wines – especially the Gamay de Touraine, Cabernet de Touraine and white Sauvignon de Touraine are top quality examples of what Touraine can produce given a little more effort. Vinification is mainly in stainless steel, but some reds do spend a time in wood. Blended wines carry the brand name Baronnie d'Aignan. A creamy white sparkling Crémant de la Loire is made using Pinot Noir, Cabernet Franc and Chenin Blanc. *Open: By appointments only.*

Jean-François Dehelly

Les Archambaults, 37800 Sainte-Marie-de-Touraine. Vineyards owned: Les Archambaults 1.5ha. *Produce: 10,000 bottles.* VP-R.

The majority of the small production from this long-established firm is of a top quality red Touraine made from Cabernet Franc. One wine is made exclusively from old vines. 20% is of rosé, both still and *pétillant*. All go under the name Le Clos Neuf des Archambaults. *Open: By appointment only.*

Domaine Dutertre

20/21 Rue d'Enfer, 37530 Limeray. Vineyards owned: Touraine Amboise 30ha. *Produce: 100,000 bottles.* VP-R.

Most of the wines from this firm come under the Touraine Amboise AC, although there is also a sparkling Touraine Crémant. The style for the whites and rosés – made using the full range of Loire grapes – is modern, clean and fresh. Reds, however, are made traditionally and see some time in wood, which gives them good ageing potential. Cot, Cabernet Franc and Gamay are used in the blend. *Open: By appointment only.*

Jean-Mary Duvoux

Le Pernas, Ange, 41400 Montrichard. Vineyards owned: Ange 10ha. *Produce: 40,000 bottles.* VP-R.

The best wine to come from Duvoux is his Cabernet – made traditionally with a long, slow fermentation. Lots of cherry-like fruit and some tannin: a wine that needs time to develop. He also makes a semi-carbonic maceration Gamay which needs to be drunk young, a Cabernet Rosé and an attractive grassy Sauvignon. White and rosé *méthode champenoise* (white from Chenin Blanc) also come out of this small family firm. He has just set up a group of 20 small producers from along the Loire to coordinate export activities. *Open: By appointment only.*

Domaine de la Gabillière

13 Route de Blère, 37400 Amboise. Vineyards owned: Touraine-Amboise and Touraine 15ha. *Produce: 60,000 bottles.* VP-R.

The domaine, set around an 18th century château, is one of the French Ministry of Agriculture's viticultural training schools. A red and white are made in the Touraine-Amboise AC area, the red mainly from Gamay and Malbec with a little Cabernet Franc, the white from Chenin Blanc. A *méthode champenoise* Crémant de la Loire is made from Chenin and Chardonnay and a sparkling Touraine from 10% Chenin. All the wines are (as expected) extremely correct. *Open: By appointment only.*

Vincent Girault (Clos Château Gaillard)

41150 Mesland. Vineyards owned: Mesland 6ha. *Produce: 70,000 bottles.* VP-R.

Red wines of the Touraine-Mesland AC are the speciality of this house. The best red is Vieilles Vignes Tradition, a blend of Gamay, Cabernet Franc and Malbec. 100% Gamay wines tend to be rather short and light, although well made. A small amount of rosé is also made. One of M. Girault's stars is his dry Crémant de la Loire, Les Doucinières, full of soft, smooth Chenin fruit. *Open: Mon–Fri 8am–noon; 2–6pm.*

Domaines Girault-Artois

7 Quai des Violettes, 37400 Amboise. Vineyards owned: Mesland 28ha. *Produce: 250,000 bottles.* VP-R.

Modern techniques dominate this large estate which makes the full range of Touraine-Mesland wines. Stainless steel, mechanical harvesting and temperature control are all brought into play. They are best at a crisp Sauvignon white, Domaine des Buttelières, and the carbonic maceration Gamay Jeunes Vignes, Domaine d'Artois. *Open: Appointments preferred.*

Lucien Launay

Ange, 41400 Montrichard. Vineyards owned: Ange 10ha. *Produce: 80,000 bottles.* VP-R.

A full range of Touraine wines are made by this firm, of which the majority is from Cabernet Franc and Gamay. Other grape varieties are Pineau Aunis and Sauvignon. M. Launay also makes *méthode champenoise* wines. *Open: Mon–Sun.*

Jean Louet

3 Rue de la Paix, Monthou-sur-Bièvre, 41120 Les Montils. Vineyards owned: 8ha. *Produce: 30,000 bottles.*

Out of this tiny vineyard come a top class Cabernet/Gamay/Cot red, Tradition, and a clean, fragrant Sauvignon Blanc. The red is definitely a wine to keep for two or three years – a 1978 was tasting at its peak in 1985. M. Louet makes the full range of Touraine AC wines, including a Chenin-based *méthode champenoise* and a rosé from Gamay. He is president of the Syndicat of the Touraine AC. *Open: By appointment only.*

Henry Marionnet (Domaine de la Charmoise)

Soings, 41230 Mur-de-Sologne. Vineyards owned: Soings 45ha. *Produce: 400,000 bottles.* VP-R.

Gamay and Sauvignon are the two principal vine varieties on this large estate, and they make a red from the Gamay and a still white. A rosé is blended from Pineau d'Aunis, Cot and Cabernet Franc. The approach is modern and the Gamay is treated to carbonic maceration to bring out the colour. Everything is done in stainless steel. *Open: By appointment only.*

Jean and Jacky Martineau

La Tesniere, Pouille, 41110 St-Aignan. Vineyards owned: 11ha. *Produce: 75,000 bottles.* VP-R.

Cabernet Franc, Sauvignon and Gamay are the main wines from this estate. The wines are sold under the name of Jacky Marineau. *Open: By appointment only.*

Domaine Christian Mauduit

Le Mechimière, Mareuil-sur-Cher, 41110 St-Aignan. Vineyards owned: 14ha. *Produce: 100,000 bottles.* VP-R.

Modern techniques of temperature control are used to make a clean-tasting Sauvignon, and future vineyard expansion will concentrate mainly on this vine variety. The reds and rosés are less successful. *Open: Mon–Fri. Appointments preferred.*

J-M Monmousseau

41400 Montrichard. Vineyards owned: 62ha. *Produce: 1.7 million bottles.* VP-R and N.

Most of the production from this firm, now owned by the Champagne house of Taittinger, is of sparkling wine made by the *méthode champenoise*. Brand names used include Brut de Mosny, JM Rosé and the top *cuvée* JM93. The wines are aged in large chalk cellars dug out of cliffs above the river Cher at Montrichard. *Open: In working hours.*

Domaine Yves Moreau

Fleuray, Cangey, 37530 Amboise. Vineyards owned:
Touraine-Amboise 4.9ha; Touraine-Mesland 3ha; Touraine
1.85ha. *Produce: 30,000 bottles.*

The Touraine-Amboise red, Cuvée François I, made from
Gamay (60%), Cabernet (20%) and Cot (20%) is the star from
this old family firm, founded in 1847. The Touraine-Mesland,
from 100% Gamay, is well-made, but just misses that top
quality. M. Moreau also makes a small quantity of a white
Sauvignon Touraine. These are true fine wines: vinification is
in the former village church. *Open: By appointment only.*

Gaston Pavy

La Basse-Chevrière, Saché, 37190 Azay-le-Rideau. Vineyards
owned: 3ha. *Produce: 13,500 bottles.* VP-R.

The top name in the Touraine-Azay-le-Rideau AC, operating
since 1890. M. Pavy makes only two wines. A white from
Chenin Blanc can be dry but also in good years lusciously sweet.
A rosé – made in tiny quantities – is from a blend of Grolleau,
Cot and Cabernet Sauvignon which ages well. Both wines are
matured in wood for two to three months which brings out
considerable depths – especially in the whites. *Open: By
appointment only.*

Gaston Pibaleau

Luré, 37190 Azay-le-Rideau. Vineyards owned: Azay-le-
Rideau 7.2ha. *Produce: 12,000 bottles.*

This is a young firm, which has adopted traditional techniques
– vinifying in wood, for example. This approach surprisingly
benefits the white and rosé as much as the red: the white,
especially, is a wine that needs some ageing, being characteristi-
cally acid in youth and developing honeyed depths in older
vintages. A small amount of white and rosé *méthode
champenoise* is also made. *Open: Appointments preferred.*

Jacky Preys

Le Bois Pontois, 41130 Meusnes. Vineyards owned: Touraine
46ha; Valencay 20ha. *Produce: 300,000 bottles.* VP-R.

With vineyard holdings in the Touraine AC and Valençay, this
large grower is able to produce a full range of wines, using
Sauvignon and Pinot Blanc in white; Gamay, Cabernet Franc,
Cot in red and rosé. They also make a Crémant de Loire. Plans
are to plant Pinot Noir and Chardonnay which should give
some interesting results. *Open: By appointment only.*

Jean-Jacques Sard

La Chambrière, 37320 Esvres. Vineyards owned: 1ha.
Produce: 3,000 bottles. VP-R.

M. Sard makes only one wine: a fine dry rosé, Noble Joué,
described by the producer as a *vin gris*, made from free-run juice
which is then put back on to the skins for 24 hours and then
fermented in wood. It is pale salmon-pink in colour and very
fresh to taste. Noble Joué is an old term for this style of wine and
a number of producers in the area are aiming to revive it. Pinot
Meunier is the main grape, with additions of Pinot Gris and
Pinot Noir. M. Sard has another 14 hectares (owned since 1976)
which he is developing. *Open: By appointment only.*

Touraine: Chinon and Bourgueil

Claude Ammeux

La Contrie, St-Nicholas-de-Bourgueil, 37140 Bourgueil.
Vineyards owned: St-Nicholas-de-Bourgueil 4.5ha.
Produce: 25,000 bottles.

This estate has a small production of high quality St-Nicholas-de-Bourgueil, made from 30-year-old vines. Fermentation is in stainless steel, but the wines are aged in wood, giving them considerable flavour and quite high alcohol. Consequently the wines need more time to mature than is usual in St-Nicholas, however the wait is worth it. *Open: By appointment only.*

Audebert et Fils

Avenue Jean Causeret, 37140 Bourgueil. Vineyards owned:
Bourgueil 26ha; St-Nicholas-de-Bourgueil 4ha.
Produce: 400,000 bottles. VP-R and N.

One of the biggest producers in Bourgueil and St-Nicholas, their own vineyards supply about 30% of their needs. They make wines in stainless steel for early drinking, which go mainly to local restaurants and elsewhere in France. The main brand they sell is Domaine du Grand Clos Bourgueil, and they also sell the smaller brand of Vignoble les Marquises. The wines from St-Nicholas are sold under the brand name La Contrie. *Open: Mon–Fri 8am–noon; 1:30–6:30pm. Appointments preferred.*

Pierre Caslot

Le Domaine de la Chevalerie, Restigné, 37140 Bourgueil.
Vineyards owned: Bourgueil 18ha.
Produce: 53,000 bottles. VP-R.

This family firm has been making wine here since 1650 – descending from father to son. Today, they have introduced some stainless steel into their attractive old cellars, and do half the fermentation in the new style, and half still in wood, blending together later. The wine is traditional in style and ages well, rich and with a good colour. *Open: Appointments preferred.*

Guy Caille

37220 Panzoult. Vineyards owned: Chinon 10ha.
Produce: 30,000 bottles. VP-R.

M. Caille makes red and rosé Chinon in traditional style from his Vignoble de la Poelerie. His rosé is a find – often better in cool years such as 1984, crisp fresh and delicate in flavour. The red is firmer, made in wood and can last quite some time. *Open: By appointment only.*

Caslot-Galbrun

La Hurolaie, Benais, 37140 Bourgueil. Vineyards owned:
11 ha. *Produce: 30,000 bottles.* VP-R.

A long-established producer whose wines have considerable depth and quality. Although fermentation is now in stainless steel, all the wines see some wood. They always seem to need some years before being attractively drinkable: in their youth they have deep colour and a fair amount of stalky tannin. *Open: By appointment only.*

Max Cognard-Taluau

Chevrette, St-Nicholas-de-Bourgueil, 37140 Bourgueil.
Vineyards owned: St-Nicholas 7ha.
Produce: 50,000 bottles. VP-R.

There are two qualities of wine coming from this producer: a standard St-Nicholas wine – red or rosé – firm but full of fruit, for reasonably early drinking. And a more serious red from older vines, called Les Malgagnes. Even with this wine, though, the fruit comes through well. *Open: Mon–Fri 9am–7pm.*

Anne-Marie Donabella (Domaine du Roncée)

Panzoult, 37220 Ile-Bouchard. Vineyards owned:
Chinon 25ha. *Produce: 130,000 bottles.* VP-R.

A considerable holding, established in 1964, making light soft reds and rosés, most of which are for early drinking. Some, from older vines in Le Clos des Marronniers and Le Clos des Folies are aged in wood for a short period to give greater longevity and some depth. *Open: By appointment only.*

Couly-Dutheil

12 Rue Diderot, 37502 Chinon. Vineyards owned: Chinon
39ha. *Produce: 700,000 bottles.* VP-R and N.

Mainly modern-style wines, from the flat plain of Chinon, under the names Domaine de Turpenay and Domaine René Couly. But there are quantities of finer wines, for ageing, from Clos de l'Echo and Clos de l'Olive on the higher plateau vineyards. Vinification and techniques are modern here, and the only traditional sights are the 11th century *caves*. The winemaker, Jacques Puisais, is a local consultant who works for other producers. The firm acts as négociant for other Touraine red and white wines and Saumur-Champigny. *Open: By appointment only.*

René Gouron et Fils

Cravant-les-Coteaux, 37500 Chinon. Vineyards owned:
Chinon 18ha. *Produce: 100,000 bottles.* VP-R.

Stainless steel fermentation and ageing in wood keeps these wines clean and ready to drink comparatively young. The quality is high. Sparkling and still rosé are also produced. *Open: By appointment only.*

Anselme et Marc Jamet

Clos du Vigneau, 37140 St-Nicholas-de-Bourgueil. Vineyards
owned: St-Nicholas 20ha. *Produce: 40,000 bottles.*

The low productive figure from the comparatively large vineyard gives a clue to the age (25 years) of the vines in this old family holding, founded in 1847. While they are attractive in a cool, stalky way when young, the wines (all red St-Nicholas) improve with some ageing. Methods are traditional with some fermentation in wood, although stainless steel has also put in an appearance. *Open: By appointment only.*

Pierre Jamet et Fils

Le Fondis, St-Nicholas-de-Bourgueil, 37140 Bourgueil.
Vineyards owned: St-Nicholas 20ha.
Produce: 80,000 bottles. VP-R.

Of the two Jamet firms (see above), this is the more modern

operating only since 1970 and making wines which can be drunk young and fresh. There is a small quantity of Cabernet Sauvignon in the vineyard which tends to give the wine some body and tannin. The firm is likely to expand into the négociant business. *Open: Mon–Fri, appointments preferred.*

Lame-Delille-Boucard

37140 Ingrandes de Touraine. Vineyards owned: Bourgueil 28ha. *Produce: 150,000 bottles.*

A traditional firm, using wood for vinification and leaving the red Bourgueil for up to three years in wood. They have been experimenting with new clones of Cabernet Franc to improve quality at the expense of yield (a rare phenomenon – to be applauded). A small amount of Bourgueil rosé is made from Cabernet Sauvignon, and a Rosé de Touraine is made from Grolleau and Gamay. A red Vin de Pays du Jardin de la France is also produced. The brand name is Domaine des Chesnaies. *Open: No.*

Jean-Claude Mabileau

La Jarnoterie, St-Nicholas-de-Bourgueil, 37140 Bourgueil. Vineyards owned: St-Nicholas 10ha. *Produce: 25,000 bottles.* VP-R.

M. Mabileau makes a light red, from vineyards on the coteaux of St-Nicholas, using carbonic maceration techniques and vinifying in cement tanks, subsequently passing them through wood for a short period. Although they can be drunk young, he argues that they will age for anything up to 30 years and has old vintages in his spectacular tufa cellars back to 1893 to prove his point. *Open: By appointment only.*

Jean-Paul Mabileau

St-Nicholas-de-Bourgueil, 37140 Bourgueil. Vineyards owned: St-Nicholas 14ha. *Produce: 70,000 bottles.* VP-R.

Red and rosé are made here, under the name Domaine du Bourg. The red has been highly praised and it is claimed to age well. *Open: By appointment only.*

Pierre Manzagol

Domaine de la Noblaie, Ligré, 37500 Chinon. Vineyards owned: Chinon 8ha. *Produce: 50,000 bottles.* VP-R.

This is one of the few firms to make a little white Chinon, using Chenin Blanc. The style is more of an Anjou than a Touraine wine, initially a hard, acid wine which demands ageing. The red is aged in wood and considered at its best after 10 years. The vineyard is high on the coteaux of Chinon on the left bank of the Vienne river. *Open: By appointment only.*

James Morisseau

Domaine de la Caillardière, St-Nicholas-de-Bourgueil, 37140 Bourgueil. Vineyards owned: St-Nicholas 12ha. *Produce: 20,000 bottles.*

An old established (1840) firm with vineyards on the coteaux of St-Nicholas, which has just moved into the modern age with temperature control and some stainless steel. The wines tend to have some tannin when young and need at least four to five years before they open out. M. Morisseau only makes a red wine. *Open: By appointment only.*

Plouzeau et Fils (Château de la Bonnelière)

37500 Chinon. Vineyards owned: Touraine 20ha; Chinon 3ha. *Produce: 900,000 bottles.* VP-R and N.

The biggest firm in Chinon, making wines from all over Touraine and Anjou. Their own vineyards (once owned by the Duc de Richelieu) produce Sauvignon de Touraine and Cabernet de Touraine, plus a small quantity of an early-drinking style Chinon. Other wines which they handle are Saumur-Champigny, Cabernet d'Anjou, Vouvray, Saumur and Coteaux du Layon. Few excitements here. *Open: Mon–Fri 9am–noon; 2–6pm. Appointments necessary for groups.*

Clos des Quarterons-Amirault

St-Nicholas-de-Bourgueil, 37140 Bourgueil. Vineyards owned: St-Nicholas 20ha. *Produce: 100,000 bottles.* VP-R.

Clos de Quarterons is the name of the single red St-Nicholas produced by this family firm, founded in 1893. The wine is kept in the tufa *caves* for up to 12 months and are at their best after four years. Another cuvée is given a short fermentation and sold at Easter as a "Vin de Pâques". *Open: Appointments preferred.*

Jean-Maurice Raffault

La Croix, Savigny-en-Véron, 37420 Avoin. Vineyards owned: Chinon 35ha. *Produce: 200,000 bottles.* VP-R.

One of the great characters of Chinon (and one of its chief propagandists), M. J-M Raffault specializes in wines with considerable ageing ability. His enormous tufa *caves* are stacked high with old casks of maturing wines – back to the 1940s and 1950s – which are still extraordinarily drinkable in a mature way. M. Raffault's family vineyard holdings date back to 1693. He vinifies, matures and bottles wines separately from his different holdings. Different *crus* include Les Picasses, Domaine d'Isore, Le Clos du Gallon and Le Clos des Lutinières. *Open: Appointments preferred.*

Domaine Thouet-Bosseau

37140 Bourgueil. Vineyards owned: Bourgueil 12ha. *Produce: 70,000 bottles.* VP-R.

The firm owns two estates, of which the more famous is the Clos de l'Abbaye. Here vines (average age 38 years) produce excellent Cabernet Franc Bourgueil. Made partly in wood and partly in stainless steel it is then blended and can age for up to 10 years. In Restigne, the five-hectare Domaine Thouet-Bosseau makes a lighter style of wine, using more stainless steel and extracting considerable freshness. *Open: By appointment only.*

Touraine: Cheverny

Bernard & François Cazin

Le Petit Chambord, 41700 Cheverny. Vineyards owned: Cheverny 12ha. *Produce: 50,000 bottles.* VP-R.

The bulk of production is of a fruity carbonic maceration Gamay, but there is also a small quantity of the rare white from the Romorantin grape. Look also for the well-made *méthode champenoise* from Chardonnay. Other wines made include still whites from Sauvignon and Chardonnay, and a rosé and red from Pinot Noir. *Open: By appointment only.*

Domaine Gendrier

Les Huards, 41700 Cour-Cheverny. Vineyards owned:
Cheverny 21.5ha. *Produce: 100,000 bottles.* VP-R.

A modern cellar producing mainly white wines (half of
Romorantin, half of Sauvignon). There is also a less astringent
Romorantin-based wine, Cuvée François I (François was the
King who introduced the grape to the area). Reds come from
Gamay and Pinot Noir and there is a top *cuvée*, Cuvée de
Trophée, which blends the two. One of the most important
firms in the area. *Open: Mon–Fri 8am–8pm.*

Touraine: Jasnières

Jean-Baptiste Pinon

12 Promenade du Tertre, 41800 Montoire-sur-Loir.
Vineyards owned: Jasnières 4.5ha; Coteaux du Vendômois
1ha; Vouvray 1ha. *Produce: 25,000 bottles.*

This may be a small holding of Jasnières – but it represents
about a tenth of the appellation total. M. Pinon's wine is dry,
almost harsh when young, and matures slowly. The small
portion of Coteaux du Vendômois produces a red from Gamay
and Pineau d'Aunis, and a little medium-dry Vouvray com-
pletes the range. *Open: By appointment only.*

Touraine: Vouvray and Montlouis

Berger Frères

135 Rue de Chenonceaux, Saint Martin le Beau, 37270
Montlouis-sur-Loire. Vineyards owned: St Martin 20ha.
Produce: 100,000 bottles. VP-R.

A well-run, modern firm which makes some attractive wines.
The demi-sec Montlouis is particularly good in better years,
and the Pétillant is lighter than the same style of wine in
Vouvray. They make a Crémant de Loire from Chenin Blanc,
Chardonnay and Cabernet Franc, which is aged for two to three
years in bottle before release. *Open: Appointments preferred.*

Bernard Bongars

Coteau de Venise, Noizay, 37210 Vouvray. Vineyards
owned: Vouvray 6.6ha; Touraine 0.4ha.
Produce: 36,000 bottles. VP-R.

Still and *pétillant* Vouvray is made by this family producer
whose vineyards in Noizay are at the eastern end of the Vouvray
AC area. Fermentation is in wood, producing dry and medium-
dry styles. A small amount of *pétillant* rosé, AC Touraine, is
produced. *Open: By appointment only.*

Claude Boureau

1 Rue de la Résistance, 37270 St-Martin-le-Beau. Vineyards
owned: Montlouis 5ha. *Produce: 25,000 bottles.* VP-R.

A traditional producer who ferments his wine in wood, and
makes high quality still and sparkling Montlouis. The wine can
be either dry or medium sweet (in good years) – and it ages well
"the more it ages, the better it is", says M. Boureau. He also
produces Touraine rouge from Cabernet Franc, rosé (Cot and
Grosleau) and white (Sauvignon). *Open: By appointment only.*

G. Delétang et Fils

St-Martin-le-Beau, 37270 Montlouis. Vineyards owned:
Montlouis 12ha; Touraine 6ha. *Produce: 100,000 bottles.* VP-R.

The cellars of M. Delétang in the centre of St-Martin-le-Beau
are filled with old bottles of wine gathering cobwebs. But
modern techniques have been applied to fermentation. His still
Montlouis can be dry or sweet, depending on the quality of the
year. The sparkling wine is aged for two years in bottle before
sale and is slightly off dry and full. He also makes Touraine AC
wines from Sauvignon, Cabernet Franc, Gamay and Groslots.
Open: Mon–Sat 10am–noon; 3–6pm.

André et Philippe Foreau (Domaine du Clos Naudin)

37210 Vouvray. Vineyards owned: Vouvray 12ha.
Produce: 50,000 bottles. VP-R.

One of the top Vouvray producers, now in its third generation,
making still and sparkling wines. All the still wines are
fermented and aged in wood, the *méthode champenoise* in
stainless steel. They age their still wine from a considerable time
– especially the sweet wine, made only in good years. The
results are well worth the wait. *Open: By appointment only.*

Maison Fouquet

47 Rue Gambetta, 37210 Vouvray. Vineyards owned:
Vouvray 19.2ha. *Produce: 80,000 bottles.* VP-R.

A medium-sized producer who makes a fine sweet still Vouvray
in years like 1985, using traditional techniques and maturing in
wood. He sells some wine to négociants and makes a dry and
sweet Vouvray and a *méthode champenoise* wine in more acid
years like 1984. *Open: Appointment preferred.*

Domaine Freslier

37210 Vouvray. Vineyards owned: 4ha.
Produce: 25,000 bottles. VP-R.

A small, traditional producer, making still and sparkling
Vouvray, using wood for fermentation. The vineyard, known
as the Quarts de Moncontour, is near the Château de
Moncontour, in one of the top sites of Vouvray. The Freslier
family makes a little of the rare Vouvray Pétillant. *Open: Mon–
Fri 9–7pm. Appointments necessary for groups.*

Jean-Pierre Gilet

5 Rue de Parçay, Parçay-Meslay, 37210 Vouvray. Vineyards
owned: Vouvray 7ha. *Produce: 30,000 bottles.* VP-R.

Much of this producer's wines are sold to local négociants, but
he does bottle some of his still and *méthode champenoise* wines.
The most attractive is a medium-dry *pétillant* wine (delicious in
1983). *Open: By appointment only.*

Sylvain Gaudron

59 Rue Veuve, Vernou 37210 Vouvray. Vineyards owned:
Vernou, Noizay, Chançay 9.4ha. *Produce: 30,000 bottles.*

Typical Vouvray cellars, carved out of rock in the 14th century.
M. Gaudron is a traditionalist who vinifies at least part of his
wine in wood. He makes all the Vouvray styles – from dry through
to *méthode champenoise*. His 1985 sweet wine will be a classic –
in about 15 years' time. *Open: Mon–Sat, during working hours.*

Benoît Gautier & Germain Gautier-Peltier

La Recauderie, Parçay-Meslay, 37210 Vouvray. Vineyards
owned: Rochecorbon: Chenin Blanc 20ha; Grolleau 1.5ha.
Produce: 80,000 bottles. VP-R.

The domaine is first recorded in the family in 1669 and it is now
divided between Germain (the father) and Benoît (the son),
although the cellars are still shared. Both men work in a
traditional way, using the natural cool air of the *caves* to control
fermentation. Over half the production goes to a *méthode
champenoise* wine. Like other Vouvray producers, the finest
year recently for sweet wines was 1985. They have only recently
started bottling and selling themselves – previously the wine
was sold to négociants. *Open: Mon–Fri 8am–8pm. Appointments necessary for groups.*

Gaston Huet

Domaine du Haut-Lieu, 37210 Vouvray. Vineyards owned:
Vouvray 32ha. *Produce: 130,000 bottles. VP-R.*

M. Huet is Mayor of Vouvray and a great propagandist for the
wines. Luckily he is also one of the best producers in the area,
making wines from some of the finest sites – Le Haut Lieu, Le
Clos du Bourg and Le Mont, which are vinified and sold
separately. He uses a judicious mix of traditional techniques
and modern stainless steel equipment, but his best wines are all
matured in small wood casks. The extensive cellars, carved out
of the tufa rock of Vouvray, are crammed with half a million
bottles, and some of the sweet still wines are of amazing
antiquity; the most recent two vintages are 1976 and 1985.
These are the finest wines, but M. Huet also makes sparkling
and *pétillant* medium dry wines. He makes very little dry wine,
believing that Vouvray's vocation is as a sweet wine. *Open:
Mon–Fri 9am–noon; 2–6pm.*

Mme Claude Metivier

51 Rue Neuve, 37210 Vernou-sur-Brenne. Vineyards owned:
Vernou 7ha. *Produce: 15,000 bottles. VP-R.*

Most of Mme Metivier's production is of sparkling and
pétillant wines. Of the still wines, most are dry and medium-
dry. Her Vernou vineyards are about five kilometres to the east
of Vouvray where the tufa cliffs draw further back from the
Loire. *Open: Afternoons only; by appointment only.*

Dominique Moyer

2 Rue de la Croise des Granges, Husseau, 37270 Montlouis.
Vineyards owned: Husseau 12ha.
Produce: 40,000 bottles. VP-R.

The Moyer family have been in the wine business since 1830,
and some of their vines have been around since the 1920s, giving
them wines with great intensity. They take great care in picking,
going through the vineyard a number of times to ensure that the
fruit is as ripe as possible: this is the old tradition in Montlouis
but is now only carried out in a few of the best properties.
Virtually all their production is of dry or medium-dry still wines
– the medium-dry wines coming from the oldest vines. 15% of
their production is of *méthode champenoise* or *pétillant* wine.
Their house is a hunting lodge dating from 1620. *Open: By
appointment only.*

Prince Poniatowksi

Le Clos Baudoin, Vallée de Nouys, 37210 Vouvray.
Vineyards owned: Le Clos Baudoin 3.8ha; Aigle Blanc
18.3ha. *Produce: 150,000 bottles.* VP-R.

Prince Poniatowski is from an ancient Polish family which has
lived in France for many years – the Vouvray estate has been in
the family for 70 years. Wines tend to be on the dry side, of great
elegance and finesse, with intense fruit, taking some time to
mature. Clos Baudoin is one of the best sites in Vouvray, on the
top of a sheltered valley facing south. Aigle Blanc is a brand for
both still and sparkling wines – with more sparkling being made
in less ripe years. The house, like so many in Vouvray, is half
carved out of the rock. *Open: By appointment only.*

Vigneau-Chevreau

4 Rue du Clos Baglin, Chançay, 37210 Vouvray. Vineyards
owned: Chançay 20ha. *Produce: 100,000 bottles.* VP-R.

The production in this traditional house is divided half and half
between dry and medium-dry still wines on the one hand; and
méthode champenoise on the other. The still wines tend to be
vinified in wood, the sparkling in stainless steel. *Open: Mon–
Fri 8am–noon; 2–6pm. Appointments necessary for groups.*

Anjou

Bonnin et Fils

Domaine la Croix des Loges, 49540 Martigné-Briand.
Vineyards owned: Anjou 30ha. *Produce: 200,000 bottles.* VP-R.

Modern techniques dominate this large estate which covers
mainly wines from the AC Anjou, but also produces a small
quantity of fine sweet white Bonnezeaux. The Anjou Rouge
from Cabernet Franc is a well-made wine with plenty of
youthful raspberry fruit, but also some ageing potential. Other
wines include Anjou Rosé, Cabernet Rosé, a medium dry Anjou
Blanc and Rosé de la Loire. A certain amount of sparkling
Saumur is also made. *Open: Appointments preferred.*

Les Caves de la Loire

19320 Brissac. Vineyards owned: 2,000ha.
Produce: 4 million bottles. Coop (500 members).

One of the largest cooperatives on the Loire, Les Caves de la
Loire has made a big name for itself in supplying reliable well-
made wines on an own label basis. In an ultra-modern winery,
the full range of Anjou wines is made: Anjou Rouge, Anjou
Blanc, Rosé d'Anjou, Cabernet d'Anjou, Rosé de la Loire. They
also make sparkling Crémant de la Loire and Saumur
Mousseux, and some good quality sweet Coteaux du Layon.
Open: By appointment only.

Les Charbottières

49320 Vauchretien. Vineyards owned: Anjou 15ha.
Produce: 20,000 bottles. VP-R.

70% of the production at this small firm is of Anjou Rouge,
which sees some wood ageing. A mixture of modern and
traditional methods is used. They also make Cabernet d'Anjou,
Rosé de la Loire, dry Anjou Blanc and a small amount of sweet
Coteaux d'Aubance, in which AC area the vineyards are

situated. *Open: Mon–Fri 10am–noon; 2–5pm. Appointments necessary for groups.*

Dhommé Père et Fils

Petit Port Girault, 49290 Chalonnes-sur-Loire. Vineyards owned: Anjou and Coteaux du Layon 14ha.
Produce: 20,000 bottles. VP-R.

75% of production from this firm goes to négociants, the remainder bottled at the domaine. Their range spans most of the Anjou wines: Anjou Blanc and Rouge, Anjou Gamay, Cabernet d'Anjou and Crémant de la Loire. They also own vineyards in Coteaux du Layon from which they produce about 100 hectolitres of sweet wine. The cellars are situated on a small island in the centre of the Loire which was formerly a stopping point for river boats. *Open: Appointments preferred.*

Jean Douet (Château des Rochettes)

Concourson-sur-Layon, 49700 Doué-la-Fontaine. Vineyards owned: Anjou and Coteaux du Layon 25ha.
Produce: 80,000 bottles. VP-R.

A long-established family firm which makes the full range of Anjou wines, plus some Coteaux du Layon made from old vines. They tend to use a mixture of traditional techniques for the reds (with wood ageing) and temperature controlled fermentation for other wines. The bulk of the production is of Anjou red. *Open: Appointments preferred.*

Domaine Gaudard

Chaudefonds-sur-Layon, 49290 Chalonnes-sur-Loire.
Vineyards owned: 15.1ha. *Produce: 100,000 bottles.* VP-R.

They've been expanding plantings of the noble varieties on this estate – Chardonnay and Cabernet Franc – and cutting back on the local Grolleau and Chenin. The Chardonnay is used as a *cépage améliorateur* in a *méthode champenoise* Anjou sparkler. Cabernet Franc goes into the Anjou Rouge, a well-made, long-lasting wine. Other wines include the range of Anjou wines, plus some Coteaux du Layon. *Open: Mon–Fri 8am–5pm.*

Cave Cooperative du Haut-Poitou

32 Rue Alphonse Plault, 86170 Neuville de Poitou.
Vineyards owned: 808ha.
Produce: 3.2 million bottles. Coop (625 members).

This cooperative has revived the fortunes of the Haut-Poitou vineyard area, by making a very good range of varietal wines. The best are from Chardonnay and Sauvignon, but they also make reds from Cabernet Franc and Gamay. Also produced are *méthode champenoise* wines from Chardonay and a sparkling rosé called Diane de Poitiers. All the wines are made by modern techniques, using stainless steel. *Open: By appointment only.*

Guy Gousset (Clos de l'Aiglerie)

St-Aubin de Luigne, 49190 Rochefort-sur-Loire. Vineyards owned: 12ha. *Produce: 60,000 bottles. VP-R.*

M. Gousset makes a range of wines: Anjou Rouge and Rosé from Cabernet Franc; sweet Coteaux du Layon; and some Vin de Pays de Maine et Loire. Techniques are traditional, with wood fermentation for all wines. Quality is reliable, with a few pleasant surprises, especially in the reds. *Open: Working hours.*

Jousset et Fils

Logis du Prieuré, Concourson-sur-Layon, 49700 Doué-la-
Fontaine. Vineyards owned: Anjou and Coteaux du Layon
28ha. *Produce: 200,000 bottles.* VP-R.

Temperature control and stainless steel are used here to make a
range of Anjou wines. The wines tend to be on the light side and
should be drunk young. *Open: By appointment only.*

Yves Leduc (Château Montbenault)

Faye d'Anjou, 49380 Thouarcé. Vineyards owned: Anjou
20ha. *Produce: 35,000 bottles.* VP-R.

M. Leduc specializes in sweet wines of the Coteaux du Layon
Faye AC. These wines are made cleanly using stainless steel for
vinification and tend not to last as long as some other sweet
wines of the area. Part of his Coteaux du Layon from the Clos
Poirier Bourgeau vineyard is vinified and bottled separately. He
also makes Anjou Rouge and Blanc, Rosé d'Anjou, Cabernet
d'Anjou, Rosé de la Loire and sparkling Anjou *méthode*
champenoise. *Open: Mon–Sat 9am–noon; 2-5pm.*

Vins Mottron

Rue d'Anjou 49540 Martigné-Briand. Vineyards owned:
Anjou 25ha. *Produce: 1 million bottles.* VP-R and N.

One of the largest négociants in the Anjou AC area. From their
own vineyards they make red and rosé wines in their modern
winery, using the Cabernet d'Anjou, Rosé d'Anjou, Anjou
Rouge ACs, plus Vin de Pays de la Jardin de la France. They also
produce other Loire wines: Muscadet, Saumur, Chinon,
Bourgueil, Touraine, Sancerre and Pouilly-Fumé. Brands include: Caves de Bel Air, Caves de Petit Colombier, Pierre Frain,
Louis Bret, Roger Lefèvre. *Open: By appointment only.*

Domaine Richou

Chauvigné, Mozé-sur-Louet, 49190 Rochefort-sur-Loire.
Vineyards owned: Anjou 28ha. *Produce: 90,000 bottles.* VP-R.

The white Anjou Blanc is the star from this old-established
firm. This blend of Chenin (80%) and Chardonnay (20%)
makes a dry, full of fruit, clean wine, best drunk in the year
following the vintage. They also make a Cuvée de Printemps
from young vines – a blended red of Cabernets which is
designed to be drunk early. From old vines, quantities of Anjou
Rouge and Cabernet d'Anjou are made, plus some sweet
Coteaux d'Aubance. *Open: By appointment only.*

Brault Père et Fils

Domaine de Ste-Anne, Ste-Anne, 49320 Brissac-Quincé.
Vineyards owned: Anjou 48ha. *Produce: 140,000 bottles.* VP-R.

This estate has adopted the high vine training of the Lenz Moser
method for the most part and although yields (which are
supposed to be higher under this system than conventional vine
training) are controlled by the AC laws, the quality of the fruit is
certainly good. This quality is translated into the well-made
wines which cover the range of the Anjou AC, and include some
Coteaux du Layon and Coteaux de l'Aubance. Just under half
the production is bottled, the remainder being sold in bulk to
négociants. Their best wines tend to be the reds. *Open:
Appointments preferred.*

THE GRAPE VARIETIES

Each region of France has a range of mainsteam grape varieties which make up the bulk of the wine they produce. But each region also has some unknowns or has attracted some foreign grape varieties. This list, arranged alphabetically by grape variety, shows in which AC and VDQS each grape variety is permitted.

Red

Abouriou
Southwest: Côtes du Marmandais.

Alicante
Provence: Coteaux Varois.

Aramon
Midi: Coteaux du Languedoc, Coteaux de Vérargues.
Provence: Coteaux Varois.

Braquet
Provence: Bellet

Cabernet Franc
Loire: Bourgueil, Chinon, Coteaux du Loir, St-Nicholas de Bourgueil, Touraine, Touraine Villages, Touraine-Mesland; Coteaux du Vendômois, Anjou, Saumur, Saumur-Champigny, Vins de Thouarsais, Coteaux d'Ancenis, Fiefs Vendéens.
Midi: Côtes de la Malapère.
Southwest: Béarn, Bergerac, Côtes de Bergerac, Côtes de Buzet, Côtes de Duras, Côtes du Frontonnais, Gaillac, Irouléguy, Madiran, Pecharmant, Côtes du Brulhois, Côtes du Marmandais, Côtes de Saint-Mont, Tursan, Vins d'Entraygues et du Fel, Vins d'Estaing, Vins de Marcillac.

Cabernet Sauvignon
Loire: Bourgueil, Chinon, Touraine, Anjou, Saumur, Vin de Haut-Poitou, Vins de Thouarsais, Fiefs Vendéens.
Midi: Cabardès, Côtes de la Malapère.
Provence: Coteaux Varois, Coteaux d'Aix en Provence, Coteaux des Baux en Provence, Côtes de Provence.
Southwest: Béarn, Bergerac, Côtes de Bergerac, Côtes de Buzet, Côtes de Duras, Côtes du Frontonnais, Gaillac, Irouléguy, Madiran, Pecharmant, Côtes du Brulhois, Côtes du Marmandais, Côtes de Saint-Mont, Tursan, Vin d'Entraygues et du Fel, Vin d'Estaing, Vin de Marcillac.

Calitor
Provence: Bandol
Rhône: Lirac

Camarèse
Rhône: Côtes du Rhône, Côtes du Ventoux.

Carignan
Midi: Coteaux du Languedoc, Coteaux du Languedoc: Cabrières, Coteaux de Méjanelle, Coteaux de Vérargues, La Clape, Méjanelle, Montpeyroux, Pic-St-Loup, Quatourze, Coteaux de St-Christol, St-Drézery, St-Georges d'Orques, St-Saturnin, Costières du Gard, Faugères, St-Chinian, Minervois, Corbières, Fitou, Cabardès, Collioure, Côtes du Roussillon, Côtes du Roussillon Villages.
Provence: Bandol, Cassis, Coteaux d'Aix en Provence, Coteaux des Baux en Provence, Côtes de Provence, Coteaux Varois.
Rhône: Côtes du Rhône, Côtes du Rhône Villages, Coteaux du Tricastin, Coteaux du Pierrevert.

Cinsault
Midi: Coteaux de Languedoc, Coteaux du Languedoc: Cabrières, Coteaux de Méjanelle, Coteaux de Vérargues, La Clape, Méjanelle, Montpeyroux, Pic-St-Loup, Quatourze, Coteaux de St-Christol, St-

Anjou: Coteaux du Layon, Quarts de Chaume, Bonnezeaux

Domaine des Baumard

8 Rue de l'Abbaye, 49190 Rochefort-sur-Loire. Vineyards
owned: Quarts de Chaume 3.5ha; Savennières 12.45ha;
Coteaux du Layon 1ha; Anjou 12ha.
Produce: 100,000 bottles. VP-R.

Quarts de Chaume and Savennières are inevitably the top two
wines from this producer. But the quality throughout the range
is high and M. Baumard makes some of the best and most
consistent wines in the region. His Quarts de Chaume has the
true intensity of this great sweet wine and really only develops
after 10 years in bottle. His Savennières (he owns part of the
Clos du Papillon) on the contrary, is a faster developer than
Savennières from other producers and is very drinkable after
four to five years. Clos de Ste-Catherine Coteaux du Layon is a
lovely contrast between intensity and lightness. Other wines
made are a Crémant de la Loire from Chardonnay and a red
Anjou, Logis de la Giraudière, from Cabernet Franc. *Open:
Appointments preferred.*

Jacques Boivin (Château de Fesles)

49380 Thouarcé. Vineyards owned: 33ha. VP-R.

One of the top producers of Bonnezeaux, which is fermented
and aged in small barrels. The wine in good years can be superb.
M. Boivin also makes standard Anjou wines: red and white,
plus Vin de Pays du Jardin de la France using Chardonnay. The
Château de Fesles itself is built on an 11th century foundation,
and the Boivin family has been there for many generations.
Open: By appointment only.

Les Vignobles de la Cour de Pierre

49190 Rochefort-sur-Loire. *Produce: 400,000 bottles.*
Coop (10 members).

A small cooperative, whose members make their own wine but
then market it jointly. They make a wide range of wines
including Quarts de Chaume, Coteaux du Layon and Coteaux
du Layon Rochefort, plus wines from the general Anjou AC:
Rosé d'Anjou, Cabernet d'Anjou, Rosé de Loire, Anjou Blanc,
Anjou Rouge, Anjou Gamay and Anjou Mousseux. They also
make a small amount of Crémant de la Loire. Standards are
good for a cooperative. *Open: By appointment only.*

Fardeau-Robin (Domaine des Hauts Perrays)

49290 Chaudefonds-sur-Layon. Vineyards owned: Coteaux
du Layon 12ha; Anjou 13ha. *Produce: 80,000 bottles.* VP-R.

The actual Domaine de Hauts Perrays produces an Anjou Blanc
from Chenin Blanc and Chardonnay (20%), the Chardonnay
cutting down on the natural harshness of the Chenin. They also
make about 40,000 bottles of a soft, medium sweet Coteaux du
Layon. Red wines include an Anjou Rouge – also Domaine des
Hauts Perrays – from Cabernet Franc (70%) and Cabernet
Sauvignon (30%). *Open: By appointment only.*

Vignobles Laffourcade (Château de Suronde)

49190 Rochefort-sur-Loire. Vineyards owned: Quarts de
Chaume 20ha. *Produce: 60,000 bottles.* VP-R.

The largest producer by far in the Quarts de Chaume. They use fermentation in stainless steel before maturation in wood to make fine examples of this superb sweet wine. Do not expect to enjoy their wine before 10 years, but then savour every mouthful. Names they use are Château de Suronde and Château de l'Echarderie. *Open: By appointment only.*

Jacques Lalanne (Château Bellerive)
49190 Rochefort-sur-Loire. Vineyards owned: Quarts de Chaume 17ha. *Produce: 20,000 bottles.* VP-R.

Expense is no object in the vineyard: picking is done over a number of weeks in a series of passes, gathering only the ripest most nobly-rotten grapes each time. Fermentation takes place in large barrels and bottling in the spring after the vintage. This means that Quarts de Chaume matures in the bottle, taking upwards from 10 years to do so. The rewards are there for those willing to wait. Quarts de Chaume is the only wine made. *Open: By appointment only.*

Fernand Moron
8 Rue de Perinelle, St-Lambert du Lattay, 49190 Rochefort-sur-Loire. Vineyards owned: Coteaux du Layon 11ha; Anjou 12ha. *Produce: 120,000 bottles.* VP-R.

M. Moron makes a whole range of wines: from the sweet Coteaux du Layon St-Lambert and Coteaux du Layon, through Anjou Blanc and Rouge and Rosé Cabernet d'Anjou to Rosé d'Anjou and Rosé de la Loire. Half the vineyard is of Chenin Blanc, but he also has Cabernet Franc, Chardonnay, Grolleau and Gamay. His best wine is inevitably the Coteaux du Layon St-Lambert which shares some of the intensity of Quarts de Chaume in good years and ages well. *Open: By appointment only.*

René Renou
Place du Champ de Foire, 49380 Thouarcé. Vineyards owned: Thouarcé 18ha. *Produce: 100,000 bottles.* VP-R.

Top of M. Renou's production is his Bonnezeaux, made in wood and matured in bottle. It's a family firm – the seventh-generation René Renou is now eight years old – and methods are traditional, especially for the sweet wines. M. Renou is president of the Bonnezeaux growers and a keen supporter of his *cru*, joining with others in marketing it, and luckily, his wines live up to its reputation. He also makes dry Anjou Blanc, Rosé de la Loire, Rosé d'Anjou and Anjou Rouge. *Open: By appointment only.*

Henri Rochais et Fils (Château de Plaisance)
49190 Rochefort-sur-Loire. Vineyards owned: Coteaux du Layon Chaume 13.5ha; Anjou 1.5ha. *Produce: 50,000 bottles.* VP-R.

Not to be confused with Quarts de Chaume, Coteaux du Layon Chaume is nevertheless one of the best of the Coteaux du Layon Villages from vineyards just up the hill from Quarts de Chaume and sharing some of the microclimate. M. Rochais picks the grapes ripe after successive passes through the vineyard, vinifies in tank and then gives the wine a short period in wood before bottling. He also makes dry Anjou Blanc and Anjou Rouge from Cabernet Sauvignon (60%) and Cabernet Franc (30%). *Open: Appointments preferred.*

LOIRE: Anjou

André Sorin (Domaine de Lamotte)

31 Avenue d'Angers, 49190 Rochefort-sur-Loire. Vineyards owned: Rochefort 17ha. *Produce: 130,000 bottles.* VP-R.

While Rosé d'Anjou is M. Sorin's largest production, he also makes a Coteaux du Layon Rochefort from a south-facing slope, which is a fine example of this sweet white wine – and one with which he obviously takes considerable care. Apart from these wines, he makes the usual range of Anjou wines, including an Anjou Sec Clos des Belles Mères from Chardonnay and an Anjou Mousseux from Chenin Blanc. *Open: Appointments preferred.*

Pierre-Yves Tijou (Domaine de la Soucherie)

Beaulieu-sur-Layon, 49190 Rochefort-sur-Loire. Vineyards owned: 35ha. *Produce: 200,000 bottles.* VP-R.

A large landowner is an area of small holdings, the bulk of M. Tijou's wine is of Coteaux du Layon and Coteaux du Layon Chaume. However, he tends not to use wood for his white wines, preferring to make a wine that is fresher and matures more quickly than some of the sweet wines of the area. He also makes the full range of Anjou AC wines, including a superior Crémant de la Loire sparkler. All the wines carry the name Domaine de la Soucherie. *Open: By appointment only.*

Anjou: Savennières

Vignoble de Coulée de Serrant, Mme Joly

Château de la Roche-aux-Moines, 49170 Savennières. Vineyards owned: Savennières-Coulée-de-Serrant 7ha; Savennières-Roche-aux-Moines 2ha; Coteaux de la Loire 2ha. *Produce: 20,000 bottles.*

Low yields, intense fruit and high quality are the reasons for the low production at this famous estate. Mme Joly is one of the few owners in France who controls an entire AC (Coulée-de-Serrant): the other well-known example is Château Grillet on the Rhône. Coulée de Serrant is an ancient monastic vineyard, Roche-aux-Moines was planted first in the 12th century. Wines are treated as naturally as possible with few chemicals. They are vinified in wood and bottled with the minimum of filtration. Despite their dryness, these Savennières wines need a minimum of five years in bottle before drinking, and will survive seemingly for ever. The risks are high: for three years in the 1970s production was well below normal and in 1972 nothing was made at all. Demand, though, is enormous and prices have followed demand upwards. Mme Joly also makes a Coteaux de la Loire Rouge from Cabernet Franc and Cabernet Sauvignon – with the same extreme care. *Open: Mon–Sat 8:30am–noon; 2–5:30pm.*

Mme de Jessey (Domaine du Closel)

49170 Savennières. Vineyards owned: Savennières 12ha; Anjou 2ha. *Produce: 60,000 bottles.* VP-R.

Another of the top Savennières estates to be run by a woman. Mme Jessey makes a classic dry white Savennières, vinified and matured in wood and needing a considerable time before it is ready to drink. This is probably the truest Savennières, lacking sometimes the intensity of Coulée-de-Serrant but with what the

74

French call *nervosité* and poised balance. Mme Jessey also makes red Anjou from Cabernet Franc and Cabernet Sauvignon, again matured in wood. *Open: By appointment only.*

Société Bizard (Château d'Epiré)

Epiré, 49170 Savennières. Vineyards owned: Savennières 10ha. *Produce: 50,000 bottles.* VP-R.

Stock turnover is obviously not a consideration here. The Savennières really isn't drinkable for 10–12 years, and will last for up to 30 or more. Like other Savennières producers, they need to pass through the vineyard two or three times to get the grapes at their ripest – even though they are making a dry wine. Vinification and maturation of the wines are all in wood. They also make small quantities of Anjou Rouge and Rosé de la Loire – probably to keep the money coming in. *Open: Appointments preferred.*

François Roussier

Clos de Coulaine, 49170 Savennières. Vineyards owned: Savennières 8ha. *Produce: 50,000 bottles.* VP-R.

About a third of production here is of Savennières, while the rest is of Anjou Rouge made from Cabernet Franc. Like most other Savennières producers, methods are traditional with vinification in wood and long ageing in bottle required. The red is well-made, less interesting than the white but certainly one of the better Anjou Rouge. M. Roussier's estate has been in the family since 1860. *Open: By appointment only.*

Pierre et Yves Soulez (Château de Chamboureau)

49170 Savennières. Vineyards owned: Savennières 21ha; Anjou 3ha. *Produce: 120,000 bottles.* VP-R.

One of the most technically advanced of the Anjou producers, who yet contrives to make a Savennières that really needs time in bottle. Most of the production is of Savennières and the three sections of the estate are bottled separately: Domaine de la Bizolière, Clos du Papillon, Château de Chamboureau. Of the three, I prefer the Clos du Papillon, of which the Soulez family own two hectares. They also make a small amount of the superior Savennières-Roche-aux-Moines, under the Château de Chamboureau name. The other wine they produce is an Anjou Rouge, 50/50 Cabernet Franc/Cabernet Sauvignon. *Open: Mon–Sat 8am–12:30pm; 1:30–6:30pm.*

Anjou: Saumur and Saumur-Champigny

Ackerman-Laurance

St Hilaire-St Florent, 49400 Saumur. Vineyards owned: None. *Produce: 3.3. million bottles.* N.

A négociant and producer specializing in sparkling wines. The oldest producer of Saumur, and still one of the largest. The bulk of production is of good quality sparkling white and rosé Saumur, all made in stainless steel, but in a range of qualities, including the top Cuvée Privilège and Cuvée Privée. They also make considerable quantities of very good Crémant de Loire. *Open: Mon–Fri 9:30am–noon; 2:30–5pm. Appointments necessary for groups.*

Bouvet Ladubay

St-Hilaire-St Florent, 49400 Saumur. Vineyards owned: no
land. *Produce: 1.6 million bottles.* N.

Producers of some of the best sparkling Saumur, the firm has
contracts with 150 growers in the Saumur region, from which it
draws all of its wine requirements. They make two qualities of
Saumur – a standard range and the Excellence range, which
includes the Crémant Brut Saphir and the vintage Crémant
d'Or. Other wines in their portfolio include white, red and rosé
brut sparkling using the general Anjou AC. Overall, the
standard is high. The firm is part of the Taittinger Champagne
group. *Open: Mon–Fri 8am–noon; 2–6pm.*

Domaine Vinicole de Chaintres

Dampierre-sur-Loire, 49400 Saumur. Vineyards owned:
Saumur 20ha. *Produce: 130,000 bottles.* VP-R.

The Château de Chaintres is a red wine estate, producing wine
for the firm's classic Saumur-Champigny. Methods are traditional and wood is used for maturation, giving wines with
some lasting power and extra tannin. The style seems to have
become lighter in recent years, probably because stainless steel
is being used as well. Owner Bernard de Tigny also makes a
white Saumur Blanc. *Open: By appointment only.*

Claude Daheuiller

28 Rue du Ruau, Varrains, 49400 Saumur. Vineyards
owned: Saumur 23ha. *Produce: 130,000 bottles.* VP-R.

Main production here is of a good Saumur-Champigny made
from the estate of Domaine de Varinelles. Half the wine is made
in wood, the other half in stainless steel and then the two are
blended, giving some firmness and structure but allowing for
early drinking and plenty of instant fruit. They also make
Saumur still white and a little sparkling Saumur Brut. Small
amounts of Sauvignon and Rosé de la Loire are also produced.
Open: By appointment only.

Denis Duveau

27 Rue de la Mairie, Varrains, 49400 Saumur. Vineyards
owned: Saumur-Champigny 10ha.
Produce: 50,000 bottles. VP-R.

Producer of one of the more intense, rich Saumur-Champigny,
principally because at least 20% of the wine comes from old
vines. Vinification and maturation are all in wood. The family
has been on the land for four generations and sticks entirely to
the one wine. *Open: By appointment only.*

Gratien, Meyer, Seydoux

Château de Beaulieu, Route de Chinon, 49400 Saumur.
Vineyards owned: Saumur 20ha.
Produce: 2.5 million bottles. VP-R and N.

Gratien & Meyer is the brand name for a range of sparkling
Saumur wines – brut, demi-sec and rosé. They also make a red
sparkling wine from 100% Cabernet Franc. The quality is very
reliable (they consider that "behind the mousse there should be
a pleasant wine") and the wines are widely distributed
throughout the world. The firm owns the champagne house of
Alfred Gratien. *Open: Mon–Sun 9am–noon; 2–6pm.*

Langlois-Château

BP6, 3 Rue Leopold Palustre, St-Hilaire-St-Florent, 49416
Saumur. Vineyards owned: Saumur 27ha; Sancerre 15ha.
Produce: 200,000 bottles. VP-R and N.

One of the famous names in sparkling Saumur, Langlois-Château also produce red and white still wines from the same AC and Sancerre red and white wines from their estate at Château Fontaine-Audon. Production is quite modern in approach, using stainless steel. The firm is owned by the Champagne house of Bollinger. *Open: Summer only, Mon–Fri 10:30am–12:30pm; 3–6:30pm.*

Edouard Pisani–Ferry (Château Targé)

49730 Parnay. Vineyards owned: Saumur-Champigny 20ha.
Produce: 100,000 bottles. VP-R.

The château has been in the family since 1655, but methods are modern, with stainless steel and temperature control used for fermentation. The total production is of Saumur-Champigny, which is then matured for six months in wood. The blend employs 10% Cabernet Sauvignon to top up the Cabernet Franc and the results are a wine which is most attractive in the second year after vintage. *Open: Mon–Fri, during working hours.*

Rémy-Pannier

St Hilaire-St Florent, 49400 Saumur. Vineyards owned:
none. *Produce: 15 million bottles.* VP-R.

Probably the largest négociant in the Loire Valley, buying in all their requirements. They make wines from virtually every AC in the Loire, all to a standard, if uninspiring, quality. Their Saumur wines are probably their best. Their marketing techniques are highly sophisticated. *Open: No.*

Robert Chevallier (Château de Villeneuve)

Souzay-Champigny, 49400 Saumur. Vineyards owned:
Souzay-Champigny 25ha. *Produce: 170,000 bottles.* VP-R.

While the bulk of production here is of red Saumur-Champigny, the most interesting wine is the rich, dry, aromatic Saumur Blanc, with a slight touch of *pétillance*, but the ability to age well. The red is at its best in warm years, such as 1983 and 1985, and other vintages are to be avoided. Vinification takes place in controlled temperature stainless steel. *Open: Mon–Fri 9am–noon; 2–6pm. Appointments necessary for groups.*

Western Loire: Muscadet de Sèvre et Maine

Aubert Frères

49270 La Varenne. Vineyards owned: Muscadet 59ha; Anjou
13ha. *Produce: 7 million bottles.* VP-R and N.

One of the major négociants of the Muscadet/Anjou area, but whose main vineyard holdings are in Muscadet. Their range of wines includes lesser ACs like Coteaux d'Ancenis, but their interests cover the whole Loire: from Sancerre and Pouilly-Fumé in the east to Vin de Pays de Maine et Loire and Muscadet in the west. They also produce wines from further afield: Côtes de Provence, Côtes de Duras and Côtes du Rhône. The techniques are modern and their cellars well run. *Open: By appointment only.*

Jérome and André Batard

La Bigotière, 44690 Maisdon-sur-Sèvre. Vineyards owned:
Muscadet de Sèvre et Maine: Domaine le Rossignol 15ha.
Produce: 50,000 bottles. VP-R.

Nine-tenths of production is of Muscadet de Sèvre et Maine,
with a small amount of Gros Plant. The vineyard has been run
by the family for many generations, but now techniques are
modern with stainless steel and temperature controls. There is a
Cuvée de Prestige, Carte Noire. *Open: Appointment preferred.*

Joseph Bosseau

12 Rue des Vignes, Le Pallet, 44330 Vallet. Vineyards
owned: Muscadet de Sèvre et Maine. Le Pallet 8.5ha; La
Chapelle-Heulin 0.4ha; Vallet 0.6ha.
Produce: 60,000 bottles. VP-R.

While the bulk of production is of Muscadet de Sèvre et Maine,
there are small amounts of Gros Plant, plus Cabernet and
Grolleau used to make Vin de Pays des Marches-de-Bretagne.
Mechanical harvesting is used in the vineyard. Brands are
Domaine des Chausselières, Cuvée de l'Ecole (Muscadet de
Sèvre et Maine), Les Saints Vincents (Gros Plant) and Le
Gabbro (Vin de Pays). *Open: By appointment only.*

Henri Bouchaud

Le Bois Joly, Le Pallet, Vallet. Vineyards owned: Muscadet
et Sèvre et Maine: Le Pallet 13ha.
Produce: 85,000 bottles. VP-R.

Domaine du Bois Joly is the name for the Muscadet de Sèvre et
Maine produced here. There is also some Gros Plant VDQS and
red Vin de Pays du Jardin de la France Cabernet Franc. *Open:
By appointment only.*

Jean Bouyer

49 Rue d'Anjou, La Charouillère, 44330 Vallet. Vineyards
owned: 11.5ha. *Produce: 20,000 bottles.* VP-R.

Domaine de la Pingossière and Domaine du Clos Julienne are
the two names used by this young producer. M. Bouyer makes
Muscadet de Sèvre et Maine, plus a little Gros Plant and
Gamay-based Vin de Pays des Marches de Bretagne. 50% of production is sold to négociants. *Open: Appointments preferred.*

André-Michel Brégeon

Les Guisseaux-Gorges, 44190 Clisson. Vineyards owned:
7.5ha. *Produce: 48,000 bottles.* VP-R.

Traditional techniques (including a short period of wood
maturation) are used here and the wines are bottled at the estate
sur lie. This gives a fuller style of wine and also an attractive
prickle on the palate. M. Brégeon's Gros Plant is a very good
example. He also makes a small quantity of Vin de Pays des
Marches de Bretagne from Cabernet Franc and Cabernet
Sauvignon. *Open: Mon–Fri 10am–7pm.*

L. Brosseau and J. Hervouet

Vignoble de la Foliette, 44690 La Haie Fouassière.
Vineyards owned: 16ha. *Produce: 60,000 bottles.* VP-R.

The estate is divided into two: 11 hectares of Vignoble de la
Foliette in Haye-Fouassière; five hectares of Les Ferrieres in

Haute-Goulaine. The Muscadet de Sèvre et Maine is bottled *sur lie*. This producer is linked in with the Louis Métaireau grouping (q.v.). *Open: By appointment only.*

Robert Brosseau (Domaine des Mortiers Gobin)
44690 La Haie Fouassière. Vineyards owned: 9ha.
Produce: 50,000 bottles. VP-R.

The wines, sold under the Domaine des Mortiers Gobin name are bottled *sur lie* and methods are traditional, with some wood maturation before bottling. M. Brosseau's family has owned the land "for ever". *Open: By appointment only.*

Le Cellier des Ducs
Rue de Sèvre et Maine, 44450 La Chapelle-Basse-Mer.
Produce: 1 million bottles. N.

Large-scale négociant making a range of wines from the Pays Nantais. They sell wines from a number of Muscadet de Sèvre et Maine estates: Domaine des Morines, Château de la Bigotière, Château de Richebourg and Domaine de Bigotière. *Open: By appointment only.*

Guy Charpentier
Les Noues, 44430 Le Loroux-Bottereau. Vineyards owned:
12ha. *Produce: 40,000 bottles. VP-R.*

Three-quarters of production here is of Muscadet de Sèvre et Maine, with smaller amounts of Gros Plant and Vin de Pays du Jardin de la France (from Gamay), plus Vin de Pays des Marches de Bretagne (from Cabernet Franc). The vineyard holdings are in four communes: Le Loux-Bottereau, Le Landreau, La Chapelle-Heulin and La Chapelle-Basse-Mer. M. Charpentier also makes a *méthode champenoise* called La Belle Folie. *Open: By appointment only.*

Ets Chéreau-Carré
Château du Chasseloir, St-Fiacre-sur-Maine, 44690 La Haie-Fouassière. Vineyards owned: 74ha.
Produce: 505,000 bottles. VP-R.

The Chéreau family is one of the biggest landowners in Muscadet de Sèvre et Maine, with five estates in some of the best vineyard land in the area. Château du Chasseloir (17 hectares) is the centre of operations. The other estates are: Château du Coing (30 hectares); La Bournaire (five hectares); Moulin de la Gravelle (12 hectares); and Château de l'Oiselinière de la Ramée at Vertou (10 hectares). Each estate makes a straight Muscadet de Sèvre et Maine and a cuvée de prestige, but all are bottled *sur lie* at the individual estate under the name of the estate. Quality of the wines is high, although Château de Chasseloir is generally regarded as the best. *Open: Apply to Château de Chasseloir.*

Bernard Pichon (Domaine des Croix)
44330 Vallet. Vineyards owned: 17ha.
Produce: 120,000 bottles. VP-R.

80% of production here is of Muscadet de Sèvre et Maine, with smaller amounts of Gros Plant (15%) and Vin de Pays du Jardin de la France (from Gamay and Cabernet Franc). The wines are bottled by Le Cellier du Prieuré at St-George-sur-Loire. *Open: By appointment only.*

Léon Dollet

Le Verger, 44690 La Haie Fouassière. Vineyards owned:
10ha. *Produce: 70,000 bottles.* VP-R.

Muscadet de Sèvre et Maine and Gros Plant are the two wines
from this small estate of mainly old vines. Production techniques use glass-lined tanks and the wines are bottled *sur lie*
from the tank. The wines have a consequent full body and
natural earthy taste. *Open: By appointment only.*

Donatien Bahuaud

La Loge, La Chapelle-Heulin, 44330 Vallet. Vineyards
owned: 18ha. *Produce: 412,00 bottles.* VP-R and N.

Two main brands come from this firm. Le Master de Donatien
is the négociant brand, launched with the 1984 vintage. This is
sold in a painted specially-designed bottle. Quality is reliable if
unexciting. More interesting is the estate-bottled Château de la
Cassemichère which is bottled *sur lie* and has some wood
maturation. The firm has undertaken extensive marketing for
its wines and has gained widespread publicity. They also make
a good Chardonnay vin de table, called Le Chouan. *Open: By
appointment only.*

Domaine des Dorices

La Touche, 44330 Vallet. Vineyards owned: 31ha.
Produce: 200,000 bottles. VP-R.

The Boullault family has run this ancient vineyard since the
1930s, making wines using no chemicals in the winery. They are
particularly proud of their Domaine des Dorices which,
unusually for Muscadet needs two years' ageing. They also
make a younger style Muscadet, Château la Touche, plus a
Gros Plant and a *méthode champenoise* called Leconte. Quality
is high here. *Open: By appointment only.*

Jean Douillard

La Fruitière, 44690 Château Thébaud. Vineyards owned:
20ha. *Produce: 100,000 bottles.* VP-R.

A modern producer who makes a light, fresh and elegant
Muscadet de Sèvre et Maine, named Domaine de la Fruitière.
Open: By appointment only.

Joseph Drouard

La Hallopière, 44690 Monnières. Vineyards owned: 13ha.
Produce: 80,000 bottles. VP-R.

As serious a producer as is possible to find with Muscadet,
making wine traditionally and bottling *sur lie* at the domaine.
The wine is full-bodied and needs a little time in bottle. M.
Drouard allows no other wines to distract him. *Open: By
appointment only.*

Domaine de la Févrie

La Févrie, Maisdon-sur-Sèvre, 44690 La Haie Fouassière.
Vineyards owned: 13ha. *Produce: 70,000 bottles.* VP-R.

Three generations of the Branger family have worked this land.
They now employ modern techniques of temperature control,
but continue to bottle *sur lie* to protect the wine's "gaiety and
youth". The result is a classic Muscadet which can take some
bottle ageing. *Open: By appointment only.*

Gabare de Sèvre

Le Pé de Sèvre, Le Pallet, 44330 Vallet. Vineyards owned:
8oha. *Produce: 160,000 bottles.* VP-R.

This grouping of nine small landowners was set up in 1982 and
already it has become a powerful force in the region. Each
member of the group vinifies and bottles his own wine, while
the group then sells the wine. The 70% of wine not sold in bottle
goes to négociants. The bulk of production is of Muscadet,
which goes under the Gabare de Sèvre label, the remainder is of
Gros Plant. The name Gabare refers to the barges which used to
transport wine along the Sèvre. *Open: By appointment only.*

Château de la Galissonière

Le Pallet, 44330 Vallet. Vineyards owned: 39ha. VP-R.

The estate consists of two properties, Château de la
Galissonière and Château de la Jannière, both of which produce
lively, fresh Muscadet of good quality. The family of Pierre
Lusseaud, the owner, has been at the estate since 1912. Modern
techniques are very much to the fore here, making wine that is
delicious in the summer following the vintage. M. Lusseaud
also makes Gros Plant and Vin de Pays des Marches de Bretagne
from Cabernet Franc and Chardonnay. *Open: By appointment
only.*

Gautier Audas

La Douarderie, 7 Rue du Château, Haute-Goulaine, 44115
Basse-Goulaine. Vineyards owned: 23ha.
Produce: 600,000 bottles. VP-R and N.

95% of this firm's requirements are made up of bought-in wine,
which they then bottle. They make wines from their four
estates, but do not sell it separately. Quality is average rather
than exciting. *Open: By appointment only.*

Isabelle Godineau-Piou

Bouaguignon, 44330 Vallet. Vineyards owned: 33ha.
Produce: 88,000 bottles. VP-R.

Muscadet de Sèvre et Maine and Gros Plant are both produced
on this estate. Much of the wine is sold to négociants, but some
is bottled. They also make red and white Vin de Table in small
quantities. *Open: By appointment only.*

Marquis de Goulaine (Château de Goulaine)

Haute-Goulaine, 44115 Basse-Goulaine. Vineyards owned:
30.7ha. *Produce: 350,000 bottles.* VP-R and N.

The château of Goulaine is a 15th century building. The estate
has been in the family for 1,000 years. When you're that well
established, it's a good thing that the wine is setting an example
to the neighbours. Much of the wine is of a modern style, which
needs early drinking, but the Cuvée du Millenaire, made from
old vines, repays a couple of years' keeping. Gros Plant is also
made. *Open: The château is open from 2–6pm. The winery by
appointment only.*

Guilbaud Frères

Les Lilas, Mouzillon, 44330 Vallet. Vineyards owned:
17.5ha. *Produce: 2.5 million bottles.* VP-R and N.

About 5% of production here is from the three estates owned by this large négociant firm. They bottle Domaine de la Pingossière, Domaine de la Moutonnière and Clos du Pont separately. Other Muscadet de Sèvre et Maine goes under a variety of brand names: Le Soleil Nantais, Cuvée Grand Or, Cuvée du Lion. Wines tend to a soft style. *Open: By appointment only.*

Domaine de la Hautière

44690 St-Fiacre-sur-Maine. Vineyards owned: 10ha.
Produce: 90,000 bottles. VP-R and N.

The Thébaud family has run this small négociant and farm for many generations and today buy in 50% of their stock as grapes from vineyards owned by other members of the family. They make one estate wine: Domaine de la Hautière, bottled *sur lie* in the March following vintage; they also make a négociant Muscadet, Les Doyennes and a Gros Plant. *Open: Appointments preferred.*

Michel et Jean Claude Lebas

38 Rue de Bazoges, 44330 Vallet. Vineyards owned: 15ha.
Produce: 60,000 bottles. VP-R.

Domaine de la Rouxière is the estate, but Réserve des Noes Gueréts is the name of the best wine to come from this small family firm. It is a comparatively sophisticated wine, which is quite soft and with an attractive tingle from being bottled *sur lie.* They also make Gros Plant. *Open: By appointment only.*

Pierre and Rèmy Luneau (Domaine de la Grange)

44430 Le Landreau. Vineyards owned: 30ha.
Produce: 150,000 bottles. VP-R.

The Muscadet here is bottled *sur lie.* The style is quite traditional (the family have been *vignerons* since 1680) and tends to fullness. They also make a small quantity of Gros Plant. Interestingly, they like to bottle the different sections of the vineyard separately and lable them accordingly: Clos de Rochettes, Clos de la Claretiere, Clos des Allèes, Cuvée Domaine. *Open: By appointment only.*

Château de la Mercredière

Le Pallet, 44330 Vallet. Vineyards owned: 36ha.
Produce: 220,000 bottles. VP-R.

The vineyard surrounds a beautiful 14th century château on the banks of the River Sèvre. The winemaking, though, is modern, with stainless steel and bottling under inert gas. The wine is smooth, not too acid, and with plenty of fruit. It responds to a little ageing. *Open: Mon-Fri 9am-noon 2-6pm.*

Louis Metaireau

La Fevrie, 44690 Maisdon-sur-Sèvre. Vineyards owned: 107ha. *Produce: 210,000 bottles.* Group of producers.

Louis Metaireau has organized a group of nine producers who pool resources and make *cuvées* which are sold under M. Metaireau's name. The wines are selected jointly, but bottled *sur lie* at each producer's own cellars. The group also owns one vineyard, the Grand Mouton, as a joint venture. The success of this enterprise lies in the high quality of the wines. *Open: By appointment only.*

Château la Noë

44330 Vallet. Vineyards owned: 60ha.
Produce: 150,000 bottles. VP-R.

The Comte de Malestroit, whose family property this is, produces a classic Muscadet, unusually full-bodied, intended for some ageing. It is not bottled *sur lie*. The estate, set around a classical mansion, has been in the family since 1740. *Open: By appointment only.*

Château de l'Oiselinière

Gorges, 44190 Clisson. Vineyards owned: 32ha.
Produce: 200,000 bottles. VP-R.

The heart of the estate is a 19th century Italianate villa, but the Aulanier family has owned the land since 1765. It is divided into four parcels, mainly producing Muscadet de Sèvre et Maine. There is also some Gros Plant. The winemaking is a mixture of traditional and modern. *Open: Mon–Fri 9:30am–noon; 3–6pm.*

Château Plessis Brezot

Monnières, 44690 La Haie Fouassière. Vineyards owned: 11ha. *Produce: 65,000 bottles. VP-R.*

This is a small estate whose production of Muscadet de Sèvre et Maine is distributed by the négociants Barre Frères. *Open: No.*

Château de la Ragotière

Le Regrippière, 44330 Vallet. Vineyards owned: 29ha.
Produce: 190,000 bottles. VP-R.

The château is an old property, with a 14th century chapel, but the present owners, the Couillaud family, have only been in charge since 1979. They are moving away from traditional techniques to stainless steel. The Muscadet de Sèvre et Maine is very clean, penetrating and citrus: very attractive when drunk young. They also make a Gros Plant. *Open: By appointment only.*

Clos des Rosiers

44330 Vallet. Vineyards owned: 13ha.
Produce: 70,000 bottles. VP-R.

This is a traditional producer, who uses some wood for maturation, making a fragrant wine with plenty of fruit, and which takes some ageing. About two thirds of the production is of Muscadet de Sèvre et Maine, the rest is of Gros Plant. The vineyards title, Clos des Rosiers, is used as a brand name. *Open: By appointment only.*

Marcel Sautejeau (Domaine de l'Hyvernière)

Le Pallet, 44330 Vallet. Vineyards owned: 70ha.
Produce: 450,000 bottles. VP-R and N.

As the vigneron at Domaine de l'Hyvernière, Marcel Sautejeau produces Muscadet de Sèvre et Maine, which is bottled *sur lie* at the estate. As the négociant, they handle wines from Anjou, Saumur and Vouvray. The domaine's history goes back to medieval times when it was visited by the French king Henri IV when he came to sign the Edict of Nantes in 1598. *Open: By appointment only.*

Sauvion et Fils (Château de Cléray)
44330 Vallet. Vineyards owned: 35ha.
Produce: 700,000 bottles. VP-R and N.

The Château de Cléray estate is the heart of a négociant business which produces a range of qualities of Muscadet. The négociant side takes 80% of production and they make Carte d'Or and Laureat brands, as well as Château du Cléray which is bottled *sur lie* and the prestige *cuvée*, Cardinal Richard. Quality is high with all these wines, the style generally being soft, with attractive earthy overtones. They pay great attention to the quality of each different vineyard from which they buy wine. La Nobleraie is a brand name for wine produced from grapes which are bought in. *Open: During working hours.*

André Vinet
12 Rue du Progres Uilbaud, 44330 Vallet. Vineyards owned: None. *Produce: 3 million bottles.* N.

A négociant specializing in the wines of the Pays Nantais. They make Muscadet de Sèvre et Maine and some Gros Plant, plus a sparkling Blanc de Blancs. The range varies, with the wines from some estates being bottled separately – one of them, Château la Touche, is run on organic lines. *Open: By appointment only.*

Western Loire: Muscadet

Pierre et Luc Choblet (Domaine des Herbauges)
Herbauges, 44830 Bouaye. *Produce: 145,000 bottles.* VP-R.

New techniques are used to make straightforward, slightly *pétillant* Muscadet and also some Gros Plant. The vineyard contains some 35-year-old vines. The wines are bottled *sur lie*. There are two brand names: Domaine des Herbauges and Clos de la Senaigerie. They also make some rosé Vin de Pays du Jardin de la France from Grolleau and red from Gamay, plus a *méthode champenoise* called Perlant Ste Cecile. *Open: By appointment only.*

René Erraud (Château de la Roulière)
44310 St-Colomban. Vineyards owned: St-Columban 30ha. *Produce: 30,000 bottles.* VP-R.

Muscadet, Gros Plant and Vin de Pays (from Gamay, Cabernet Franc and Grolleau) are all produced by this traditional grower. 45% of production is of Muscadet, 45% of Gros Plant and 10% of Vin de Pays. Much of it is sold in bulk to négociants. What is bottled is sold under the Château de la Roulière name. *Open: By appointment only.*

Auguste Bonhomme
1 Rue de la Roche, Gorges, 44190 Clisson. Vineyards owned: Muscadet 25ha. *Produce: 960,000 bottles.* VP-R and N.

Fief de la Brie and Domaine du Banchereau are the two estate bottled wines from this négociant. 80% of their sales come from wine which is bought in from the area, the bulk of it from Muscadet AC. A smaller amount of Gros Plant is also sold. Techniques are quite traditional. *Open: Mon–Fri 8am–noon, 2–6pm.*

Western Loire: Ancenis

Jacques Guindon

La Couleuverdière, Saint-Géréon, 44150 Ancenis. Vineyards
owned: Ancenis 8ha; Muscadet Coteaux de la Loire 14ha;
Gros Plant 3ha. *Produce: 200,000 bottles.* VP-R and N.

Inevitably, Muscadet and Muscadet Coteaux de la Loire *sur lie*
are the largest production from the négociant side of the firm –
representing 20% of requirements. But the interest lies in 8,000
bottles of sweet Malvoisie wine made under the Coteaux
d'Ancenis VDQS: a honeyed dessert wine with a good balance.
They also make rosé Coteaux d'Ancenis from Gamay and red
from Cabernet Franc and Cabernet Sauvignon. Some of the red
is matured in wood. *Open: Mon–Sat.*

Les Vignerons de la Noëlle

BP 102, 44150 Ancenis. Vineyards owned: 459ha.
Produce: 2 million bottles. Coop (300 members).

One of the few cooperatives in the Muscadet area, this produces
large quantities of simple Muscadet from 220 hectares under a
number of different brand names. Other wines they make
include red Coteaux d'Ancenis from 50 hectares of Gamay,
Gros Plant and red Vin de Pays du Jardin de la France. They also
make some red and white wines under the Anjou AC, plus a
small amount of Crémant de la Loire from Chardonnay grapes.
Standards are improving with the installation of new equipment. *Open: By appointment only.*

Western Loire: Fiefs Vendéens

Mercier Frères (Domaine de la Chaignée)

La Chaignée, 85770 Vix. Vineyards owned: Fiefs Vendéens
Vix 25ha. *Produce: 9,000 bottles.* VP-R.

All the wines at this small estate are made in stainless steel.
White comes from a blend of Chenin Blanc, Sauvignon and
Chardonnay; rosé from Gamay, Pinot Noir and Cabernet
Franc. Red wine from Gamay, Cabernet Franc and Cabernet
Sauvignon is made by a semi-carbonic maceration method.
Open: No.

Ph. et X. Coirier

La Petite Groie, Pisotte, 85200 Fontenay-le-Comte.
Vineyards owned: Fiefs Vendéens Pisotte 16ha.
Produce: 50,000 bottles. VP-R.

Over half the production here is of red and rosé wines – a blend
of Gamay, Pinot Noir and Cabernet Sauvignon. The red is a
light coloured wine, best drunk chilled and at its best a year
after the vintage. The white is a fragrant blend of Colombard
with Chenin Blanc and Muscadet. *Open: Appointments
preferred.*

Arsene Rambaud

Follet, Bosnay, 85320 Mareuil-sur-Lay. Vineyards owned:
Fiefs Vendéens 4ha. *Produce: 6,000 bottles.* VP-R.

Red and rosé Fiefs Vendéens are produced from a range of
grapes: Gamay, Pinot Noir, Cabernet Franc and Cabernet
Sauvignon and Négrette. About 40% of production is sold to
négociants. *Open: By appointment only.*

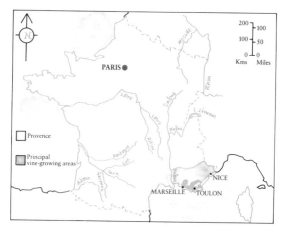

Provence was the first area of France to be planted with vines. They were already growing when Greek traders from Asia Minor arrived at the Phoenecian city of Marseilles in 600BC. The Greeks set about consolidating what they found and the Romans carried on from there. It was from Provence – the Roman Provincia – that vines were carried north up the Rhône valley to the rest of France.

Provence is natural vine growing country. Long hot, dry summers and mild winters provide ideal conditions. The cool winds from the sea keep temperatures from soaring too high, while the mountains of Lubéron protect the region from the worst effects of the Mistral wind.

It is a beautiful part of the country to visit. Inland from the strip of resorts along the coast, the landscape is relatively unspoilt. The Massif des Maures looms huge over the Côtes de Provence vineyards and the Massif de Ste-Baume backs the coastal vineyards of Bandol. The vineyards of Les Baux are inside the spectacular circle of jagged mountains called Les Alpilles. The Alps stretch in a line to the north.

The market has always been there for the wines. The Mediterranean coast was colonized first by traders and, more recently, by holidaymakers. Vast quantities of local wine are washed down by the visitors who throng to the fashionable resorts of the Côte d'Azur or stay on the camp sites behind the beaches. Because it is so much a part of local society, wine is not treated very seriously in Provence. It is something to be enjoyed and not talked about too much. The general quality of wine is adequate rather than inspiring, although there are pockets of higher quality production. Out of four million hectolitres made each year, about 20% is of AC status, under the French average of 25%.

The main concentration of vines is in the département of Var, the central part of Provence. Here they cover over half the agricultural land, two thirds producing rosé, the remainder almost all red. Provence is by far the biggest producer of rosé wine in France: much of it is alcoholic, heady stuff with surprisingly little taste but quite a kick. In the past it has been consumed unconcernedly by tourists, but, increasingly, producers have found a resistance to the old-fashioned heavy style.

Modern equipment has certainly helped to lighten the rosés, giving greater freshness and less risk of oxidation. The new ability to control fermentation has also made it possible to increase the planting of vines for white wines, which everybody realizes are the fashion of the decade. But with 4,500 producers in the Côtes de Provence AC alone, it's going to take a while for the message to get through that white is in and rosé is out.

So there's a vast area of wine production that, certainly before the creation of AC Côtes de Provence, was churning out some fairly mediocre stuff, with only a few producers trying somewhat harder. The best wines of Provence came from a much smaller area in the west – Bandol, Cassis and Pallette – and in the east – Bellet – with decent producers also to be found around Aix-en-Provence and Les-Baux-en-Provence. Good wine still comes from these areas; but, certainly in Bandol and Bellet, the prices are often high, perhaps unnecessarily so.

Things have improved since 1977 with the creation of the AC Côtes de Provence. Tasting panels now control the quality to an extent, tasting upwards of 3,000 wines a year. New grape varieties from the north – the Syrah and Cabernet Sauvignon – are being planted and used to give the wines more taste. The Tibouren, already grown in Provence, is being boosted as a grape to give a deliciously herby taste to dull rosés based on Grenache and Cinsault.

Elsewhere in Provence, things are changing too. The two VDQS areas of Coteaux d'Aix-en-Provence and Coteaux des Baux-en-Provence have been promoted to AC status, and, to my mind, are the best source of good Provençal reds: apart from one or two top estates, they are not too expensive either.

Between Aix-en-Provence and the Côtes de Provence is a new VDQS area, Coteaux Varois. This promises well, especially for the reds, where Cabernet Sauvignon and Syrah have been introduced. Production is huge – around 30 million bottles – and the price is good. While much of the wines goes through cooperatives, it is the few private estates which are doing the hard work.

The Appellations
AC

Bandol: Red, white and rosé wines made in vineyards on the coast between Toulon and Marseilles. The total production area is 1,000 hectares on limestone soil. The approved grape varieties for the reds and rosés include Mourvèdre (which has about 50% of the red vineyard), Grenache, Cinsault, Calitor, Carignan, Syrah and Tibouren. For whites, the grapes are: Bourboulenc, Ugni Blanc, Clairette and Sauvignon. The reds (by far the greatest production) and rosés are the more famous, often commanding high prices. Reds, which have to spend at least 18 months in wood, are deep, intense, described as spicy and peppery on the palate (the Mourvèdre has characteristics of the Syrah). Rosés are often aged before bottling and can acquire a mature orange colour: an acquired taste, but much appreciated in France. Whites are generally less interesting. Vintages: For red, 1976, '78, '80, '81, '82, '83. For rosés and whites, drink generally as young as possible.

Bellet: A tiny AC, to the north of Nice, where most of it seems to be consumed. About 40 hectares are planted. The wine can be red, rosé or white, but here it is the white which is best. Grapes for the whites are the local Rolle with Roussanne, Chardonnay, Clairette and Bourboulenc, producing an attractive almondy wine. For reds and rosés, grapes are the local Braquet (Italian Brachetto) and Folle Noire (Italian Fuella Nera) – after all this is almost Italy – Cinsault and Grenache. Price for all Bellet are high – undeservedly so. Drink young.

Cassis: Not to be confused with blackcurrant liqueur, this is an area producing red, rosé and white wines, situated around the small port of Cassis between Marseilles and Bandol. There are 150 hectares producing 700,000 bottles each year. The white is the most famous, made from a blend of Marsanne, Ugni Blanc, Clairette, Grenache Blanc (locally Doucillon) and Sauvignon, with Marsanne the most important. The wine is dry, normally pale yellow in colour (because of slight oxidation), and quite tangy – like light fino sherry. Reds and rosés are from Grenache, Cinsault, Mourvèdre and Carignan. Vintages: Drink whites as young as possible. For reds, 1976, '78, '80, '81, '82, '83, but drink sooner than Bandol.

Coteaux d'Aix-en-Provence: Promoted to AC with the 1985 vintage, this is an area producing some of the best-value wines in Provence. Reds, rosés and whites are all made on 3,000 hectares of chalky soil lying mainly to the south and east of Aix-en-Provence. Reds are made from Cinsault, Grenache, Counoise, Carignan and Mourvèdre with Cabernet Sauvignon. The Cabernet has an immense influence on the taste (it can give up to 60% of the blend) in some estates, producing a wine akin to a deep-coloured, intense-tasting Bordeaux. Other reds resemble Côtes du Rhône – they are certainly not like red Côtes de Provence. The rosés are lighter in colour than Côtes de Provence. Whites (5% of production) are made from Grenache Blanc, Sémillon, Ugni Blanc and Sauvignon: it is the touch of Sauvignon that gives these wines their class and style and freshness, even if they do tend to lack acidity. Vintages: For reds, 1978, '81, '82, '83, '85. Drink whites and rosés as young as possible.

Coteaux des Baux-en-Provence: A much smaller area than Coteaux d'Aix-en-Provence, lying in a circle of mountains near the hilltop resort of Les-Baux-en-Provence. Virtually all the production is red, although rosé and white are permitted. The general quality of the wines – although similar in style to Aix-en-Provence – is even higher, partly because production is smaller and is all in the hands of private estates. At the moment prices are very good. The grape varieties are the same as for Aix-en-Provence. The AC was created for the 1985 vintage. Vintages: 1978, '81, '82, '83, '85, although wines age a little longer.

Côtes de Provence: By far the largest AC in Provence, covering 18,000 hectares producing red, rosé and white wine. There are three main areas in this huge expanse: the coastal vineyards running from St-Tropez to Toulon; the valley north of the Massif des Maures around Les Arcs and the vineyards further northeast and west of Draguignan. By far the largest production (55%) is of rosé wines. The old style was for heavily alcoholic, full-bodied wines made mainly from Carignan and Grenache. Newer style wines are lighter with some input of Mourvèdre and Tibouren, lower in alcohol and cleaner and younger to taste. Reds are the next most important style in Provence. Made from Grenache, Cinsault, Mourvèdre and Carignan, they now also include Syrah and Cabernet Sauvignon to an increasing degree. As with rosés, there has been a change of style to bring in these northern grapes and the wines have become fresher and less prone to oxidize. They now have some tannic structure and a firmer, spicy, stalky taste which have replaced the somewhat soft heavy taste of old style reds. Whites make up 10–15% of production. Permitted grape varieties are Clairette, Ugni Blanc, Rolle and Sémillon. Early picking and controlled temperature fermentation are improving these whites beyond all recognition. Vintages: For reds, 1982, '83, '85. Drink rosés and whites as young as possible.

Palette: A tiny AC area, just to the east of Aix-en-Provence which really consists of one property: Château Simone. Here old vines on 15 hectares of limestone soil produce red, rosé and white wines. The reds are the finest: made from Mourvèdre, Grenache and Cinsault, they are aged in wood, to produce an austere wine, lean and quite tannic, which needs keeping for some time before drinking. The rosés are made from the same grapes. The whites are made from Clairette, Grenache Blanc and Ugni Blanc: but despite these "southern" grapes, they are surprisingly lively and steely to taste. Drink as young as possible.

VDQS

Coteaux Varois: A large area of vines around the town of Brignoles, making over 30 million bottles a year. Red, rosé and white are made. Red grapes are: Cinsault, Grenache, Mourvèdre, Carignan, Alicante and Aramon (the grapes that have contributed most to the French portion of the European wine lake) with, now, Cabernet Sauvignon and Syrah. They tend to be heavy, slightly too full and a little dull. But quality is improving. Whites comes from Grenache Blanc, Ugni Blanc, Clairette and Malvoisie. It is the Malvoisie which gives them character and some fragrant flavour, but on the whole they lack acidity. The area was promoted from Vin de Pays to VDQS in 1985.

Provence: Bandol

Domaine de Frégate

Domaines Notre-Dame de Port d'Alon, Route de Bandol,
83270 Saint-Cyr-sur-Mer. Vineyards owned: Domaine de
Frégate 22ha. *Produce: 100,000 bottles.* VP-R.

Red is the major part of production here. The wine is aged for
the statutory 18 months, but not sold until three years old. They
are at their best after five to six years. Whites (of which
production is 10% of the total) and rosés are sold in the year
after the vintage. The estate is situated next to the sea, with a
cellar cut into the rock. *Open: Mon–Fri 8am–noon; 2–6pm.*

Domaine le Galantin

83330 Le Plan de Castellet. Vineyards owned: 14ha.
Produce: 60,000 bottles. VP-R.

M. Pascal is only a part-time *vigneron*, but he produces a
fragrant red from 60% Mourvèdre, 20% Grenache and 20%
Cinsault (which he buys in). White and rosé are made in
stainless steel from free-run juice only; the red is made in
stainless steel, then aged in wood for the 18-month minimum.
All the wines tend to the light and fresh side. *Open: By
appointment only.*

Domaine de l'Hermitage

Le Rouve, 83330 Le Beausset. Vineyards owned: 36ha.
Produce: 180,000 bottles. VP-R.

Gerard Duffort, who owns the estate, has restored it completely
since he acquired it in 1974. Half of his production is in red
(which includes small amounts of Syrah), about 45% in rosé,
and the remaining 5% in white (made from Ugni Blanc and
Clairette). Equipment is modern, and the reds are vinified in
stainless steel before going into wood in an air-conditioned
cellar for 18 months. The whole operation is highly profes-
sional and the results expensive. *Open: Mon–Fri 8am–noon;
2–6pm.*

Domaine Lafran Veyrolles

83740, La Cadière d'Azur. Vineyards owned: 8ha.
Produce: 25,000 bottles. VP-R.

Traditional techniques, avoiding chemicals in the vineyard, are
to the forefront here. Mme Jouve-Férec, a descendant of the
family which has owned the estate since 1541, ages her reds for
22 months in wood, while whites and rosés stay in tanks. About
60% of production is of red, 30% rosé and 10% white. Quality,
especially of the red, is high. *Open: By appointment only.*

Domaine la Laidière

GAEC Estienne, Ste-Anne-d'Evenos, 83330 Le Beausset.
Vineyards owned: 18ha. *Produce: 90,000 bottles.* VP-R.

A long slow fermentation after de-stalking is one of the secrets
behind the very fine wines to come from this estate. Stainless
steel is used for vinification, but reds (which account for 60% of
production) are then aged in oak. The red is a wine that lasts a
long time, the whites and rosés often have more fruit than the
average Bandol. The Estienne family was involved in the
creation of the Bandol AC in 1941. *Open: Mon–Fri 8am–noon;
2–6pm.*

Moulin des Costes

Mas de la Rouvière, 83740 La Cadière d'Azur. Vineyards
owned: 75ha. *Produce: 350,000 bottles.* VP-R.

The Bunan family have owned this estate since 1962 after their
return from Algeria. The production is split almost equally
between red and rosé Bandol, with a smaller amount of white.
The wines are made using a mix of modern and traditional
technology, and the results are some superb wines, with a very
high percentage of Mourvèdre in the red. This is one of the few
estates in Bandol which also has a little Cabernet Sauvignon,
used to produce a Vin de Pays de Mont Caume. *Open: Summer:
8am–noon; 2–7pm. Winter: 8am–noon; 2–5:30pm*

Domaine de la Noblesse

83740 La Cadière d'Azur. Vineyards owned: 15ha.
Produce: 90,000 bottles. VP-R.

Jean-Pierre Gaussen is the owner of this small estate, making
powerful reds and a little rosé and white. The style is modern,
with stainless steel being used for fermentation. *Open: By
appointment only.*

Domaines Ott

22 Boulevard d'Aguillon, 06601 Antibes. Vineyards owned:
140ha. *Produce: 550,000 bottles.* VP-R.

One of the largest producers in Provence, founded in 1896.
They own estates in Côtes de Provence (Château de Selle and
Clos Mireille) as well as Bandol (Château Romassan). They are
most famous for their highly sought after Bandol Rosé Coeur de
Grain, which is fermented and aged in wood, giving an orange-
coloured wine which, while it may lack freshness, compensates
with its range of flavours. Small amounts of red and white
Bandol are also made. The Clos Mireille estate produces a white
Côtes de Provence from Ugni Blanc and Sémillon. The Château
de Selle estate produces rosé and red in which there is a high
proportion of Cabernet Sauvignon; the white is dominated by
Sémillon. *Open: Each estate Mon–Fri 8am–noon; 2–6pm.*

Château de Pibarnon

83740 La Cadière d'Azur. Vineyards owned: 30ha.
Produce: 130,000 bottles. VP-R.

The vineyards of Comte Henri de Saint Victor at Château de
Pibarnon are situated 270 metres up, on limestone soil,
dominating the Bandol area. A mix of modern and traditional
techniques are used, with stainless steel for vinification. The red
(60% of production) is aged for a maximum of two years in
wood. It has typical Bandol richness and tannin, and needs
seven to eight years before maturity. Rosé, too, is a wine for
keeping. The white (with 40% of the rare Bourboulenc) needs
to be drunk young. *Open: Mon–Sat 8am–noon; 2:30–7pm.*

Château Romassan

See Domaines Ott.

Château Ste Anne

Ste Anne d'Evenos, 83330 Le Beausset. Vineyards owned:
20ha. *Produce: 100,000 bottles.* VP-R.

There are two estates owned by François Dutheil de la Rochère.

The 12 hectares of Château Ste Anne, a 16th century building, produce Bandol; while the eight-hectare Château de la Tourelle produces Côtes de Provence. Methods are traditional, avoiding the use of chemicals in vinification. The reds are aged for up to 22 months in wood. A light rosé and white Bandol are also made. The Côtes de Provence wine is all rosé. *Open: Mon–Fri 8am–noon; 2–6pm.*

Domaine des Salettes

83740 La Cadière d'Azur. Vineyards owned: 29ha.
Produce: 150,000 bottles. VP-R.

Half the production of Jean Pierre Boyer's Domaine des Salettes, on the slopes of Mal Passe, is of Bandol rosé, a light, fresh style of wine. 45% is of a full, smooth red which has less Mourvèdre than some other producers. This is a solid, reliable producer, even if great heights are not reached. The vineyard has recently expanded by 15 hectares. *Open: By appointment only.*

Domaine Tempier

GAEC Peyraud, Le Plan de Castellet, 83330 Le Beausset.
Vineyards owned: 26ha. *Produce: 90,000 bottles.* VP-R.

The use of chemicals is minimal in this vineyard which was originally established in 1834. Lucien Peyraud, the owner, works hard to support the wines of Bandol, and continues traditional methods, using wood for some of his fermentation, and ageing the reds in wood for up to 30 months. The results are tannic wines, which need plenty of time, but mature well, with complex flavours. Red and rosé are the only two wines made. The blend of the rosé includes a little Carignan from old vines. *Open: By appointment only.*

Château Vannières

83740 La Cadière d'Azur. Vineyards owned: 27ha.
Produce: 150,000 bottles. VP-R.

The vineyard of Vannières dates back to the 16th century, when it was the property of André de Lombard, Seigneur de Castellet. Today the owners are the Boisseaux family, who use traditional methods, vinifying in wood. They make a red Bandol and a red Côtes de Provence, both with the same *cépage* which includes 6% Syrah. The Bandol can be very long-lasting with splendid rich, ripe fruit. *Open: By appointment only.*

Provence: Bellet

Château de Bellet

St Roman de Bellet, 06200 Nice. Vineyards owned: 9ha.
Produce: 30,000 bottles. VP-R.

One of a handful of Bellet producers, Ghislain de Charnacé makes white, red and rosé wines at the historic castle of Bellet in the hills above Nice. The whites are made from Rolle (Ugni Blanc) and Chardonnay; the reds and rosés from Braquet, Folle Noire, Cinsault and Grenache. Methods are traditional. The white is to my mind the most interesting of the three wines: the Chardonnay gives it considerable depth, balancing the simple rather bland freshness of the Rolle. The rosé is fruitier than many Côtes de Provence rosés – but is also more expensive. *Open: By appointment only.*

Provence: Cassis

Clos Ste Magdelaine

Avenue du Revestel, 13260 Cassis. Vineyards owned: 10ha.
Produce: 50,000 bottles. VP-R.

Three quarters of the production is of a white straw coloured wine, with a nutty bouquet and a tinge of greenness from the small amount of Sauvignon in the blend. The remainder is of a rosé, made from Cinsault, Grenache and Mourvèdre. The vineyard runs almost out to sea on a narrow spit of land jutting into the bay of Cassis. *Open: By appointment only.*

Provence: Coteaux d'Aix

Château Barbebelle

Rognes, 13840. Vineyards owned: 34ha.
Produce: 150,000 bottles. VP-R.

Red, rosé and white wines are made on this large estate, in the hands of the Herbeau family for several generations. The top quality red *cuvée* is the called Château Barbebelle Jas d'Amour, a blend of Cabernet Sauvignon, Syrah and Grenache. The standard red and rosé Château Barbebelle are made from Grenache, Cinsault and Carignan. The white is made from Ugni Blanc and Sauvignon. *Open: Mon–Fri 9am–noon; 2–7pm.*

Domaine les Bastides

St Canadet, 13610 Puy-Ste-Réparade. Vineyards owned: 20ha. *Produce: 100,000 bottles.* VP-R.

Organic methods are used in this vineyard, which produces a red and rosé Coteaux d'Aix, using traditional grape varieties. The red Rouge Tradition is a blend of Grenache, Mourvèdre and Cinsault. There is also a Cuvée Spéciale which has 50% Cabernet Sauvignon. The house speciality is a Vin Cuit, a dessert wine made from Grenache, Cinsault, Ugni Blanc and Clairette. *Open: By appointment only.*

Château de Beaulieu

13840 Rognes. Vineyards owned: 300ha.
Produce: 1.2 million bottles. VP-R.

The largest estate in the Aix-en-Provence AC, owned by the Touzet family. A modern winery produces red, white and rosé wines from vines on volcanic soil to the east of Aix. The red is made from Grenache, Cabernet Sauvignon, Syrah, Mourvèdre. The rosé from Cinsault and Carignan; the white from Sauvignon, Clairette, Ugni Blanc and Sémillon. The estate has been largely created in the past decade by the Touzet family who now live in the well-restored house. *Open: By appointment only.*

Commanderie de la Bargemone

RN7, 13760 Saint-Cannat. Vineyards owned: 60ha.
Produce: 350,000 bottles. VP-R.

This estate has been spectacularly restored by the Rozan family, wealthy industrialists from northern France. Techniques rely on tradition, but there is some carbonic maceration for the reds, and stainless steel fermentation for the whites. The top red Cuvée Tournebride, made with 50% Cabernet Sauvignon, spends some time in wood. The standard red Commanderie de la Bargemone is a blend of Grenache (45%) with Cinsault, Syrah, Cabernet Sauvignon and Carignan. A rosé is made from Grenache and Cinsault; the white is a blend of Sauvignon, Grenache Blanc and Ugni Blanc. High standards have been achieved since the estate was bought by M. Rozan in 1977. *Open: By appointment only.*

Château la Coste
13610 Puy Ste Réparade. Vineyards owned: 180ha.
Produce: 1.3 million bottles. VP-R.

The largest estate in Aix-en-Provence and one of the largest in Provence. The Bordonado family owns Château la Coste and two associated estates Domaine de la Grande Séouve and Domaine de la Boulangère. The techniques are modern for rosés and whites, but traditional for reds. Nearly half the production is of red, with 40% rosé and 15% white. For such large scale production, the quality of the wines is very high – especially for the reds. They have just purchased a new 30 hectare estate, Château de Costefriede, whose wines will be available from the 1987 vintage. *Open: By appointment only.*

Château de Fonscolombe
13610 Puy-ste-Réparade. Vineyards owned: 160ha.
Produce: 1 million bottles. VP-R.

The Marquises de Saporta have owned this estate since 1720, but now modern equipment is used to make some of the best value wines from Coteaux d'Aix AC. The red Château de Fonscolombe is the bulk of production: a wine which is fruity, aromatic and can be drunk young, although it will age for some years. Other brands used are Domaine de la Cremade and Marquis de Saporta. They also make a Vin de Pays des Bouches du Rhône, called Domaine de Boullery. *Open: Mon–Fri 8am–noon; 2–6pm.*

Château Grand Seuil
13540 Puyricard. Vineyards owned: 47ha.
Produce: 250,000 bottles. VP-R.

This medieval château is now owned by the Carreau Gaschereau family, which bought the estate in 1973. They have renovated the estate and installed modern equipment in a brand new 6,000 hectolitres capacity cellar. They produce red, rosé and white; the red is a blend of Cabernet Sauvignon, Syrah and Grenache. They also make a Blanc de Blancs *méthode champenoise* wine. The wines reach a reliable quality. *Open: By appointment only.*

Château Vignelaure
Route de Jouques, 83560 Rians. Vineyards owned: 55ha.
Produce: 160,000 bottles. VP-R.

In the days before Coteaux d'Aix was promoted to AC this was probably the most expensive VDQS wine in France. Now Vignelaure is simply the most expensive wine from Coteaux d'Aix. It's still the best: Georges Brunet, who restored the Bordeaux château of La Lagune, has created the nearest thing to a red Bordeaux in Provence, using a blend of 60% Cabernet Sauvignon, 30% Syrah and 10% Grenache. The wine is made using modern technology, stays in wood for up to 32 months, producing an elegant wine, with finesse even though the fruit is full and rich. In Bordeaux manner, a second wine, Le Page de Vignelaure, is made from young vines. *Open: Mon–Sat 8:30am–12:30pm; 2–6:30pm. Sun 10:30am–12:30pm; 2–6:30pm.*

Château Vignerolles

13700 Gignac-la-Nerthe. Vineyards owned: 80ha.
Produce: 500,000 bottles. VP-R.

This property, owned by Charles Sardou, is to the west of Aix-en-Provence, and operates using modern technology and stainless steel vinification. 65% of production is of red, with 30% rosé and 5% white. The brand names used are Château Saint Jean de l'Hôpital and Cuvée Margot. The white and rosé are better than the red – the white, with its touch of Sauvignon, especially attractive. *Open: By appointment only.*

Provence: Coteaux des Baux en Provence

Domaines de Lauzières

Le Destet, 13890 Mouriès. Vineyards owned: 60ha.
Produce: 400,000 bottles. VP-R.

This well-established family estate produces only one wine: a red Coteaux des Baux, using 70% Grenache, plus Cinsault, Carignan, Syrah and Mourvèdre to make up the difference. The wine is hard in youth, but mellows after four to five years. *Open: By appointment only.*

Mas de la Dame

13520 Les Baux-en-Provence. Vineyards owned: 55ha.
Produce: 300,000 bottles. VP-R.

Rosé and red wine is made here in one of the best Baux-en-Provence estates. Stainless steel is used. The high (14%) percentage of Syrah in the Rouge Réserve red gives it good ageing ability, and the introduction of 23% Cabernet Sauvignon produces considerable elegance. The rosé has 25% Syrah and 25% Cabernet Sauvignon. The wines are not – yet – expensive for their quality. *Open: By appointment only.*

Mas de Gourgonnier

Le Destet, 13890 Mouriès. Vineyards owned: 35ha.
Produce: 200,000 bottles. VP-R.

A new vineyard on an old family estate, run by Nicolas Cartier who operates the vineyard organically, producing excellent wines, red, rosé and white. His best wine is the Reserve du Mas, a blend of Cabernet Sauvignon (30%), Syrah (30%) and Grenache (40%). His other red introduces 10% Mourvèdre. The white, a freshly made wine, has 40% Sauvignon Blanc. A very serious estate. *Open: Mon–Fri 8am–noon; 2–6pm.*

Mas de Sainte-Berthe

13520 Les Baux-en-Provence. Vineyards owned; 33ha.
Produce: 25,000 bottles. VP-R.

Carbonic maceration and stainless steel produce easy-drinking fruity wines at this estate, situated in a spectacular position under the cliff-top village of Les-Baux. Almost two thirds of the production is red, one third rosé, with a few thousand bottles of white. The brand Cuvée Louis David is their top quality wine, and is designed for some ageing. *Open: Mon–Sun 9am–noon; 2–6pm.*

Domaine des Terres Blanches

RN99, 13210 Saint-Rémy-de-Provence. Vineyards owned:
40ha. *Produce: 200,000 bottles.* VP-R.

Organic farming methods are used on this model estate and few
chemicals are used in the making of the wine. Noël Michelin,
the owner, and his cellarmaster Georges Dutel are both strong
advocates of this method of winemaking, which has gained
ground in other Baux-en-Provence estates. They produce a
white, a rosé and a red. The red is sometimes described as
austere, and certainly it needs time: then it becomes very poised
and elegant. *Open: Mon–Sat 8am–noon; 2–6pm.*

Domaine de Trévallon

13150 St-Etienne. Vineyards owned: 15ha.
Produce: 65,000 bottles. VP-R.

The vineyards of this producer are in the centre of the strange
basin surrounded by Les Alpilles mountains. This is another of
the estates in Les-Baux which practises organic methods. In the
winery, stainless steel is used, but then the wine is aged in wood.
The red – the sole wine from the estate – is a blend of 60%
Cabernet Sauvignon and 40% Syrah, a splendid combination
which produces a wine that is well structured but has
considerable ageing ability. *Open: By appointment only.*

Domaine de la Vallongue

13810 Eygalières. Vineyards owned: 35ha.
Produce: 130,000 bottles. VP-R.

Red and rosé wine is produced at this estate. The wines are
mainly based on traditional varieties in the area: Carignan,
Cinsault and Grenache, with only a little amelioration from
Cabernet Sauvignon and Syrah. The red is full-bodied, southern
tasting but not overblown. The rosé tends to mature quickly
and needs to be drunk young. *Open: By appointment only.*

Provence: Palette

Château Simone

Palette, 13100 Aix-en-Provence. Vineyards owned: 15ha. VP-R.

By owning three quarters of the vineyards of the AC area, the
Rougier family are entitled to regard themselves as synonymous
with Palette. They make red, rosé and white. To my mind – on
the rare occasions when I have tasted the wines – the red (from
Grenache, Mourvèdre, Cinsault, and local varieties
Manosquan, Caster, Brun-Fourca and Teoulier) is wood-aged
and needs six or seven years to be ready. The white is herbily
aromatic. *Open: By appointment only.*

Provence: Côtes de Provence

Jean Bagnis et Fils

83390 Cuers. Vineyards owned: 13ha.
Produce: 3.5 million bottles. VP-R and N.

By far the largest production from this firm is of the branded
L'Estandon Côtes de Provence wine. They also own a small
vineyard in the Bellet AC area at Château de Crémat, where
they make red, rosé and white wines. *Open: By appointment
only.*

Château Barbeyrolles
Gassin, 83990 St-Tropez. Vineyards owned: 10ha.
Produce: 65,000 bottles. VP-R.

Organic methods are used in the small vineyard owned by Régine Sumeire, a PhD in history who is researching the history of viticulture in the area. She makes a very fine red and rosé – the red a blend of a third each of Grenache, Mourvèdre and Syrah, which then spends 10 to 18 months in wood. The rosé is surprisingly delicate for Provence. A small amount of white will also be made from Ugni Blanc, Rolle and Sémillon planted in 1983. *Open: By appointment in winter only.*

La Bastide Neuve
Le Cannet des Maures, 83340 Le Luc. Vineyards owned: 12ha. *Produce: 70,000 bottles.* VP-R.

Unusually for Provence, M. Brochier makes 100% varietal wines – red, rosé and white. The reds – from Syrah, Mourvèdre and Grenache – are made in a traditional way, before ageing for one year in large barrels. The other wines are made in enamel-lined tanks: a Tibouren-based rosé of great character and a white from Ugni Blanc. *Open: Mon–Sat 8am–noon; 2–7pm.*

Commanderie de Peyrassol
SCEA Rigord, Flassans, 83340 Le Luc. Vineyards owned: 55ha. *Produce: 160,000 bottles.* VP-R.

Modern technology is used at this large estate to make red, white and rosé wine. The red is then aged in new wood, the time varying according to vintage. There are two ranges: a standard range, Cuvée Eperon d'Or of Blanc de Blancs, rosé and red (the red having 33% Cabernet Sauvignon). A red and white special *cuvée*, Cuvée Marie Estelle, are produced from lower yielding vines: the red in this case has 60% Cabernet Sauvignon. A rosé is also made – Le Rosé d'Art. *Open: Mon–Sun 9am–noon; 2–5pm. Appointments necessary for groups.*

La Bernarde
83340 Le Luc. Vineyards owned: 33ha.
Produce: 200,000 bottles. VP-R.

M. and the late Mme Meulnart bought this vineyard in 1974 and invested considerable sums of money to produce top quality wines. The vineyard is situated 300 metres up, north of Les Maures. Reds include the special *cuvée*, Clos Bernarde St-Germain, made from 55% Syrah, 40% Cabernet Sauvignon and 5% Grenache, and Clos de la Bernarde, which contains 30% Grenache. Both reds are matured in bottle rather than wood. The estate produces a delicate rosé made with 30% Tibouren plus Grenache and Cinsault, and white wines made from Ugni Blanc and Sémillon. *Open: By appointment only.*

Domaine Castel Roubine
BP 117, RD 562, 83510 Lorgues. Vineyards owned: 65ha.
Produce: 300,000 bottles. VP-R.

Soundly-based red, rosé and white Côtes de Provence, the red is made in wood, the white and rosé in stainless steel. The rosé is made attractive by a touch of Tibouren, and the red has a good percentage of Cabernet Sauvignon, with some Syrah and Mourvèdre. *Open: Mon–Fri 8am–noon; 2–5pm.*

Vignobles Crocé-Spinelli

Domaine des Clarettes, 83460 Les Arcs. Vineyards owned:
31ha. *Produce: 60,000 bottles.* VP-R.

M. Crocé-Spinelli owns three estates: Domaine des Clarettes
near Les Arcs, and Domaine du Saint-Esprit and Domaine de
Fontselves near Draguignan. The wine from Domaine du Saint-
Esprit has a high percentage of Syrah, while Domaine des
Clarettes relies more on Mourvèdre. At Domaine de Fontselves
there is a planting of Cabernet Sauvignon. Rosé wines are also
made. *Open: Appointments preferred.*

Domaine de la Croix

83420 La Croix Valmer. Vineyards owned: 100ha.
Produce: 540,000 bottles. VP-R.

A long-established vineyard in the St-Tropez peninsula which
has been completely reconstructed in recent years. They
produce a red, white, rosé, Blanc de Blancs and a Gris de Gris.
They also produce 100% Cabernet Sauvignon and 100%
Mourvèdre wines. *Open: By appointment only.*

Domaine de Curebeasse

Km 4, Route de Bagnols, 83600 Fréjus. Vineyards owned:
18ha. *Produce: 100,000 bottles.* VP-R.

Low temperature fermentation is used here for rosés and
whites: the whites stay on their lees after fermentation to retain
their freshness. There are three styles of red and two of rosé.
The top red is Roches Noires, which comes from vines on
volcanic soil; it is matured in wood and made from 50%
Mourvèdre, 30% Cabernet Sauvignon and 20% Syrah. Other
reds use Cinsault, Carignan and Grenache. The white is a blend
of Rolle and Ugni Blanc: an attractive, fresh wine that needs to
be drunk young. *Open: By appointment only.*

Domaine de Deffends

83660 Carnoules. Vineyards owned: 29ha.
Produce: 50,000 bottles. VP-R.

Red and rosé take 90% of production at this traditional estate.
A white is made from Ugni Blanc and Clairette. Nearly 60% of
production goes to négociants in bulk. *Open: In working hours
only.*

Domaine du Dragon

Route de Montferrat, 83300 Draguignan. Vineyards owned:
25ha. *Produce: 130,000 bottles.* VP-R.

The three wines – red, white and rosé – produced here all bear
the Domaine du Dragon name. The red has 30% Cabernet
Sauvignon and a proportion of Syrah, and is made using a semi-
carbonic maceration method, giving it considerable colour even
if it lacks depth. The white is slightly sweet and soft, with 30%
Clairette. Vinification methods are traditional at M. Garro's
estate. *Open: Mon–Sat 9am–noon; 3–7pm.*

Domaine des Féraud

Route de la Garde Freinet, 83550 Vidauban. Vineyards
owned: 60ha. *Produce: 190,000 bottles.* VP-R.

High quality winemaking goes on at this large estate. The red, a
blend of 60% Cabernet Sauvignon, 25% Syrah and 15%

Grenache is a strange Bordeaux creature in the middle of Provence, big and tannic and requiring some ageing. The rosé and white are well-made if less unusual. The vineyard has been owned by the Laudon-Rival family for three generations. *Open: By appointment only.*

Domaine des Fougues

83400 Hyères. Vineyards owned: 26ha.
Produce: 40,000 bottles. VP-R.

Changes in this vineyard have increased the planting of Syrah, Tibouren and Grenache. They make red, rosé and white Côtes de Provence and red and rosé Vin de Pays du Var. The two brand names are Domaine les Fouques and Les Restanques. *Open: Mon–Fri 8am–noon; 1–6pm.*

Château de Gairoird

83390 Cuers. Vineyards owned: 30ha.
Produce: 80,000 bottles. VP-R.

Half M. Pierrefeu's production is of rosé, for which there is a good export market. It is made in small refrigerated tanks of epoxy-lined resin: the 30% Mourvèdre holds it together and gives it some elegance. The white contains 40% Clairette, plus Rolle and Ugni Blanc. Reds contain Syrah and Grenache. A second label is called Domaine St-Jean. *Open: Mon–Fri 8am–noon; 2–6pm.*

Domaine de Galoupet

83250 La Londe les Maures. Vineyards owned: 65ha.
Produce: 450,000 bottles. VP-R.

Perhaps the most interesting wine made on this estate is a rosé made with 95% Tibouren, a fresh, very fragrant wine, quite unlike traditional heavy Provence rosés. The red Cuvée Spéciale, made from Mourvèdre, Syrah and Grenache, is aged in wood. The white is a blend of Rolle and Sémillon. *Open: By appointment only.*

Vignobles Gasperini

42 Avenue de la Libération, 83260 La Crau. Vineyards
owned: 15ha. Produce: 85,000 bottles. VP-R.

The estate has been in the Gasperini family's possession since 1834 and is now run by Alain and Guy who preserve traditional methods. The red, called Cuvée des Commandeurs, is matured in wood, which enhances the ageing potential of the Cabernet Sauvignon in the blend. There is also a rosé made from Grenache and Cinsault called Cuvée Dame Jardin. *Open: Mon–Fri 8am–noon; 2–7pm.*

Château Grand'Boise

BP No 2, 13530 Trets. Vineyards owned: 40ha.
Produce: 165,000 bottles. VP-R.

A well-maintained estate southeast of Aix-en-Provence, dating from the 17th century, which has been in the Gruey family since 1879. A combination of techniques is used: cement tanks for white and rosé, and carbonic maceration for reds, followed by some wood ageing. The red is meaty, savoury on the palate, which is quite soft, despite its blend of Cabernet Sauvignon, Syrah and Grenache. Some of the grapes used for the white wine are bought in. *Open: Mon–Sat 8am–noon; 1:30–5:30pm.*

Domaine de Grandpré
83390 Puget-Ville. Vineyards owned: 15ha.
Produce: 40,000 bottles. VP-R.

A traditional estate, based – for reds and rosés – on Carignan and Grenache, with Ugni Blanc and Clairette for white. The red is the best wine. *Open: Mon–Sat 9am–8pm.*

Domaine du Jas d'Esclans
Route de Callas, 83920 La Motte. Vineyards owned: 50ha.
Produce: 125,000 bottles. VP-R.

The red is the best wine from this old-fashioned estate, owned by M. Lorgues. It's matured in wood and has smooth, firm fruit, which can take some ageing. The blend is of Mourvèdre, Syrah and Grenache with 50% Cinsault. Sémillon and Clairette in the white give the wine an attractively perfumed bouquet, but it tends to heaviness. The rosé is classic Provençal rosé. *Open: By appointment only.*

Mas de Cadenet
13530 Trets. Vineyards owned: 50ha.
Produce: 100,000 bottles. VP-R.

The Negrel family have owned this pretty estate since 1813. Syrah, Cabernet Sauvignon and Grenache are used for the red, while rosé wines are made from Cinsault and Grenache. Techniques are a combination of traditional and modern. The red is the best wine: spicy and rich, it ages well, and also comes through well when young. *Open: By appointment only.*

Luc and Louis Maille
42 Avenue Ferrandin, 83570 Carces. Vineyards owned: 19ha.
Produce: 100,000 bottles. VP-R.

There are three sections to this estate: Domaine St-Jean, on limestone soil, is the best, and produces a good red based on Syrah, Cabernet Sauvignon and Grenache. The two other vineyards are Domaine de Canebieres and Bastide de la Rimade. In total, half the vineyards are now planted with noble grape varieties for red wines, leaving Carignan and Cinsault for the rosés and a little Ugni Blanc and Rolle for whites. They also make Vin de Pays du Var. *Open: By appointment only.*

Les Maitres Vignerons de la Presqu'ile de Saint-Tropez
83990 St-Tropez. Vineyards owned: 168ha.
Produce: 2.7 million bottles. Coop (12 members).

This cooperative choose only the wines from its members that it wishes to bottle and sell. Hence its quality is high. Stainless steel is used for whites and rosés: the white (a blend of Ugni Blanc and Rolle) is particularly attractive. The two brand names used are Château de Pampelonne and St-Roch les Vignes. There is also a top quality range of red wines under the name Cuvée de Chasseur. Distinctive marketing tactics include an association with local Michelin 3-star chef Roger Vergé and painted bottles. *Open: Mon–Fri 8am–noon; 2–6pm.*

Domaine de la Malherbe
83230 Bormes-les-Mimosas. Vineyards owned: 25ha.
Produce: 100,000 bottles. VP-R.

A vineyard in a spectacular setting by the sea, facing the Fort de

Bregancon, an island castle now a residence of the French President. Madame Serge Ferrari, the owner, has invested considerable sums to create a modern winery which produces wines benefiting from the cool air of the coast. Three brand names are used: Reine Jeanne, Pointe du Diable and, for the top *cuvées*, Domaine de la Malherbe. The rosé is especially fine. *Open: By appointment only.*

Château Miraval

83143 Le Val. Vineyards owned: 19ha.
Produce: 40,000 bottles. VP-R.

85% of production is rosé, the rest red and white. They use Carignan, Cinsault and Syrah for red; Cinsault for rosé; and Ugni Blanc for some white. Some Vin de Pays du Var is also made. Jacques Loussier, the owner, is also a well-known jazz pianist. *Open: By appointment only.*

Château de Mentone

St Antonin du Var, 83510 Lorgues. Vineyards owned: 29ha.
Produce: 35,000 bottles. VP-R.

Much of the produce from this estate goes in bulk to Lyons and Paris, but a small amount is bottled on the premises. Traditional methods are used by Mme Perrot de Gasquet, whose family has owned the estate for 150 years. The estate has grown quickly recently, from 10 hectares to the present 30. *Open: By appointment only.*

Clos Mireille

See Domaines Ott, Bandol

Château Montaud

Pierrefeu, 83390 Cuers. Vineyards owned: 400ha.
Produce: 2 million bottles. VP-R.

M. Ravel returned from Algeria, and bought this large estate, where he has installed a winery with a capacity of 28,000 hectolitres, making clean, modern fresh wines. The rosé is the bulk of production: light with plenty of acidity. The red has some Syrah and Mourvèdre in the blend and is an attractive wine which needs some ageing. The white is less interesting. *Open: By appointment only.*

Château Minuty

Gassin, 83990 St-Tropez. Vineyards owned: 80ha.
Produce: 160,000 bottles. VP-R.

There are two estates owned by the Farnet family: Château Minuty and Châteauneuf à Vidauban, which is sold under the Domaines Farnet name. Grenache, Cinsault, Mourvèdre and Syrah are used in the red Château Minuty, which is aged in wood to produce an elegant wine. Rosé and white are also made under the Château Minuty name. A sparkling Blanc de Blancs is made under the Domaines Farnet name. *Open: Mon–Sat 9am–noon; 2–7pm.*

Domaine de Nestuby

83570 Cotignac. Vineyards owned: 40ha.
Produce: 300,000 bottles. VP-R and N.

The négociant side of Roubaud et Fils provides 30% of their requirements. They make red, rosé and white Côtes de

Provence, Coteaux Varois and vin de table red and rosé. Methods are traditional. Brand names used are Domaine de Nestuby, Domaine Jean Roubaud; and Roxane for Coteaux Varois wines. *Open: By appointment only.*

Domaine de Peissonnel

Route de la Garde Freinet, 83550 Vidauban. Vineyards owned: 15ha. *Produce: 60,000 bottles. VP-R.*

Unusually for Côtes de Provence, this estate only produces red wines. And, even more unusually, they make a wine from 80% Merlot with 15% Cabernet Franc: a combination which works best in cooler years, when the wine's structure shows through. The Domaine de Peissonnel red *cuvée* is a blend of 50% Syrah and 50% Cabernet Sauvignon: a strongly tannic wine which needs at least four years before drinking. *Open: By appointment only.*

Domaine des Planes

83520 Roquebrune sur Argens. Vineyards owned: 25ha. *Produce: 150,000 bottles. VP-R.*

Ilse and Christophe Rieder have owned this estate since 1980. They also own vineyards in Germany and Switzerland, and have obviously learnt much of modern techniques from those two countries. All fermentation is by grape variety in stainless steel, although the red is then aged in wood for up to 18 months. They make a full range of Côtes de Provence AC wines, including a rosé from 100% Tibouren. They also produce Vin de Pays du Var: red and rosé and a sweet 100% Muscat. Names include Domaine des Planes, Grives des Planes and Coulée du Fournel. *Open: By appointment only.*

Vignobles Poussel

Domaines le Val d'Anrieu, BP4 Gonfaron 83590. Vineyards owned: 35ha. *Produce: 60,000 bottles. VP-R.*

The vineyards are in the valleys of Arnieu, la Pellegrine and Sableu, the first two on limestone soil, the third on more sandy soil. The white is made from Rolle and Ugni Blanc; the rosé Cuvée Jean Remy from Grenache and Cinsault with a little Mourvèdre, Syrah, Carignan and Tibouren. Red grapes include Grenache, Mourvèdre, Syrah, Cabernet Sauvignon and Cinsault and the top red wine is called Cuvée Caroline. *Open: By appointment only.*

Pradel

06270 Villeneuve Loubet. Vineyards owned: none. *Produce: 1.3 million cases. N.*

This négociant is a large-scale merchant, making large-scale Côtes de Provence, Bellet and Bandol. *Open: By appointment only.*

Domaine de la Pugette

Le Thoronet, 83340 Le Luc. Vineyards owned: 23ha. VP-R.

M. Petit makes a red, rosé and white at his estate near Brignoles in the central Côtes de Provence. The vineyards stretch up to the ruins of the Abbey of Thoronet, which was a Cistercian monastery. The red, made from Grenache, Syrah and Cabernet Sauvignon is the best: aged in wood, it has firm tannin in youth and needs time to mellow. *Open: By appointment only.*

Cave de Vinification de Ramatuelle

Route de la Croix-Volmer, 83350 Ramatuelle. Vineyards
owned: 550ha.
Produce: 800,000 bottles. Coop (205 members).

A rosé and a red are the two principal wines made at this large
cooperative. The rosé is 100% Tibouren, which results in a
refreshing wine, with plenty of character. The red is a blend of
Grenache, Carignan and Syrah. Much of the wine is sold in
bulk. *Open: By appointment only.*

Vignobles F. Ravel (Château Montaud)

83390 Pierrefeu. Vineyards owned: 380ha.
Produce: 2 million bottles. VP-R.

One of the largest private estates in Côtes de Provence, built up
by M. Ravel since the 1960s. He makes a mix of Côtes de
Provence red, rosé and white and Vin de Pays des Maures, using
Cabernet Sauvignon for the red and Tibouren for the rosé.
*Open: Mon–Thur 8am–noon; 1:30–5:30pm. Fri 8am–noon;
1:30–4:30pm.*

Domaine Richeaume

13114 Puylombier. Vineyards owned: 22ha.
Produce: 100,000 bottles. VP-R.

M. Hoesch's vineyards are on the slopes of Mt Sainte-Victoire
in the east of the Côtes de Provence. He makes a red from
Cabernet Sauvignon and Syrah which is aged for two years in
wood, and believes that even his rosé and white are wines for
keeping. A Blanc de Blancs from Clairette is certainly well made
in a traditional way. *Open: By appointment only.*

Domaine de Rimauresq

83790 Pignans. Vineyards owned: 26ha.
Produce: 80,000 bottles. VP-R.

This vineyard is planted with ancient vines, has small yields but
high quality. The red, aged in wood and a blend of Syrah,
Mourvèdre, Grenache, Carignan and Cinsault, is particularly
fine, with a warmth balanced by structure and some tannin.
The rosé is 100% Tibouren, while the white is a blend of Ugni
Blanc, Clairette and Rolle. A top producer, in an estate which is
one of the oldest in the region. *Open: By appointment only.*

Saint-André de Figuière

83250 La Londe. Vineyards owned: 15ha.
Produce: 60,000 bottles. VP-R.

An organically run vineyard with modern equipment in the
winery and producing some deliciously refreshing wines. The
white is light and fresh, a blend of Sémillon, Ugni Blanc and
Rolle. The red Cuvée Spéciale is a soft, rich wine, a blend of
Mourvèdre and Carignan, which needs three to four years. The
estate also produces a Vin de Pays du Var. *Open: Mon–Fri
9am–noon; 2–6pm.*

Domaine de St-Baillon

83340 Flassans-sur-Issole. Vineyards owned: 28ha.
Produce: 150,000 bottles. VP-R.

Stainless steel for vinification and wood for maturing the reds
sit side by side in this new winery, owned by Hervé Goudard

since 1974. As much as 60% of the vineyards is devoted to Cabernet Sauvignon and Syrah, which are blended into the spicy, peppery Cuvée de Roudaï, and are joined by Cinsault and Grenache in the Rouge Traditionnel. Rosé is also made, and a Blanc de Blancs of Rolle and Ugni Blanc. Domaine du Pradon is another brand name. *Open: By appointment only.*

Château de Selle

See Domaines Ott, Bandol

Domaine de la Source Ste-Marguerite

Le Haut Pansard, 83250 La Londe les Maures. Vineyards owned: 14ha. *Produce: 65,000 bottles.* VP-R.

M. Fayard produces red, rosé and white wine from his estate which he acquired in 1977. He uses the name of La Source Ste-Marguerite for his standard wines and Oustau de Baumanière for his special *cuvée*. *Open: By appointment only.*

Provence: Coteaux Varois VDQS

Domaine du Deffends

83470 St Maximin. Vineyards owned: 10ha.
Produce: 40,000 bottles. VP-R.

Two reds and a rosé – all VDQS Coteaux Varois – are produced from this small estate. Clos de la Truffière (made from 40% Cabernet Sauvignon, 45% Syrah; 15% Grenache and Cinsault) and Rouge du Deffends (20% Cabernet and Syrah, 80% Grenache and Cinsault) are the two reds. The Rosé de la Nuit is made from 80% Cinsault and 20% Grenache. A form of carbonic maceration is used to bring out colour in the red. The rosé is almost blush pink in colour. *Open: By appointment only.*

Domaine de Saint-Jean

83930 Villecroze. Vineyards owned: 31ha.
Produce: 130,000 bottles. VP-R.

This modern firm, founded in 1975, produces Coteaux Varois and Vin de Pays du Var from a large vineyard containing a considerable proportion of Cabernet Sauvignon and some Syrah as well as the more usual Cinsault (used for rosé) and Grenache. A *méthode champenoise* Blanc de Blancs is made from Ugni Blanc. The Vin de Pays du Var are 100% varietals (from Syrah and Cabernet Sauvignon). The Coteaux Varois red is a blend of Cabernet Sauvignon, Syrah and Grenache. Red and rosé wines are also sold in bulk. The vineyard is unusual because of the training system on wires and the use of California T-budding techniques for the Cabernet Sauvignon. *Open: Mon–Fri 8am–noon; 1–6:30pm.*

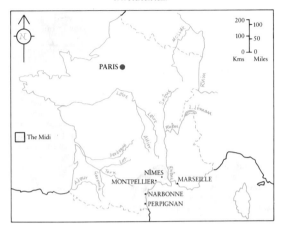

Languedoc – the land of the French wine lake – and Roussillon occupy the stretch of Mediterranean coast that sweeps in a great arc from Marseilles down to the Spanish frontier. A wide coastal plain in Languedoc is bounded by the mountains of the Massif Central to the north. In Roussillon, the mountains come closer and closer to the sea. What is not harsh, rugged hill country is flat alluvial plain interspersed with marshy tracts.

From the mountains, a series of small rivers come down to the sea. Torrents in winter and dry in the long, hot summers, they have carved out valleys on whose slopes vineyards are the natural form of agriculture.

This is the hottest part of France. The heat is dry, tempered with the winds of the Mistral and Tramontane which blow, for days on end, across the wide open spaces of the plains. Although the coastal strip is now becoming built up with the growth of tourism, inland the landscape is empty with scattered red-roofed villages and a few larger, often walled, towns commanding the heights.

Nearly 40% of all French wines comes from these two regions. Much of it is virtually undrinkable plonk – all red – which goes less and less to quench the thirst of the French peasant or factory worker and more and more to increase the EEC surplus of industrial alcohol.

But it was not always such a sad tale. Before phylloxera, the majority of the vineyards were on the hills, where decent if fairly ordinary wine was made. However those vineyards were always precarious economically. And when phylloxera struck, it was not worthwhile to replant them. Vinous activity was transferred to the plain, where enormous yields were possible and cash returns were greater. Alicante and Aramon as well as Carignan were planted – giving yields of up to 200 hectolitres per hectare of thin, watery wine which sold well to the poor and thirsty of the industrial towns of the north.

Fashions change and the traditional industries have waned in France as elsewhere. The thirst for cheap wine after a day's work in a dusty steel mill or coal mine has gone. The French want better-quality wine – and want to drink less of it. The call has gone out for a return to the hill vineyards and the abandonment of those on the plains. And, slowly but surely, this is what is happening.

The authorities are now trying to encourage quality rather than quantity. One way of doing that is to create AC and VDQS zones in the hills, which has the effect of pushing up prices – from almost nothing to not very much. And the government has also paid the farmers on the plains to grub up their vineyards and plant other crops such as cereals. The authorities have encouraged local traditional vineyards, especially those in Roussillon, where there is a long history of quality wine making. And in Languedoc, they have worked at the introduction of the noble grape varieties such as Cabernet Sauvignon, Syrah, Mouvèdre – even Chardonnay – to blend in with local grapes to give more flavour, style and aroma to often dull wines.

The authorities are also paying out grants for new equipment in the wineries. Temperature-controlled vinification and stainless steel are coming to Languedoc and Roussillon, where they are at last creating the possibility of decent white wines and un-oxidized reds. The techniques of carbonic maceration, which bring out colour and flavour from the grapes, have been introduced and encouraged. The region boasts one of the biggest viticultural and winemaking research centres at SICAREX near Montpellier, and ideas are being disseminated from there.

The message is getting through to the conservative French farmers in a number of ways. Cooperatives are important. 60% of the region's wines go through cooperatives. Most farmers have tiny holdings on which they can scarcely survive let alone become involved in the high-tech of wine. A few big négociant firms – Nicolas and Chantovent among them – are also buying wine from small holders, the best of which they bottle under individual domaine names. And a few of the larger estates are dominating their areas by example.

What this means for the wine drinker is that here is an area which is just about to burst forth with a range of good quality, cheap wines. There is rarely anything to take one's breath away – the region needs time for that. But there are certainly pockets of very good quality and larger areas where standards are getting better all the time.

It does not just mean, luckily, that what is now being offered is simply well-made "modern" style wines. Some of the new AC and VDQS areas recognize long traditions. There have been vines here since the second century BC, and Narbonne was one of the first major cities of Roman Gaul. The French are good at recognizing local character, and small vineyard areas have been given separate ACs in cognizance of their differences in style and quality.

The region also produces a range of sweet, fortified wines which, highly popular in France, are virtually unknown outside. There are potentially high alcohol wines whose fermentation is stopped by the addition of about 10% eaux-de-vie, leaving a strong, rich sweet wine. They can be either Vins

Doux Naturels (made from grape brandy from any French source) or Vins de Liqueurs (made with spirit from the region of production) and can be either red or white. Most attractive are the wines made from the Muscat grape.

The Appellations
Gard Département: AC
Clairette de Bellegarde: White wine only, made from the Clairette grape in two small areas within the larger Costières du Gard between Nîmes and Arles. 6,000 hectolitres are produced on red, pebbly soil. The wines are often fragrant, if full, with a pale gold colour. They lack acidity, tend towards flabbiness unless made with care. A few estates make good examples.

Gard Département: VDQS
Costières du Gard: Red, white and rosé wines coming from a large area southeast of Nîmes and north of the Camargue marshes. The 4,000 hectares of vineyard are on flat land, much of it quite barren, some of it sandy, partly also planted with lemon and orange groves as well as olives. Red wines form around 70% of production, rosé about 20% and white around 10%. Red and rosé wines are made from Carignan (which can constitute up to 50% of the wine, although better producers use less), Cinsault, Grenache, Mourvèdre, Syrah, Counoise and Terret Noir. Depending on the blend, the reds can be attractively simple, with southern warmth and nuttiness, topped up with a Rhône-like spicy pepperiness. Whites are made from Clairette, Bourboulenc and Ugni Blanc. Modern vinification and the picking of under-ripe grapes is helping to improve their quality and make fresh if undistinguished wines.

Hérault Département: AC
Clairette du Languedoc: Dry, medium and sweet white wines made exclusively from the Clairette grape in communes around Cabrières, Aspiran and Clermont l'Hérault in the valley of the Hérault. Much of 10,000 hectolitres produced is sold for vermouth, but other wines are aged to produce Rancio – what some might call an oxidized wine, but which others describe as maderized and profess to enjoy. High in alcohol, Clairette de Languedoc is best drunk on its own or before or after a meal.

Faugères: Red and dry white wines coming from seven communes in the foothills of the Cevennes north of Beziers. The vineyards are on steep hillsides and are difficult to work. Between 40,000 and 50,000 hectolitres are made each year. Grapes for the red wines are: principally Carignan but, increasingly Grenache and Cinsault. Full-bodied and best described as hearty with intense colour, it is a wine which needs rich food. A little white is made from the Clairette grape.

Saint-Chinian: One of the most promising AC areas in the Hérault, producing only red wines in a large area to the southwest of the Faugères AC. The vineyards cover the hillsides on both banks of the Orb river on slate soil with limestone. 80,000 hectolitres are made. The grapes are Carignan, Grenache and Cinsault, with the better producers only having a small proportion of Carignan. The wines are lighter than other reds from Languedoc and more elegant and the growth of prestigious single domaine wines is encouraging for the future.

Coteaux du Languedoc: A highly complicated region producing red and rosé wines throughout Hérault. The grapes used in both red and rosé are Carignan, Cinsault, Counoise, Grenache,

Mourvèdre, Syrah and Terret Noir. White wines are not permitted the basic Coteaux du Languedoc AC, although certain Coteaux du Languedoc Villages (see below) also produce dry white wines using Clairette, Picpoul and Bourboulenc (locally Malvoisie). Standards are improving right across the region and one or two producers are outstanding.

Coteaux du Languedoc Villages: 12 communes are allowed to add their name to the general AC Coteaux du Languedoc. Two – La Clape and Quatourze – are in the Aude département, the rest are in Hérault. They are also allowed to use the village name without the Coteaux du Languedoc prefix – just to confuse us all!

Cabrières: Rosé wines from vineyards just outside Béziers, mainly from Carignan and Cinsault with a little Grenache.

Coteaux de la Méjanelle: Red wines from Carignan, Cinsault and Grenache from near Montpellier. A small amount of dry white is also made.

Coteaux de Vérargues: Red and rosé wines, from vineyards northeast of Montpellier. Carignan, Cinsault, Grenache and some Aramon are used.

La Clape: In the Aude département, on the edge of the Corbières VDQS area, a large mound-shaped hill supports the vineyards of La Clape. Red, dry white and rosé wines are made on chalk soil. Red and rosés are from Carignan, Grenache, Cinsault and Terret Noir. Whites from Clairette, Picpoul and Bourboulence.

Méjanelle: Red wines from near Montpellier in the same general area as Coteaux de la Méjanelle.

Montpeyroux: Red and rosé from schist soil north of Béziers. The red includes some Syrah in the *cépage* which gives them some style.

Pic-Saint-Loup: Red, rosé and dry white from north of Montpellier. Fairly ordinary, straightforward wines.

Quatourze: Vineyards around Narbonne in the Aude département producing red, dry white and rosé on stony soil. The red is particularly powerful and traditionally was used to strengthen weaker brews from the plains. Now generally bottled in its own right.

Coteaux de Saint-Christol: Vineyards northeast of Montpellier producing simple red wines from Carignan, Cinsault and Grenache.

Saint-Drézery: Just west of Saint-Christol, vineyards producing red and a small amount of rosé. The usual grape varieties are used, but Carignan tends to be in higher proportion.

Saint-Georges d'Orques: Red and rosé wines from northwest of Montpellier. A high proportion of Cinsault is used, and the wines age well.

Saint-Saturnin: Stylish wines from Grenache, Cinsault, Carignan and Mourvèdre and Syrah to give the extra quality. Red and rosé are made in the hills north of the Hérault river.

Minervois: A large area of vineyards, in 61 communes, which crosses the departmental boundary between Hérault and Aude. The best vineyards are in the Hérault around Minerve and St-Jean-de-Minervois. Red and rosé are produced from Carignan (over 50%), Grenache and Cinsault. A small amount of white is also made. The reds are characterized by spicy, ripe southern fruit which makes them attractive when young, although the producers who use some wood make wines that can age. The area received the AC in 1985.

Picpoul de Pinet: Dry white wines made from Picpoul, Clairette and Terret Blanc in a small vineyard area just inland from the Bassin de Thau. The wines tend to flabbiness quite quickly and need to be drunk young and very fresh.

Blanquette de Limoux: Hilly region southwest of Carcassonne centred around the town of Limoux, producing sparkling white wine from the Mauzac Blanc, Clairette and Chardonnay made by the *méthode champenoise*. The name Blanquette comes not from the colour of the wine but from the white film that covers the underside of the leaves of the Mauzac. The producers in the area – dominated by a cooperative – claim that their sparkling wine used the *méthode champenoise* before Dom Pérignon used it in Champagne. Whether or not that's true, today the Blanquette de Limoux is one of the very best sparklers in France outside Champagne.

Corbières: The largest AC area in Languedoc and Roussillon, covering 92 communes from the coast right back to the high land of the Hautes-Corbières. Up to 650,000 hectolitres of wine are produced in an average year, of which 90% is red, 1% rosé, the rest white. Grapes for the red and rosé are Carignan, Cinsault, Grenache, Mourvèdre, Terret Noir and Syrah with a little white Picpoul. For white, grapes are Clairette and Bourboulenc. Similar in style to Minervois (see under Hérault) the wines are possibly softer and heavier with less ability to age. But the range of quality from good to bad is enormous with so much wine being made. New equipment and better practices in the vineyards are improving standards all the time. The area became an AC in 1985. Maybe in retrospect some of the vineyards should have been declassified at the same time.

Corbières Supérieures: White wine only from the same region as Corbières, but with a higher minimum alcohol than straight Corbières.

Fitou: An area of vineyard within the larger Corbières AC, by the coastal lagoon of Salses. The AC applies to red wine only, made from a minimum of 70% Carignan with Grenache and Cinsault. The result is a powerful, full-bodied red which has to be aged for a minimum of nine months in wood. They have recently achieved some popularity on the export market. The AC is one of the oldest in the Aude – established in 1948.

Cabardès or Côtes du Cabardès et de l'Orbiel: Red and rosé wines produced to the north of Carcassonne on the slopes of the Minervois. Grapes are Carignan, Cinsault, Grenache, Mourvèdre and Syrah with Cabernet Sauvignon, Cot, Fer and Merlot from the southwest region just across the hills. The reds, quite tannic in youth, are better than the rosés.

Côtes de la Malapère: Vineyards to the southwest of Carcassone on the western side of the Aude Valley. Red and rosé wines are made principally from Cinsault, Cot and Merlot with smaller amounts of Cabernet Sauvignon, Cabernet Franc, Grenache and Syrah: a heady brew which actually produces some comparatively sophisticated wines. Rosés are from Grenache and Cinsault and are better than many rosés from surrounding areas. An area to watch.

Collioure: Tiny AC area right by the Spanish border, covering the same area as the Banyuls Vin Doux Naturel AC. Red wine from Grenache, Carignan, Mourvèdre, Syrah and Cinsault are made in baking hot vineyards on the slopes of the Monts Albères as they drop down to the sea. Potentially a fine wine, especially from the old-established vineyards, it is a declining area with only about 50 hectares in four communes.

Côtes du Roussillon: Red, rosé and dry white wines from a large area of the Pyrénées-Orientales. The Côtes du Roussillon stretch south from Perpignan and vines are found on the coast and stretching inland to the foothills of the Pyrénées. Reds and rosés are made from Carignan, Cinsault, Grenache, Mourvèdre and the local Ladoner Pelut plus the white Spanish Macabeo in small amounts. Whites are made from the Macabeo and the Malvoisie. Of the four large AC areas in the Midi – Corbières, Coteaux du Languedoc and Minervois – this is the one which has shown the greatest potential.

Côtes du Roussillon Villages: The area north of Perpignan in the valley of the Aigly is regarded as producing superior wine. The soil is gravelly with some granite and schist which gives the wines a backbone and elegance as well as a range of styles. Only red wines are covered by this AC. Two villages – Caramany and Latour-de-France – on the south bank of the Aigly are allowed to add their name to the Villages AC.

Vins Doux Naturel (VDN) and Vins de Liqueur

Hérault

Clairette de Languedoc: Made from the same white wines which also produce the dry white Clairette de Languedoc.

Frontignan: Red VDN made from the Grenache grape in an area north of Sète. Also known as Vin de Frontignan. Can be a VDN or Vin de Liqueur.

Muscat de Frontignan: In the same area as Frontignan, this is a white wine, one of the best VDNs from the Muscat grape. Can be either a Vin Doux Naturel or a Vin de Liqueur.

Muscat de Lunel: From the Muscat grape in the area around St-Christol northeast of Montpellier.

Muscat de Mireval: A small area just north of Frontignan.

Muscat de St-Jean-de-Minervois: A small area just at the northern extremity of the Minervois.

Pyrénées-Orientales

Banyuls: Red and tawny VDN occupying the same area as the red Collioure, stretching down to the Spanish frontier. The wines are made from Grenache Noir, Grenache Gris, Grenache Blanc, Macabeo, Malvoisie and Muscat. The more Grenache, the better the wine seems to age.

Banyuls Rancio: Banyuls VDN which has been aged in barrels in the open air under the sun to concentrate the wine. The best Banyuls Rancio is called Banyuls Grand Cru, and is considered by some to rival tawny port.

Grand Roussillon: VDN red wine from the general area of the Pyrénées-Orientales. Can also be produced in a Rancio version.

Maury: Red and rosé VDN from the north bank of the Aigly river. It is made only from Grenache Noir. Lighter than Banyuls, it can also be aged in wood to produce Maury Rancio.

Muscat de Rivesaltes: A Muscat-based VDN from just north of Perpignan. In the same area as Rivesaltes (see below).

Rivesaltes: Red, white and rosé VDN made from Grenache Noir, Macabeo, Malvoisie and Muscat. Only 100% Muscat wines can be called Muscat de Rivesaltes.

The Midi: Banyuls/Collioure

Groupement Interproducteurs du Cru Banyuls

Route de Mas Reig, 66650 Banyuls-sur-Mer. Vineyards
owned: 4,305ha. *Produce: 3.9 million bottles.*
N and Coop (1,200 members).

This is a large-scale operation, a grouping of three cooperatives
which also acts as a négociant. They dominate the Collioure
and Banyuls AC areas (with 2,600 hectares in Banyuls). There
has been considerable investment in equipment and the general
quality is good. Brand names used include Templers and Cellier
des Templiers. They make considerable quantities of Rivesaltes
red and muscat (under the name Aphrodis) and Côtes du
Roussillon AC reds. *Open: Mon–Fri 9:30am–noon; 2–6pm. All
day in summer.*

Cave Coopérative Les Dominicains

66190 Collioure. Vineyards owned: 2,800ha.
Produce: 26,660 bottles. Coop (287 members).

Despite the address, most of the land belonging to this
cooperative produces Banyuls, but 400 hectares make
Collioure. Most of the wine is sold to négociants, but some is
bottled under Le Dominicain name. They make an attractive
Collioure Cuvée Matisse. *Open: By appointment only.*

Société Coopérative Agricole l'Etoile

26 Avenue du Puig des Mas, 66650 Banyuls-sur-Mer.
Vineyards owned: 170ha. *Produce: 290,000 bottles.*
Coop (70 members).

Virtually all the production here is of Banyuls Vin Doux
Naturel, made principally from Grenache Noir and Carignan.
They make a range of these wines: Grand Cru Select Vieux,
Grande Réserve, Doux Paille, Extra Vieux, a Muscat-based
Tuile and drier styles. They also produce a small amount of
Collioure, which is made in stainless steel. *Open: By appoint-
ment only.*

Domaine du Mas Blanc

9 Avenue Général de Gaulle, 66650 Banyuls-sur-Mer.
Vineyards owned: 13ha. *Produce: 38,000 bottles.* VP-R.

Production from this 17th century estate is split evenly between
Banyuls Vin Doux Naturel and red Collioure. The Banyuls is
made with the usual *cépage* of Grenache Noir, Mourvèdre and
Carignan with the addition of some Syrah; they rejoice in some
particularly lurid labels. The Collioure is made with 40%
Mourvèdre, 40% Syrah and 20% Grenache: a wine which can
take considerable ageing. *Open: By appointment only.*

The Midi: Clairette de Bellegarde

Domaine de l'Amarine

30127 Bellegarde. Vineyards owned: 37ha.
Produce: 250,000 bottles. VP-R.

Costières du Gard and Clairette de Bellegarde are the two styles
of wine produced on this large estate. The Costières du Gard
comes in red, rosé and white from a standard range and special
cuvées of red (Cuvée des Bernis) and rosé (Cuvée Royal).
Grenache predominates in the red with Cinsault, Carignan and

Syrah, the white is 100% Grenache Blanc. Clairette de Bellegarde is 100% Clairette. Some rosé *méthode champenoise* sparkling wine is also made (Cour de Bernis). *Open: By appointment only.*

Midi: Cabarde

Château Rivals
11600 Villemoustaussou. Vineyards owned: 19.4ha.
Produce: 30,000 bottles. VP-R.

Red and rosé Cabardes are made from Grenache, Merlot and Cabernet Sauvignon (for the red) and Grenache and Carignan (for the rosé). Despite the blend, the red is made to be drunk young. White Vin de Pays is made from 100% Maccabeu. An interesting estate, whose owner, Madame Charlotte Troncin-Capdevila is experimenting with Bordeaux style wines. *Open: By appointment only.*

The Midi: Corbières

Château de la Baronne – Domaine des Lanes
11700 Fontcouverte. Vineyards owned: 40ha.
Produce: 150,000 bottles. VP-R.

Carbonic maceration, with temperature control, is used for reds at both these estates. The Château de la Baronne also produces a rosé, while Domaine des Lanes (Vin de Pays des Hautes Rives) makes a white. *Open: Appointments preferred.*

Société Coopérative Agricole de Vinification Castelmaure
11360 Embres et Castelmaure. Vineyards owned: 285ha.
Produce: 380,000 bottles. Coop (125 members).

Red Corbières made with carbonic maceration is the main production at this cooperative, one of the best in the region, in the southern part of the Corbières AC. The top red is the Cuvée Pompadour, made with Carignan, Grenache and Syrah and aged in small barrels, which impart a bouquet of truffles and mushrooms and give the wine good ageing ability. Standard red, rosé and white Corbières are also made. Cold fermentation is used for rosé and white. The cooperative has been bottling for five years, and hopes to bottle most of its production in five years' time. *Open: Mon–Fri 8am–noon; 2–pm.*

Union de Caves Coopératives des Corbières Maritimes
11490 Portel. Vineyards owned: 3,600ha.
Produce: 900,000 bottles. Coop (1,300 members).

This is the grouping of the cooperatives of Peyriac de Mer, Portel and Sigean. The vineyards are on the flat land adjoining the Etangs de Bage, a large shallow inlet from the sea. 90% of the enormous production is of Corbières, with small amounts of rosé and white. Some of the red is given carbonic maceration vinification and sold as Corbières Primeur, some is produced for ageing. The top Cuvée Grand Opera is aged in wood for a time. *Open: Mon–Fri 8am–noon; 2–6pm.*

Société Coopérative Agricole Vinicole Fraisse des Corbières
11360 Fraisse des Corbières. Vineyards owned: 297ha.
Produce: 20,000 bottles. Coop (121 members).

One of the oldest cooperatives in the region, which sells 87% of its production in bulk to négociants. They bottle two carbonic maceration red Corbières: one with 5% Syrah in a blend of Carignan and Grenache, the other straight Carignan (80%) and Grenache. The carbonic maceration is new and has certainly improved the quality here. They also make Vin de Pays de la Vallée du Paradis and Vin de Pays de l'Aude. *Open: Mon–Fri 8am–noon; 2–6pm.*

Château de Lastours

11490 Portel des Corbières. Vineyards owned: 99ha. *Produce: 450,000 bottles.* VP-R.

Red, Gris de Gris rosé and white Corbières are made on this estate. The red is the best of the three, with the top *cuvée*, Simone Descamps, an interesting blend of Carignan, Grenache and Cinsault, with a little Syrah and Merlot thrown in. This particular wine needs around five years before it is ready but a new *cuvée*, Arnaud de Berre, is designed to be drunk young. The Gris de Gris is 100% Grenache, the white 100% Malvoisie – a very attractive wine. *Open: Mon–Fri 8am–4pm.*

Château les Ollieux

Montséret, 11200 Lézignan. Vineyards owned: 45ha. *Produce: 200,000 bottles.* VP-R.

Mme Surbézy-Cartier, who owns this vineyard, makes wine the modern way. She has modernized part of the vineyard as well, introducing Syrah and Grenache where previously there was only Cinsault and Carignan. Red and rosé are made under the name of the château and under the Domaine Surbézy-Cartier name. The château itself is old: a Cistercian monastery from medieval times, it came into the family in 1855. Merlot de Françoise is a Vin de Pays des Coteaux de la Cabrerisse. *Open: By appointment only.*

Domaine de la Voulte-Gasparets

Boutenac, 11200 Lézignan-Corbières. Vineyards owned: 50ha. *Produce: 250,000 bottles.* VP-R.

Two *cuvées* of red Corbières are the main production from this family owned estate. The vines are old, with a low yield and consequent high quality. The standard *cuvée* comes from Carignan, Grenache, Cinsault and Syrah. For the Cuvée Réserve, the proportion of Syrah is increased and there is no Cinsault: the wine is deeper, more perfumed and one to keep. A rosé is also made. This is one of the few estates in the area where exports are more important than local sales. *Open: Mon–Sun, in working hours.*

The Midi: Faugères

Domaine du Fraïsse

Autignac, 34480 Magalas. Vineyards owned: 17ha. *Produce: 80,000 bottles.* VP-R.

Jacques Pons uses carbonic maceration for his red Faugères, made from Carignan, Grenache, Syrah and Cinsault. He vinifies the different *cépages* separately, and only blends them together before bottling. At the moment, he only makes a red wine, but new plantings of Bourboulenc, Marsanne and Grenache Blanc will come on stream in 1987 or 1988. *Open: By appointment only.*

Cave Coopérative de Laurens
34480 Laurens. Vineyards owned: 1,600.
Produce: 700,000 bottles. Coop (400 members).

Most of the production from this cooperative is of Vin de Pays des Coteaux de Laurens and vin de table, much of which is sold in bulk. However they also produce some AC Faugères, made using carbonic maceration for the 50% Carignan in the blend, and adding Grenache, Syrah and Cinsault. New plantations of Cabernet Sauvignon and Merlot will change the look of the vin de pays. *Open: By appointment only.*

The Midi: Fitou

Paul Colomer
11350 Tuchan. Vineyards owned: 19ha.
Produce: 40,000 bottles. VP-R.

This small property produces both Fitou and Rivesaltes Vin Doux Naturel. The Fitou is made in stainless steel, using some carbonic maceration, giving a powerful wine which is better drunk within three years of the vintage. The sweet Rivesaltes Rouge is 100% Grenache. M. Colomer, whose family have owned the estate for generations, also produces a white, honeyed Muscat de Rivesaltes. *Open: By appointment only.*

Cave Coopérative de Fitou
11510 Fitou. Vineyards owned: 444ha.
Produce: 300,000 bottles. Coop (185 members).

Fitou is the main production here, made with carbonic maceration and using stainless steel. Their Fitou Terre Natale is an attractively spicy wine, benefiting from a dash of Mourvèdre and Syrah. Other wines produced are Rivesaltes Rouge Vin Doux Naturel, much of which is sold in bulk, and a good example of a Muscat de Rivesaltes. Also produce Corbières red, white and rosé. *Open: Mon–Fri 8am–noon; 2–7pm.*

Les Producteurs de Mont Tauch
11350 Tuchan. Vineyards owned: 1,015ha.
Produce: 3.5 million bottles. Coop (550 members).

The largest cooperative in the Fitou region, producing Fitou, Corbières and Rivesaltes wines. It's a highly mechanized operation, with controlled temperature fermentation and carbonic maceration. A whole range of brands is produced: d'Aguilar and Don Neuve being the best known. The cooperative has been developed over the past few years so that now 80% of their production is bottled. Vin de Pays des Coteaux de Cathares and vin de table are also produced. *Open: Mon–Fri 8am–noon; 2–6pm.*

Château de Nouvelles
11350 Tuchan. Vineyards owned: 88ha.
Produce: 150,000 bottles. VP-R.

One of the few private producers in the Fitou area, a property in the family since 1834. The wines are made in stainless steel without any wood ageing and are intended for drinking young – none the worse for that. Apart from the Fitou, they make a range of Corbières wines and Rivesaltes (including an aged Royal Rancio, which is an attractive apéritif wine). Plans at this estate include the planting of Mourvèdre to add to the *cépage* of the Fitou. *Open: Mon–Sat 8am–noon; 2–5pm.*

Cave Coopérative des Viticulteurs de Paziols
11530 Paziols. Vineyards owned: 750ha.
Produce: 600,000 bottles. Coop (215 members).

Fitou and Corbières are the main production at this cooperative, which takes in virtually all the producers in the commune of Paziols. Some carbonic maceration is practiced, but methods are traditional. An interesting touch with the Fitou is the use of 10% white Macabeo to lighten the wine. Red and Muscat Rivesaltes are also made. *Open: By appointment only.*

The Midi: Costières du Gard

Château de Belle Coste
30132 Caissargues. Vineyards owned: 53ha.
Produce: 250,000 bottles. VP-R.

Bertrand du Tremblay's family has run this estate for more than a century and they produce red, rosé and white Costières du Gard. The red (matured in wood) uses Syrah and Mourvèdre with Grenache Noir, and the rosé uses 100% Grenache Noir. There are two whites, one with Ugni Blanc and Grenache Blanc, the other Grenache Blanc alone. *Open: 9am–noon; 2–7pm.*

Château Roubaud
30600 Valivert. Vineyards owned: Costières du Gard 70ha.
Produce: 150,000 bottles. VP-R.

This estate has been owned by the Molinier-Thomas family since 1927. Much of the wine from this estate – out of a total of 4,300 hectolitres each year – is sold in bulk. Red, white and rosé Costières du Gard are made, using stainless steel fermentation. The usual *cépage* includes some Syrah for red and Ugni Blanc for whites. *Open: By appointment only.*

Château de St-Vincent
Jonquières St-Vincent, 30300 Beaucaire. Vineyards owned:
Costières du Gard 36ha. *Produce: 250,000 bottles.* VP-R.

This is a traditional estate, making red and rosé, using wood for ageing the reds. The grapes for both styles are Grenache, Cinsault, Carignan and some Merlot. *Open: Mon–Fri.*

Domaine Viticole Salin du Midi
68 Cours Gambetta, 34063 Montpellier. Vineyards owned:
Côtes de Provence 123ha; Coteaux Varois 139ha; Vin de
Pays 1,750ha. *Produce; 25.4 million bottles.* VP-R.

The largest wine producer in France has vineyards in Côtes de Provence (Château La Gordonne, Domaine de Saint-Hilaire), a négociant business (Bernard Camp Romain) and the huge vineyard area in the Gard département making Vins de Pays des Sables du Golfe du Lion. Quality for such vast production is high and the brand name is Listel. *Open: Visits to the Côtes de Provence vineyards only.*

Château de la Tuilerie
30000 Nîmes. Vineyards owned: Costières du Gard 74ha.
Produce: 110,000 bottles. VP-R.

An immaculately maintained estate owned by Mme Chantal

Comte. The property, which she inhertied from her husband, includes another 200 hectares of fruit trees. She makes red, rosé and white Costières du Gard, the white with 100% Grenache Blanc, the red a blend of Grenache, Syrah and Cinsault and the rosé 100% Cinsault. The red is the best of the three and ages well. *Open: By appointment only.*

The Midi: Coteaux du Languedoc

Georges Bonfils

20 Quai d'Alger, 34200 Sète. VP-R and N.

This firm is mainly a négociant for wines from the Coteaux du Languedoc and the Vin de Pays de l'Hérault. They also have a Coteaux du Languedoc estate, Domaine de Lavabre which produces a fairly standard red from Cinsault, Grenache, Syrah and Carignan. Other Coteaux du Languedoc wines are estates for which they have exclusive rights: Château de Beauregard and Château de St-Series. Their Vins de Pays – especially a Chardonnay Vin de Pays d'Oc are better than their AC wines. *Open: By appointment only.*

Château le Condamine Bertrand

Avenue d'Ormesson, 34120 Lézignan la Cebe. Vineyards owned: 100ha. *Produce: 200,000 bottles.* VP-R.

Stainless steel has been installed at this family owned estate and whites and rosés are vinified at controlled temperatures. Reds – the bulk of production – go through carbonic maceration which brings out the fruit and colour. Red and rosé are made with the Coteaux du Languedoc AC, the white has the Clairette du Languedoc AC. A range of wines in the interesting Vin de Pays de Thongues includes reds from Syrah, Mourvèdre, Merlot and Cabernet Sauvignon. *Open: Mon–Fri 8am–noon; 2–8pm.*

Château de l'Engarran

34880 Laverune. Vineyards owned: 53ha.
Produce: 200,000 bottles. VP-R.

The estate of Château de l'Engarran only makes red Coteaux du Languedoc St-Georges d'Orques from Carignan, Cinsault, Grenache and 10% Syrah. This is aged in wood for 18 months and produces rich, slightly spicy wine which takes some ageing. The Domaine de l'Engarran produces a white Blanc de Blancs Vin de Pays d'Oc from Ugni Blanc. *Open: By appointment only.*

Domaine Martin-Pierrat

Saint-Christol, 34400 Lunel. Vineyards owned: 20ha.
Produce: 90,000 bottles. VP-R.

Red and rosé Coteaux du Languedoc St-Christol are produced on this small estate, using traditional methods. The red is a rich, smooth wine which matures quickly. Some Syrah is used in the blends, including a Cuvée Spéciale. They also produce a white Vin de Pays de la Bénovie from Chardonnay, Grenache Blanc and Ugni Blanc. *Open: By appointment only.*

Château de Nizas

34320 Roujan. Vineyards owned: 43ha.
Produce: 180,000 bottles. VP-R.

Red Coteaux du Languedoc Château de Carrion-Nizas is produced here using carbonic maceration and some wood ageing, resulting in a typical southern taste which is improved with a touch of Syrah. Perhaps more interesting is the estate's Vin de Pays de Caux: the red is made from 10% Cabernet Sauvignon and 15% Merlot, plus the usual local varieties. Small amounts of Vin de Pays rosé and white are made also. *Open: Mon–Fri 8am–noon; 2–7pm.*

Château Notre Dame du Quatourze

11100 Narbonne. Vineyards owned: 45ha.
Produce: 180,000 bottles. VP-R.

One of the bigger private producers from the small Quatourze area near Narbonne, M. Yvon Ortola makes red, white and rosé Coteaux du Languedoc using some stainless steel for vinification and aiming to get highly aromatic wines. He has been planting Mourvèdre, Syrah and Grenache to replace the Carignan. The white Coteaux du Languedoc is made from Macabeo. *Open: Mon–Sat 8am–noon; 2–6pm.*

Château Pech-Céleyran

Salles d'Aude, 11110 Coursan. Vineyards owned: 90ha.
Produce: 300,000 bottles. VP-R.

The vineyard is owned by the Comte de Saint-Exupéry. They produce red and rosé Coteaux du Languedoc La Clape, some of which has up to two years in wood. They have also planted Cabernet Sauvignon, Merlot and Chardonnay, which are used as part of the blend for Vin de Pays des Côtes de Perignan, red, rosé and white. A vineyard that obviously takes trouble with its wines. *Open: Mon–Sun 8am–6pm.*

Château Pech-Redon

11100 Narbonne. Vineyards owned: 41ha.
Produce: 300,000 bottles. VP-R.

Cabernet Sauvignon and Merlot form 15% of this vineyard, and it shows in the red Coteaux du Languedoc La Clape which Jean Demolombe makes. He uses two names – that of the château and also Domaine de l'Abbaye de Valfernière; an abbey which was discovered while the vineyard was being created. In addition to the reds, M. Demolombe makes a rosé La Clape, using 25% Syrah and 25% Grenache. He also makes a Blanc de Blanc Vin de Pays Coteaux de Narbonne from Chardonnay and a Blanc de Noir vin de pays from Cinsault. Because the vineyard is high up on the slopes, the vines get a slower, longer growing season than those on the plain. *Open: By appointment only.*

Raoul et ses Fils

Domaine des Grès-Ricards, 34150 St-André-de-Sangonis.
Vineyards owned: 23ha. *Produce: 20,000 bottles.* VP-R.

A red Coteaux du Languedoc is produced with Syrah (15%), Grenache and Cinsault, rather high in alcohol but not unpleasant. Another red is a more unusual Vin de Pays de l'Hérault made from Merlot (60%), Cabernet Sauvignon (30%) and Carignan: quite stylish, aged in wood and needs some time in bottle. *Open: By appointment only.*

Cave Coopérative St Félix de Lodez

34150 St Félix de Lodez. Vineyards owned: 710ha.
Produce: 300,000 bottles. Coop (250 members).

This cooperative was set up in 1942 to take in wines from a

number of communes around St-Félix de Lodez. The quality is
reliable, helped by new stainless steel equipment. The bulk of
production is of red Coteaux du Languedoc, but they also make
the pale red Vin d'Une Nuit and white AC Clairette du
Languedoc and a number of different vins de pays. One of their
more unusual wines produced is a sweet *pétillant de raisin*, a
low alcohol wine made with Clairette grapes. *Open: By
appointment only.*

Domaine St-Jean d'Aumières

34150 Gignac. Vineyards owned: 26ha.
Produce: 180,000 bottles. VP-R.

While the bulk of Daniel Delclaud's production is of Vin de
Pays, he also produces some Coteaux du Languedoc from
Grenache, Cinsault and Syrah. Modern vinification in stainless
steel is used, but M. Delclaud's aim, he says, is to produce red
wines for keeping. His vins de pays include Vin de Pays de
l'Hérault made from 50% Cabernet Sauvignon, plus Grenache,
Cinsault and Syrah. Probably his most interesting wine is a
100% Cabernet Sauvignon Vin de Pays des Gorges de l'Hérault,
which is matured in wood. *Open: By appointment only.*

Château de Ricardelle

Route de Gruissan, 11104 Narbonne. Vineyards owned:
47ha. *Produce: 400,000 bottles.* VP-R.

Organic methods in the vineyard – no chemical sprays – and
modern equipment in the winery produce some attractive
Coteaux du Languedoc La Clape wines. The vineyard is on the
western slopes of the hill of La Clape facing out over the city of
Narbonne. The red is a blend of Carignan, Grenache, Syrah and
Cinsault. The rosé (or gris) omits the Syrah. Vin de Pays de
l'Aude red and rosé, which include some Merlot, are also made.
Open: Mon–Fri 8am–noon; 2–6pm.

Château de Salles

Salles d'Aude, 11110 Coursan. Vineyards owned: 28ha.
Produce: 200,000 bottles. VP-R.

The Château de Salles has been in the Hue-Bellaud family since
the 18th century. Now they make a range of wines, including
AC Coteaux du Languedoc La Clape. The Grenache dominates
the blend for this wine which is partly made by carbonic
maceration. There is a small proportion of Syrah, Terret Noir
and Carignan as well as Cinsault. They also make Vin de Pays
des Côtes de Perignan; the red has 80% Merlot, 10% Syrah and
is an interesting and successful wine. *Open: By appointment
only.*

Les Vins de Saint-Saturnin

Route d'Arbaras, 34150 Saint-Saturnin. Vineyards owned:
820ha. *Produce: 3 million bottles.* Coop (182 members).

The main cooperative in the Coteaux du Languedoc Saint-
Saturnin AC area, specializing in the rosé Vin d'une Nuit brand
(a blend of Carignan, Cinsault, Grenache and Syrah), so called
because the skins remain on the must for only one night. In
addition to the Vin d'une Nuit they also make a large number of
brands of red Coteaux du Languedoc, of which the best is the
Cuvée Spéciale. Vin de Pays de l'Herault and Vin de Table are
also made. *Open: Mon–Fri 8am–noon; 2–5pm.*

The Midi: Minervois

Domaine Barroubio

Saint-Jean-de-Minervois, 34360 St-Chinian. Vineyards
owned: 10ha. *Produce: 25,000 bottles.* VP-R.

A 15th-century estate in the Minervois AC area which produces
an attractive red for drinking young. They also make a
Minervois rosé and Muscat de St-Jean-de-Minervois. *Open:
Mon–Fri 9am–noon.*

Dominique de Berthier (Château de Paraza)

11200 Lézignan. Vineyards owned: 72ha.
Produce: 440,000 bottles. VP-R.

Good red and rosé Minervois, using the Château de Paraza
label. *Open: No.*

SCAV Costos Roussos

11160 Trausse-Minervois. Vineyards owned: 430ha.
Produce: 270,000 bottles. Coop (210 members).

The bulk of the bottled production here is of Minervois, sold
under two names: Traussan and Costos Roussos. The methods
used here are traditional but with the use of some carbonic
maceration for the Carignan used in the Minervois. Some Vin
de Pays de l'Aude and Coteaux de Peyriac is also made. There is
a strong feeling at this estate that time has stood still. *Open: By
appointment only.*

Domaine Daniel Domergue

Trausse-Minervois, 11160 Caunes. Vineyards owned: 5ha.
Produce: 25,000 bottles. VP-R.

A small producer who is doing interesting things. Over half the
vineyard is planted with Syrah, which dominates three of M.
Domergue's wines, Cuvée Noire (100% Syrah), Cuvée d'Or
(75% Syrah) and Cuvée Canteperdrix (80% Syrah). Another
Minervois, Cuvée des Clos du Bosc is 100% Mourvèdre.
Although the quantities are small, the quality is high. *Open: By
appointment only.*

Château de Fabas

11800 Laure-Minervois. Vineyards owned: 40ha.
Produce: 300,000 bottles. VP-R.

There's quite a high percentage of Syrah and Mourvèdre in this
vineyard – and there's more to come. But the red Minervois is
dominated at present by Grenache, giving a typical southern
taste and warm, rounded finish. Jean-Pierre Ormières uses
temperature-controlled fermentation and a long maceration,
and his Cuvée Spéciale gets some wood ageing. Rosé and a small
amount of white wine are also made. *Open: By appointment
only.*

Châteaux Gibalaux

Laure-Minervois 11800 Trèbes. Vineyards owned: 60ha.
Produce: 60,000 bottles. VP-R.

New plantings of Mourvèdre and Syrah have improved the
quality and style of the wine since M. Bonnet took over in 1969.
He makes Minervois red from Carignan and Grenache with
20% Syrah; rosé has 50% Carignan and 50% Mourvèdre. Vin
de Pays des Coteaux de Peyriac red and white are also made (the

white has 50% Chardonnay). The use of stainless steel produces very clean wines. *Open: By appointment only.*

Château de Gourgazaud
La Livinière, 34210 Olonzac. Vineyards owned: 68ha.
Produce: 500,000 bottles. VP-R.

This is the showplace vineyard of the giant Chantovent organization, which acts as a major négociant in Languedoc and Roussillon. The vineyard is planted with a considerable proportion of Syrah, which is blended with Carignan, Merlot and Cabernet Sauvignon to produce a highly drinkable red, good when young but able to age. Minervois Blanc, made from Sauvignon, Macabeo and Marsanne is well-made but much less interesting. New plantings of Cabernet Sauvignon, Syrah and Chardonnay are proposed. *Open: Mon–Sat 9am–noon; 3–6pm.*

Cave Coopérative des Coteaux du Haut-Minervois
34210 La Livinière. Vineyards owned: 650ha.
Produce: 300,000 bottles. Coop (180 members).

A variety of vinification techniques are used at this cooperative which was established in 1924. They use carbonic maceration, heating of the must, and de-stalking before fermentation. The best wine – the Cuvée Jacques de la Jugie AC Minervois – is made by carbonic maceration, and then given some ageing in wood. No white wines are made, but about a third of production is of vin de pays and vin de table. *Open: By appointment only.*

Paul Herpe et Fils (Château de Vergel)
11120 Ginestas. Vineyards owned: 22ha.
Produce: 220,000 bottles. VP-R.

Red Minervois is produced here, with 30% Syrah giving it attractive, firm fruit. Techniques are traditional, with wood maturation. They also make a Vin de Pays at this estate. The firm of Paul Herpe also owns vineyards in Corbières and Coteaux du Languedoc La Clape. *Open: Appointments preferred.*

Domaine de l'Herbe Sainte
Mirepeisset, 11120 Ginestas. Vineyards owned: 40ha.
Produce: 60,000 bottles. VP-R.

Guy Rancoule has owned this vineyard since 1965, and has installed stainless steel and planted some Cabernet Sauvignon, Cot and Merlot to add to his Minervois and Vin de Pays du Val de Cesse. He uses organic methods both in the vineyard and the winery, vinifying in stainless steel but cutting the use of sulphur to a minimum. Although only a small production is bottled at the domaine at the moment, M. Rancoule is planning to bring the figure up to 400,000 bottles soon. *Open: June–Sept 9am–noon; 3–7pm. Otherwise by appointment only.*

Les Vignerons Coopératives de Malves en Minervois
11600 Conques sur Orbiel. Vineyards owned: 453ha.
Produce: 50,000 bottles. Coop (132 members).

Only a small proportion of the wine going through this cooperative is bottled – most is sold in bulk. They are trying though: stainless steel and temperature-controlled fermentation have put in an appearance, and the Minervois Château de Malves, which contains 33% Syrah, is a well-made wine. Other names they use are Domaine de Parazols and Menhir. Vins de Pays des Coteaux de Peyriac and Coteaux de la Cité de Carcassonne are other wines also produced. *Open: By appointment only.*

Château de Mandourelle

11360 Villesque des Corbières. Vineyards owned: 67ha.
Produce: 400,000 bottles. VP-R.

Red and rosé Corbières are made here. There is a special *cuvée*, Henri de Monfroid. Carbonic maceration is used for the reds. The Latham family also owns the 43 hectare Château de Saint-Esteve, another Corbières estate. *Open: By appointment only.*

Domaine Jacques Maris

34210 La Livinière. Vineyards owned: 52ha.
Produce: 190,000 bottles. VP-R.

Red, rosé and white Minervois are the main production at this large estate in the heart of the Minervois AC, north-west of Olonzac. While wine is still sold in bulk, the proportion of wine sold in bottle has gone up in the last five years. Some carbonic maceration is used for the Carignan which forms 70% of the red and 50% of the rosé. Syrah is used in the Cuvée Spéciale, giving a distinct perfume to the wine. Whites are made from 100% Macabeo. There are plans to plant some Cabernet Sauvignon. *Open: By appointment only.*

Jacques Meyzonnier

Pouzols-Minervois, 11120 Ginestas. Vineyards owned: 10ha.
Produce: 65,000 bottles. VP-R.

M. Meyzonnier only produces one wine on this small estate. His red Minervois is made from carbonic maceration and contains 50% Carignan, 25% Cinsault, 10% Syrah and 15% Grenache. A special Cuvée du Vigneron is sometimes produced. *Open: By appointment only.*

Château de Paraza

Paraza, 11200 Lézignan. Vineyards owned: 130ha. VP-R.

Two styles of Minervois are made on this large private estate: a Rouge Tradition, which is vinified traditionally; and a Cuvée Spéciale, made with carbonic maceration, and containing some Syrah. The Cuvée Spéciale is a more attractive style – with a deep colour and intense concentrated fruit and a perfumed taste. Mme de Girard also makes a rosé, which is designed for drinking young. *Open: By appointment only.*

Domaine du Pech d'André

Azillanet, 34210 Olonzac. Vineyards owned: 19ha.
Produce: 80,000 bottles. VP-R.

The estate, at the base of the hill of the town of Minerve, produces two red Minervois: one based around 50% Mourvèdre with Carignan and Grenache, the other replacing the Mourvèdre with Syrah. Both are excellent examples of the quality that Minervois can now produce, the Syrah wine perfumed and peppery, the Mourvèdre softer, warmer and ready to drink younger. Smaller amounts of rosé and white are also made. *Open: Mon–Sun 8am–8pm.*

Cave Coopérative de la Region de Peyriac-Minervois
11160 Peyriac-Minervois. Vineyards owned: 320ha.
Produce: 50,000 bottles. Coop (250 members).

Only a small amount of Minervois is bottled at this cooperative, the rest being sold in bulk. The wines are dominated by the traditional Carignan, but they do use carbonic maceration to give freshness and colour. Tour St-Martin is the cooperative's top Minervois *cuvée*, which has 50% Syrah, Grenache and Mourvèdre with 50% Carignan. Vin de Pays des Coteaux de Peyriac is also made. Much of their wine is sold to the big négociant firm of Chantovent. *Open: By appointment only.*

Les Vignerons du Haut-Minervois
34210 Azillanet. Vineyards owned: 301ha.
Produce: 35,000 bottles. Coop (250 members).

The members at this long-established cooperative have vineyards in Azillanet, Cesseras and Minerve, mainly producing Carignan, but with a smaller amount of Syrah, Grenache, Cinsault and Terret Noir. Most of the production here is of Vin de Pays des Côtes du Brian and Vin de Pays de l'Hérault, much of which is sold in bulk. Winemaking is modern, with temperature control and carbonic maceration used. *Open: By appointment only.*

Château Villerambert-Julien
11160 Caunes-Minervois. Vineyards owned: 60ha.
Produce: 120,000 bottles. VP-R.

Marcel Julien uses both traditional vinification and carbonic maceration to make his red Minervois at his château whose foundations are Roman. His top *cuvée*, Cuvée Tradition, has 50% Carignan, 25% Syrah and 25% of Grenache and Mourvèdre, giving a wine with plenty of raspberry fruit and should be drunk within three years. The other red is Cuvée Liberté (named to commemorate the centenary of the Statue of Liberty). M. Julien also makes a rosé. *Open: By appointment only.*

Château de Villerambert
11160 Caunes-Minervois. Vineyards owned: 80ha.
Produce: 240,000 bottles. VP-R.

There are two Minervois estates owned by the Moureau family: the Château de Villerambert and the Château Villegly. The Villegly wines have more character and depth, but both are well made. They also make red and rosé Vin de Pays des Coteaux de Peyriac and a Cabernet Sauvignon/Syrah vin de pays, Domaine Moureau. *Open: Mon–Fri 8–11am, 2–7pm.*

The Midi: Picpoul de Pinet

Claude Gaujal
BP No 1, 34850 Pinet. Vineyards owned: 60ha.
Produce: 80,000 bottles. VP-R.

The estate has been in the Gaujal family since 1791. Most of the production of wine in bottle is of citrusy Picpoul de Pinet, made using modern techniques, with fermentation at 17° in stainless steel. Other bottled wines include a Sauvignon Blanc and red Merlot Vin de Pays des Côtes de Thau. The rest of the production is sold in bulk. *Open: By appointment only.*

The Midi: Côtes du Roussillon

Société Coopérative Vinicole de Bélesta
66720 Bélesta. Vineyards owned: 350ha.
Produce: 50,000 bottles. Coop (140 members).

This old-established cooperative, founded in 1925, makes both Côtes du Roussillon and the superior Côtes du Roussillon Villages Bélesta. The Villages wine is made using carbonic maceration. The cooperative also makes a small amount of Vin Doux Naturel, some based on Muscat. *Open: Mon–Sat 8am–noon; 2–6pm.*

Domaine de Canterrane
66300 Trouillas. Vineyards owned: Domaine de Canterrane 102ha; Domaine du Clos Saint Georges 48ha.
Produce: 920,000 bottles. VP-R.

These two estates have adapted modern techniques to traditional methods, with the use of stainless steel and temperature control fermentation. Both make a range of Roussillon wines including Côtes du Roussillon, Rivesaltes red Vin Doux Naturel and Muscat de Rivesaltes. Large-scale production does not seem to harm quality. *Open: Mon, Wed–Sat 8am–noon; 2–6pm.*

Château de Corneilla
66200 Corneilla-del-Vercol. Vineyards owned: 60ha.
Produce: 381,000 bottles. VP-R.

Red Côtes du Roussillon is the most important wine to come from this ancient estate (the château dates from the 15th century). Philippe Jonquères d'Oriola, the owner, makes a top *cuvée* of the red which he ages in wood – a full-bodied wine with a touch of spice. He also makes white and rosé Côtes du Roussillon. Other wines from the estate include Rivesaltes Vin Doux Naturel and Muscat de Rivesaltes and a red Vin de Pays de Corneilla, called Domaine de la Chapelle du Paradis, made from Syrah, Merlot, Cabernet Sauvignon and Grenache: a surprisingly sophisticated wine from the French deep south. *Open: June–Sept, Mon–Sat 4–7pm.*

Société Coopérative Vinicole de Lansac-St Arnac
66720 Latour-de-France. Vineyards owned: 188ha.
Produce: 20,000 bottles. Coop (65 members).

A small cooperative which produces mainly Côtes du Roussillon Villages, 70% of which is sold to local négociants. Smaller amounts of straight Côtes du Roussillon red and rosé are also made, and there's some Vin de Pays du Val d'Aigly red and white. The cooperative is a member of the Vignerons Catalans grouping of producers. *Open: Mon–Fri 8am–noon; 2–6pm.*

Société Coopérative Vinicole Lesquerde
66220 St Paul de Fenouillet. Vineyards owned: 434ha.
Produce: 275,000 bottles. Coop (70 members).

A well-run cooperative producing Côtes du Roussillon red, white and rosé and Côtes du Roussillon Villages. Most of their production is now bottled at the cooperative. The wines are sound and break few viticultural records. They also make Vin Doux Naturel – both red and Muscat-based. *Open: No.*

Chais de l'Oratoire
Domaine de Montcalm, 66300 Thuirs. N.

A large négociant firm which buys wine from all over the Languedoc-Roussillon region. They sell Côtes du Roussillon, Corbières, Coteaux du Languedoc, Minervois, St-Chinian, Fitou and Costières du Gard under different château names. *Open: By appointment only.*

Domaine Saint-Luc
Passa, 66300 Thuir. Vineyards owned: 40ha.
Produce: 6,000 bottles. VP-R.

Most of the wine from this estate is sold in bulk around France. But they do bottle a certain amount of their Côtes du Roussillon and red and Muscat Rivesaltes Vin Doux Naturel. Methods are traditional, although some carbonic maceration is now used for some of the reds. Red vin de table forms the bulk of production. *Open: By appointment only.*

Sarda-Malet
134 Avenue Victor d'Albiez, 66000 Perpignan. Vineyards owned: 33ha. *Produce: 120,000 bottles.*

The Bulk of this estate produces Côtes du Roussillon and Rivesaltes Vin Doux Naturel. They make a cold fermentation Côtes du Roussillon white from 100% Grenache Blanc, and a range of red Côtes du Roussillon including a wood-aged Carte Noire which requires ageing for four or five years. The Vin Doux Naturel include the red Rivesaltes and the Muscat de Rivesaltes. They also produce Vin de Pays Catalans. *Open: By appointment only.*

Cazes Frères
4 Rue Francisco Ferrer, 66600 Rivesaltes. Vineyards owned: 85ha. *Produce: 400,000 bottles. VP-R.*

One of the most go-ahead private firms in the area, producing a whole range of wines – 15 in all – from Côtes du Roussillon and Côtes du Roussillon Villages, through Vin Doux Naturels to Vin de Pays Catalans. Quality on the whole is good, and most of the production is now bottled on the premises. *Open: Mon–Fri 8am–noon; 2–6pm.*

Cave Coopérative Vinicole Les Vignerons de Maury
128 Avenue Jean Jaures, 66460 Maury. Vineyards owned: 1,800ha. *Produce: 1 million bottles.* Coop (350 members).

The Vin Doux Naturel of Maury in all its forms is what matters at this cooperative. They make aged Rancio as well as the younger styles and wines like Maury Vieille Réserve. They make a small amount of Muscat de Rivesaltes, plus Côtes du Roussillon Villages and Côtes du Roussillon white. Export markets include Japan. *Open: By appointment only.*

The Midi: St-Chinian

Cave Coopérative des Rieu-Berlou
343 Avenue des Vignerons, Berlou, 34360 St-Chinian. Vineyards owned: 530ha. *Produce: 280,000 bottles.* Coop (102 members).

St-Chinian AC Berlou Prestige, the top red wine from this

cooperative, is a carbonic maceration wine made from Carignan, Grenache and Syrah and needing three years in bottle before drinking. The cooperative also makes a standard red St-Chinian and rosé and white. 70% of the production here is of vin de pays and vin de table which is sold in bulk. New plantings of Mourvèdre and Syrah should improve quality. *Open: Mon–Fri 10am–noon; 2–6pm.*

Château Coujan
34490 Murviel les Béziers. Vineyards owned: 104ha.
Produce: 170,000 bottles. VP-R.

François Guy and his sister Solange Peyre run this model estate producing one of the best St-Chinian reds from Syrah, Grenache and Cinsault. For this top wine they use the name Cuvée Marquise de Spinola, who bought wine from this estate in the 18th century. An elegant wine, it is aged for a while in 200 litre barrels, adding a layer of complexity to the wine. Another *cuvée* is Cuvée du Prieur, based on 60% Mourvèdre. The estate also produces red and white Vin de Pays des Coteaux de Murviel. *Open: By appointment only.*

Pierre et Henri Petit
Villespassans, 34360 Saint-Chinian. Vineyards owned:
21.5ha. Produce: 15,000 bottles. VP-R.

Red and rosé Saint-Chinian are produced on this small family estate, mainly from Carignan and Cinsault, but with a little Mourvèdre, Syrah and Merlot. They use carbonic maceration for the reds. *Open: By appointment only.*

Vin Doux Naturel

Coopérative du Muscat de Frontignan
14 Avenue du Muscat, 34110 Frontignan. Vineyards owned:
670ha. Produce: 2.2 million bottles. Coop (350 members).

This is by far the biggest producer of the sweet Muscat de Frontignan, the only wine they make. They operate traditionally, with some ageing of the wine in wood, and the result is a good commercial wine which preserves the grapey taste of Muscat and adds a touch of honeyed sweetness. *Open: By appointment only.*

Cave de Rabelais
BP 14, 34840 Mireval. Vineyards owned: 150ha.
Produce: 300,000 bottles. Coop (80 members).

Muscat de Mireval is the product from this appropriately named cooperative. They use stainless steel for vinification, but the rest of the production is traditional. Mireval is one of the smaller, less publicized Muscat areas, but its production is just as good as the better known appellations. *Open: Mon–Fri 8am–noon; 2–6pm. Closed March.*

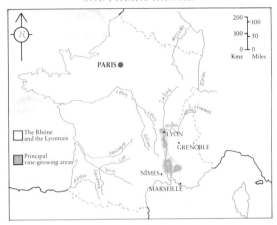

The red wines of the Rhône were traditionally regarded as some of the finest in France. Hermitage had pride of place long before Bordeaux achieved its present eminence. Today, the best wines from the Rhône can achieve equal quality with Bordeaux, and certainly provide much greater reliability than Burgundy can offer.

The Rhône vineyards are currently the most exciting source of red wine in France. Exciting, because we – the consumers – are rediscovering the greatness of Hermitage and Côte Rôtie and Cornas; and exciting because the vast sprawl of Côtes du Rhône vineyards has come to life with wines that have the rare combination – quality and value. Even white wines – not normally considered an important part of the Rhône Valley wine spectrum – have improved with the arrival of new equipment. The two small areas of Condrieu and Château Grillet command, with their rarity value, extravagantly high prices.

Conventionally, the Rhône vineyards are divided into two areas: the northern Rhône and the southern Rhône. The northern Rhône starts south of Lyons at the ancient Roman city of Vienne, which faces the first vineyards of the northern Côtes du Rhône and Côte Rôtie.

In this first stretch of Rhône vineyards, the valley is narrow, with the eastern edge of the Massif Central cut in two by the fast-flowing river. Vineyards are steeply terraced, expensive to work and spectacular to see.

The red wine Côte Rôtie vineyards, facing east and south-east, run into the small AC white areas of Condrieu and the tiny plot of Château Grillet. Immediately after this white interlude, the northern end of the St-Joseph AC is reached, while before long – on the opposite bank – the vineyards of Crozes-Hermitage begin.

The vineyards of Crozes-Hermitage lap round the edge of the huge dome-shaped hill of Hermitage which marks the end of the steep slopes on the eastern bank of the river. On the western bank, the town of Tournon faces Tain l'Hermitage. Behind Tournon are the terraced vineyards which produce the best St-Joseph; only a short gap divides them from Cornas and then St-Péray. And here the northern Rhône stops.

Nothing happens in the way of vineyards round the nougat town of Montélimar: maybe the smell of all that sweet sticky stuff does not agree with the vines. South of Montélimar the valley opens out in both directions – east towards the foothills of the Alps and west to the Cévennes. Coteaux du Tricastin is on the east bank. Next, the vast Mistral-swept plain of the Côtes du Rhône begins, the boundary of the ancient Roman Provinçia (Provence) is passed – and you are in the Mediterranean world.

On the eastern edge of the Côtes du Rhône, where the Alps begin, are the prime hillside vineyard sites of the Côtes du Rhône Villages and Gigondas and the new AC of Côtes du Ventoux which runs along the southern edge of Mont Ventoux. Facing Mont Ventoux and hard on the eastern bank of the Rhône is the outcrop of rolling hills which marks Châteauneuf-du-Pape, facing, on the western bank, Tavel and Lirac. By the time the city of Avignon has been reached, the Côtes du Rhône has run its course. The only vineyards left are the outliers like Côtes du Lubéron and the Coteaux de Pierrevert away to the east, grouped in this section because they are in the Vaucluse département but possibly more akin to Aix-en-Provence from which they are hardly separated.

In the past the division between north and south has not only been a question of convenience, but one of styles of wine. The northern Rhône vineyards were dominated by the Syrah grape; the southern by a mélange of grape varieties, of which Grenache and Cinsault were perhaps the most important.

Today the differences are becoming a little more blurred. The change has come from the movement of grape varieties – in particular the Syrah. The Syrah fulfils the same role in the Rhône as the Cabernet Sauvignon does elsewhere. It has become what the French call a *cépage améliorateur* – a noble grape variety which is used to lift the quality of a local wine. And it is the increasing use of the Syrah in southern Rhône vineyards which is one of the chief reasons for the improvement in quality of Côtes du Rhône.

Another has been the development of new techniques of winemaking. Some producers are now blending together wine made from free-run juice with wine that is the result of a long maceration of the grapes, stalks and all. The maceration brings out the colour and fruit (with the stalks adding some tannin) while the free-run juice gives elegance and freshness.

The other reasons are standard. There has been considerable investment in new equipment, the cellars tend to be cleaner than they used to be, and many of the younger generation of wine producers have been to colleges and universities to study their craft. The Rhône Valley has also been given its very own Université du Vin. Housed in a spectacular château in the village of Suze-la-Rousse, in the middle of the Côtes du Rhône vineyards, this runs courses particularly for local producers but also for producers from other parts of France. It has a fine library and tasting rooms. For any visitors to the area, a tour around the château is a must (telephone (75) 04 86 09).

While the Côtes du Rhône is the heart of the southern Rhône vineyards, there has also been a development of vineyards in the surrounding areas. New ACs and VDQS have been created – Ventoux, Tricastin, Lubéron, Vivarais – which have brought recognition and an improvement in quality to hitherto unknown areas.

The southern Rhône has the potential for a range of quality wines at prices we can all afford. A very different situation applies in the north, where demand regularly outstrips supply. Here the vineyard area is long-established and in some areas the best quality hillside vineyards have already been planted, leaving little room for expansion without a diminution of quality. Prices for the northern Rhône wines, especially Hermitage and Côte Rôtie, a few years ago represented superb value but are now rocketing. Much of the running has been made by a few of the négociant firms who dominate this area, and who argue that they are simply charging the prices the wines are worth. They have forced the individual growers along in their wake. But in the less popular ACs – St-Joseph, Crozes-Hermitage and, to a lesser extent, Cornas – the wines are still affordable.

The Appellations
AC

Côtes du Rhône: The huge area of the Côtes du Rhône AC stretches from vineyards behind the slope of the Côte Rôtie in the north to Avignon in the south. In all, there are 41,000 hectares of vines in six départements: Rhône, Loire, Ardèche, Drôme, Vaucluse and Gard. The bulk of the vineyards are in the wide plain east of Orange and north of Avignon, but areas of good quality are also found on the edges of the Crozes-Hermitage AC area in the north and around the edges of Tavel and Lirac in the south. Red, rosé and white wines are made under this general AC. The red and rosés must have at least 70% of the noble grape varieties: Cinsault, Grenache, Mourvèdre and Syrah, with Carignan allowed up to 30% and Camarèse, Counoise, Muscardin, Vaccarèse and Terret Noir also permitted. Whites are made from Bourboulenc, Clairette, Grenache Blanc, Marsanne, Roussanne and Ugni Blanc. The reds are to be drunk comparatively young – probably within three years of the vintage, although in great years, some wines will age very well. Vintages: 1980, '83, '84, '85, '86.

Côtes du Rhône Villages: See under southern Rhône AC.

Northern Rhône: ACs

Château Grillet: The smallest AC in France, and one of only two which are entirely owned by one producer (the other is Coulée de Serrant in the Loire). Here white wine is produced from the rare Viognier grape in limited quantities from a 2.6 hectare vineyard arranged in a semi-circle high above the Rhône, south of the town of Condrieu. Some years (such as 1978) may produce only about 4,000 bottles, others (such as 1980) may yield as much as 16,500. The taste of the wine is like an intense version of Condrieu – apricots, honey and ripe fruits are often cited, but the wine is dry. It is bottled in brown flute bottles – the only wine on the Rhône to use this shape and colour. It can live for anything up to 10 years in good vintages –

sometimes even longer. Vintages: 1978, '81, '83, '85, '86.

Condrieu: A slightly larger area than Château Grillet with 200 hectares available for planting, although only a little over 20 are actually in use. The vineyard has declined because of the attraction of local industry and the notoriously low yield and unreliability of the Viognier grape. Unlike Château Grillet, there are two styles of Condrieu – a sweet and a dry. I prefer the dry, which, although somewhat more obvious than Château Grillet has many of the same attractions, with its intense spicy fruit and the same apricots and honey bouquet. The wine does not keep for as long as Château Grillet – it reaches maturity after three to four years and rarely goes beyond 10. Vintages: 1981, '83, '85, '86.

Cornas: 100% Syrah wine from the steep hillside on the western bank of the Rhône, south of Tournon and Tain l'Hermitage. The vineyard area was once 25% larger, but now has only 60 hectares planted on the slope above the village of Cornas. New housing, low prices and the sheer physical difficulty of working the land were the main reasons for the decline. A rise in price after the 1983 and 1985 vintages has put this situation into reverse. The wine is fuller than a Côte Rôtie, very closed up and tannic when young, but in good years the fruit of the Syrah breaks through with intense earthy, spicy, violet flavours; often the equal of Hermitage. Some lighter wines are made lower down the slope on sandy soil. Top wines are not ready for drinking until 10 years, lighter wines are maturing after four to five. Vintages: 1971, '76, '78, '79, '81, '83, '85, '86.

Côte-Rôtie: The success story vineyard of the northern Rhône, Côte Rôtie has been taken up in the past six years with great enthusiasm and a consequent rise in price. The vineyards start just south of Vienne on the west bank on steep hillsides, facing south and southeast, and with ideal exposure – hence the name of "roasted slope". The core of the vineyard level with the village of Ampuis is divided into the Côte Brune (on clay soil) and the lighter soil (and hence lighter wine) of the Côte Blonde. Some wines are labelled as a blend of the two vineyards, but most Côte Rôtie is a blend from a larger number of sites than just these two. A small amount of white Viognier is normally blended with the Syrah to lighten its tannic intensity, and about 5% of the vineyard has the white vine. New plantings on the plateau above the hill have brought the total area under vine up to 130 hectares. Most tasters, however, agree that the plateau does not produce the right style of wine for good Côte Rôtie and the best growers will have nothing to do with these new plantings. The wine is rich, very smooth when mature with the characteristic spicy fruit of the Syrah, but toned down and lightened by the presence of the Viognier. Vintages: 1971, '76, '78, '80, '82, '83, '85, '86.

Crozes-Hermitage: Long-regarded as the poor relation of Hermitage, this large vineyard area is now coming into its own, following the price rise in Hermitage and the improvement of quality in Crozes. The village of Crozes-Hermitage itself lies behind the Hermitage hill, but the vineyards stretch along the Rhône's eastern bank, around the base of the hill and out into the plain as far as Roch-de-Glun and Pont d'Isère to the south. The total area is now over 800 hectares. Red is from the Syrah, while the small proportion of white comes from the Marsanne and Roussanne grapes. Some producers are now bottling single estate wines, although in the past most Crozes-Hermitage has been bought in by the négociants. Quality of the top estates is very good, approaching that of Hermitage, but there is still some indifferent wine under anonymous labels. Good wines have a spicy aroma, with the presence of blackcurrant fruit when young. They develop comparatively fast – within three to four years – and age up to between six and eight years for better wines. Vintages: 1981, '83, '85, '86.

Hermitage: The superb position of the vineyards on the hill of the Hermitage, which receive the sun virtually the whole day, guarantee the high quality of this AC. The Hermitage is a small chapel at the top of the hill once occupied by a crusading knight and now a magnificent viewing point. The band of Hermitage vineyards stretch around the hill from the top almost into the town of Tain l'Hermitage. They are divided into a number of smaller sections, which sometimes appear on the labels – Chante Alouette, la Chapelle, les Bessards, les Greffieux and le Méal are among the best known. The total AC Hermitage area is small – 125 hectares – and almost completely planted. While nearly all the granitic soil of the vineyard is planted with Syrah, a small amount of Marsanne and Roussanne are grown which can be added to the red (up to 15%) or used to make a white Hermitage. All attention, though, is focused on the reds with their superb keeping powers, their intense blackcurrant fruit when young and their chocolatey richness when mature. Along with fine Côte Rôtie, and the occasional Cornas, Hermitage is the finest wine on the Rhône. The wines from good years seem capable of surviving almost for ever – and really should not be touched before 10 years. Vintages: 1971, '73, '76, '78, '80, '83, '85, '86.

Côtes du Rhône Villages: Superior (in alcohol and generally quality) Côtes du Rhône which can either be simply AC Côtes du Rhône Villages (if it's a blend from a number of different, specified, communes) or can come from a specific one of 17 communes – in which case the name of the commune will appear on the label. Red, rosé and dry white wines are made. Reds and rosés come from Grenache (maximum 65%), Carignan (maximum 10%) and at least 25% in total of Syrah, Mourvèdre and Cinsault. Whites are made from Bourboulenc, Clairette and Roussanne. The 17 Villages communes are mainly on the eastern edges of the Côtes du Rhône plain: Rousset-les-Vignes, St-Pantaléon-les-Vignes, Valréas, Visan, Vinsobres, St-Maurice-sur-Eygues, Roaix, Cairanne, Rochegude, Rasteau, Séguret, Sablet, Vacqueyras and Beaumes de Venise. Three communes (St-Gervais, Chusclan and Laudun) are on the west side of the Rhône, opposite Orange. The red wines last a little longer than ordinary Côtes du Rhône – up to eight to nine years for good vintages. Vintages (red): 1978, '79, '80, '81, '83, '85, '86.

Côtes du Ventoux: The huge mass of Mont Ventoux dominates the eastern edge of the Côtes du Rhône plain. Along its southern slopes, round the corner from the Côtes du Rhône Villages, are the 6,400 hectares of Côtes du Ventoux vineyard. Red, rosé and dry white are made on sedimentary soil. The red and rosé are made from Grenache, Syrah, Mourvèdre, Cinsault, with smaller amounts of Camarèse, Counoise, Muscardin, Terret Noir and Vaccarèse. Whites come from Bourboulenc, Clairette, Grenache Blanc, Marsanne and Roussanne. The reds are lighter in style than Côtes du Rhône and are best drunk two or three years after vintage. The whites can be very fresh if made with modern equipment. Vintages (reds): 1985, '86.

Gigondas: Lies between the two Côtes du Rhône Villages of Sablet and Vacqueyras and shares many of the characteristics of each (it was a Villages wine until 1971). Only red and rosé wines are made from 1,200 hectares. Grapes are: Grenache (maximum 80%), Syrah, Mourvèdre and Cinsault. Clay soil produces very rich reds, with spicy fruit and often a vegetal farmyard smell. Wines can last seemingly for ever, and are not really drinkable for four to five years after vintage. Vintages: 1976, '78, '79, '80, '83, '85.

Lirac: Mainly red and rosé wines (and a tiny amount of white) from a small area (650 hectares) northwest of Avignon on the west side of the Rhône, adjacent to Tavel (q.v.). The red and rosé come from Grenache (minimum 40%), Syrah, Mourvèdre and Cinsault. Whites from: Bourboulenc, Clairette, Picpoul, Calitor and Macabeo. The reds are a sort of lighter version of Châteauneuf, more long-lasting than Côtes du Rhône, and worth keeping for five years. At the moment, they are some of the best-value red Rhônes around. Rosés are a little heavy. Whites are also very good, fresher and more acidic than many Rhône whites. Altogether, an AC that's worth watching. Vintages (reds): 1979, '81, '83, '85, '86.

Tavel: The most famous rosé AC in France, with vines planted on nearly 750 hectares of clay soil west of Avignon. The wines are made from Grenache and Cinsault, Syrah and Mourvèdre with the permitted addition of the white grapes of Bourboulenc, Picpoul and Clairette. The wine is invariably very dry, with a little fruit, more tannin, a characteristic onion-skin colour from wood and comparatively low acidity. More modern techniques are enhancing the fruit and acidity and decreasing the use of wood. They age for around four years, but are at their best after two to three years.

Northern Rhône: VDQS

Coteaux du Lyonnais: Not strictly speaking in the northern Rhône orbit because it comes from the Gamay rather than the Syrah, the Coteaux du Lyonnais is rather an outlier of the Beaujolais. The vineyards cover an area south of Villefranche-sur-Saône and around Lyons. Reds are from the Gamay, whites from Chardonnay, Aligoté and Melon de Bourgogne. They are cheap, cheerful and mainly consumed in Lyons.

Southern Rhône: ACs

Châteauneuf-du-Pape: From the road coming north from Avignon, the truncated tower of the medieval Papal palace rises over the small town of Châteauneuf-du-Pape and its surrounding vineyards. The vineyards – with their characteristic gnarled vines and sometimes huge stones which reflect the heat – roll up to a high plateau. Châteauneuf mainly produces red wines, although a small amount of white is also made. The vineyards are large – covering 3,000 hectares in five communes. There are 13 grape varieties permitted for the red (in order of importance): Grenache (Noir and Blanc), Syrah, Mourvèdre, Cinsault, Clairette (white), Bourboulenc (white), Roussanne (white), Picpoul (white), Counoise, Terret Noir, Vaccarèse, Muscardin and Picardan (white). Very few growers actually use more than five, although two of the best – Domaine de Mont-Redon and Château de Beaucastel – use all 13. Châteauneuf-du-Pape is a highly alcoholic wine, but the richness and smoothness of the fruit should compensate for this – if the producer is any good. White Châteauneuf comes from Grenache Blanc, Clairette, Bourboulenc and Roussanne. It tends to be flowery but on the full side. Domaine-bottled wines now come in bottles bearing the Papal coat-of-arms; négociant-bottled wines do not. Vintages (reds): 1970, '76, '78, '79, '80, '83, '85.

Châtillon-en-Diois: Away to the east of the main Rhône vineyards are two small ACs in the heart of Alpine scenery, of which this is one. Centred on the little town of Châtillon-en-Diois in the valley of the Bez (a tributary of the Drôme). Red, white and rosé wines are made. Red comes from Gamay, Syrah and Pinot Noir; whites from Chardonnay and Aligoté. The occasional Chardonnay can be attractive, but on the whole they are not exciting.

Clairette de Die: Still wines from the same area as the *mousseux* (see below). Not often seen outside Die – and really best as a base for the sparkling wines.

Clairette de Die Mousseux: Another small area only a few miles from Châtillon, back in the valley of the Drôme, but still in spectacular mountain scenery. Dry and medium sweet sparkling wines are made from Clairette and Muscat à Petits Grains. The dry sometimes uses the *méthode champenoise*, while the medium sweet uses a local *méthode dioise*, which uses the sugar left over from an arrested first fermentation to start the second fermentation. The medium sweet Clairette de Die is similar to, if a little drier than, Asti Spumante, and quite as delicious.

Coteaux du Tricastin: Red, rosé and dry white wines from a large (2,000 hectare) area south of Montélimar and at the northern end of the big Côtes du Rhône plain around Orange. The soil is clay with large stones. Reds and rosés come from Grenache, Syrah, with a little Carignan, Cinsault and Mourvèdre. Whites come from Marsanne and Bourboulenc. There is little to distinguish these wines from their Côtes du Rhône neighbours, especially with the increasing use of Syrah, and their quality, like those of the Côtes du Rhône is getting better all the time. They are best drunk within two to three years of the vintage, when their full fruit and peppery flavour are at their best. Vintages: 1983, '85, '86.

Southern Rhône: VDQS

Coteaux de Pierrevert: This is often called the highest vineyard in France. Certainly the scenery is definitely Alpine and remote. This small area of 400 hectares in the Alpes-de-Haute-Provence département on the River Durance, north of Aix-en-Provence, produces red, rosé and white. The rosé is best – made from Cinsault, Carignan and Grenache. Fresh, acid and best drunk within two years of vintage. Whites are from Clairette, Marsanne and Roussanne.

Côtes du Lubéron: Red, rosé and dry white wines from the southern slopes of the Montagne de Lubéron in the Durance Valley east of Avignon. The reds and rosés come from Grenache, Syrah, Mourvèdre, Cinsault with some Gamay. The whites are from Grenache Blanc, Clairette, Bourboulenc, Marsanne and some Ugni Blanc, with some Chardonnay and Sauvignon now being planted. The quality from the better producers here who domaine bottle is good and getting better.

Côtes du Vivarais: Red, rosé and dry white wines from the west bank of the Rhône between Pont St-Esprit and Montélimar.

Red and rosé come from the standard Côtes du Rhône grapes with the addition of Gamay. Whites (of which the production is very small) also come from Côtes du Rhône varieties. Three communes are allowed to add their name to the AC: Orgnac, St-Montan and St-Remèze. Reds are lighter than Côtes du Rhône and delicious slightly chilled.

Vin Doux Naturels

Two communes in the Côtes du Rhône Villages also produce fortified sweet Vin Doux Naturels for which they have separate ACs.

Muscat de Beaumes-de-Venise: A Muscat-based sweet white VDN, made from the Muscat de Frontignan, which has achieved greater worldwide popularity than any other VDN from the south of France. It has the grapey, honeyed, smooth taste characteristic of all these wines.

Rasteau: A VDN made from the Grenache, which can be either red or pale tawny (made by removing the skins early in the fermentation). There is also a version called Rancio which results from leaving the wine in cask.

Saint-Joseph: This vineyard runs parallel to Crozes-Hermitage on the opposite (western) bank of the river, stretching much further north to the southern edge of Condrieu and a little further south almost to Cornas – a distance in total of nearly 70 kilometres. The original area was the southern end, around the town of Tournon and into the side valleys a little to the south. But changes in the AC legislation in 1972 extended the area from the previous 240 hectares to around 600 hectares today. Sadly, as with Côte Rôtie, the new plantings do not produce such good wine as the original, and the best wines still come from the southern communes of Tournon, Mauves and St-Jean de Muzols. The style of St-Joseph – even the best – is much lighter than Crozes-Hermitage, deriving its character from the sand and gravel which are mixed in with the granite base of the vineyard soil. The style brings out the fruit of the Syrah rather than the intense flavours, and makes St-Joseph a wine to enjoy younger than some other wines from the area. After three years it is certainly mature, and very few wines go beyond 10 or 11 years. Vintages: 1978, '79, '80, '82, '83, '85, '86.

Saint-Péray: The end of the northern Rhône vineyards is marked with the appearance of a 60-hectare white wine AC. This is made in a still and sparkling style (q.v.). The still wine is from Marsanne and Roussanne grapes, and is dry with a high natural acidity, a pale gold colour and a relatively short life (two to three years).

Saint-Péray Mousseux: The more interesting version of Saint-Péray. The sparkling wine comes from the sandy, clayey soil around the small town of Saint-Péray and the surrounding villages which stretch into the side valley towards Lamastre. It is made by the *méthode champenoise* and is generally a blended non-vintage wine, although a few growers do make vintage wines. Full and fruity, the wine is popular in France but rarely seen outside.

Côtes du Rhône

For producers making Côtes du Rhône Villages from a specific village, see under Southern Rhône producers

Vignerons Ardechois

Quartier Chaussy, 07120 Ruoms. Vineyards owned: 6,363ha.
Produce: 6 million bottles. Coop (a grouping of 21
cooperatives with 4,228 members)

The largest single production unit in the Rhône, this Union des Coopératives brings together smaller cooperatives in Côtes du Rhône, Coteaux du Tricastin and Côtes du Vivarais. While the vast production of 4.2 million bottles of Vin de Pays des Coteaux de l'Ardèche (much of it as varietal wines such as Syrah, Merlot, Gamay, Chardonnay – some of which goes to Louis Latour in Burgundy) dominates the operation, they also make considerable amounts of the AC wines. The Côtes du Rhône is basic, sound wine, and there is a smaller amount of Côtes du Rhône Villages made from 80% Grenache and 20% Syrah. *Open: Mon–Sat 8am–noon; 2–6pm.*

Domaine de la Berthete

Route de Jonquières, 84150 Camaret sur Aigues. Vineyards
owned: 50ha. *Produce: 250,000 bottles.* VP-R.

Traditional and modern techniques mix in this producer's cellars, which have been owned by the same family for 200 years. They use a combination of stainless steel and lined cement tanks for vinification. Quality is good, especially for a fresh white Côtes du Rhône, made from Grenache, Bourboulenc and Clairette. They also make white Vin de Pays de la Principauté d'Orange and red Vin de Pays de Vaucluse. *Open: Mon–Sat 9am–noon; 2–7pm.*

Domaine de Bruthel

Colombier, Sabran, 30200 Bagnols-sur-Cèze. Vineyards
owned: 24ha. *Produce: 30,000 bottles.* VP-R.

Red and white Côtes du Rhône are made by this family firm whose vineyards are west of the Rhône. They make an unusual white Côtes du Rhône from 90% Ugni Blanc, which is light, refreshing and attractively green tasting. The red and rosé are more conventional. Much of the production is sold to négociants, with about a third being bottled at the estate. *Open: Mon–Sat, in working hours.*

Domaine du Cabanon

5 Place de la Fontaine, Saze, 30650 Rochefort-du-Gard.
Vineyards owned: 20ha. *Produce: 30,000 bottles.* VP-R.

M. Payan uses some carbonic maceration for his red Côtes du Rhône, which is the only wine he makes. The blend includes 10% Syrah which gives a deep long-lasting colour to the wine; not designed for ageing. *Open: Mon–Sat 9am–noon; 2–6pm.*

Coopérative Vinicole Le Cellier des Templiers

84600 Richerenches. Vineyards owned: 750ha.
Produce: 65,000 bottles. Coop (150 members).

While much of the wine here goes for bottling elsewhere, a small amount of Côtes du Rhône and Coteaux du Tricastin are bottled on site. The wine is generally on the light side, and should be drunk young. *Open: Mon–Fri 8am–noon; 2–6pm.*

Chambovet Père et Fils

Rue St-Jean Prolongée, 84100 Orange. Vineyards owned:
82ha. *Produce: 300,000 bottles.* VP-R.

The vineyards belonging to this company are near the village of
Suze-la-Rousse. They come from three estates: Château
d'Estagnol, La Serre du Prieur and Domaine Ste-Marie. All
three estates produce excellent wines – although my preference
goes to La Serre du Prieur, which is dominated by the Syrah. In
addition to reds, they also make white Côtes du Rhône,
including an unusual 100% Bourboulenc with apricot flavours and
good fresh acidity. *Open: By appointment only.*

Emile Charavin

84110 Rasteau. Vineyards owned: 30ha.
Produce: 30,000 bottles. VP-R.

Domaine Wilfried produces Côtes du Rhône Villages from
Rasteau and Cairanne. Most of the production is of red, with a
small amount of rosé and some red Vin Doux Naturel from
Grenache. Wood is used extensively in the traditional cellars.
Open: Appointments preferred.

Domaine de la Chartreuse de Valbonne

St Paulet de Caisson, 30130 Pont St Esprit. Vineyards
owned: 6ha. *Produce: 30,000 bottles.* VP-R.

This beautiful Carthusian monastery founded in 1203 is now a
medical centre which owns the surrounding vineyard. This red
Côtes du Rhône is of good quality if limited production. It has
60% Grenache and 30% Syrah although the flavours of the
Syrah dominate. *Open: Mon–Fri 9–11:30am; 2–6pm. Mon–
Sun in summer.*

Domaine de Grand-Cyprès

470 Avenue du Maréchal Foch, 84100 Orange. Vineyards
owned: 12ha. *Produce: 70,000 bottles.* VP-R.

M. Lindeperg runs this small vineyard at Sormelongue near
Orange, using traditional techniques and ageing the wine in
wood. He only makes a red (70% Grenache and 30% Syrah)
which is designed for some ageing. His label – with a row of
cypresses – is particularly attractive. *Open: No.*

Château du Grand Moulas

Mornas, 84420 Piolenc. Vineyards owned: 29ha.
Produce: 96,000 bottles. VP-R.

M. Ryckwaert's cellars are close to the Rhône surrounded by
fruit trees which are an important part of his estate. His
vineyards are on higher ground near Uchaux, where he makes
Côtes du Rhône and Côtes du Rhône Villages. He does not
make wines for keeping, but they are immediately attractive
with perfumed violet flavours that spring out of the glass. He
presses 20% of the crop and leaves the rest to ferment as whole
fruit, giving very good colour and also softening out the
tannins. *Open: By appointment only.*

A. Gras et Fils (Domaine de St-Chétin)

84600 Valréas. Vineyards owned: 25ha.
Produce: 130,000 bottles. VP-R.

Red and white Côtes du Rhône are made here. The red comes in two styles, Domaine des Hauts de St Pierre, a blend of Grenache, Mourvèdre, Cinsault and Syrah, and Le Tresor de St-Chétin, which adds some Carignan. A white, La Gloire de St-André, is also made and has a tiny amount of Viognier in the blend. The wine is bottled for the owners by the local cooperative. *Open: By appointment only.*

Edmond Latour et Fils (Domaine de l'Espigouette)
84150 Violes. Vineyards owned: 21ha.
Produce: 50,000 bottles. VP-R.

Two vineyards form this estate. One, the Domaine de l'Espigouette, produces a Côtes du Rhône, predominantly of Grenache with 10% Syrah and other varieties. The other, Plan de Dieu, makes Côtes du Rhône Villages, with 80% Grenache and 20% Syrah, Cinsault and Mourvèdre. Controlled temperatures fermentation give good colour and depth to both wines. Small amounts of white and rosé are also made. *Open: Mon–Fri 8am–noon; 2–7pm.*

Nadine Latour (Domaine de Cabasse)
84000 Séguret. Vineyards owned: 24ha.
Produce: 96,000 bottles. VP-R.

Côtes du Rhône and Côtes du Rhône Villages Séguret are the wines produced on this estate. The Côtes du Rhône is in an easy-to-drink style, while the Villages wines is more serious and takes some bottle age. *Open: By appointment only.*

Jean-Marie Lombard (Brézème)
Quartier Piquet, 26250 Liuron. Vineyards owned: 2ha.
Produce: 12,000 bottles. VP-R.

This small vineyard is planted entirely with Syrah. The wine made is aged for up to two years in wood, giving considerable depth, rich deep tannic fruit when young, maturing into spicy, vanilla roundness after four or five years. With such small quantities, it is good to see the vineyard is being expanded. *Open: By appointment only.*

Domaine Martin de Grangeneuve
84150 Jonquières. Vineyards owned: 50ha.
Produce: 75,000 bottles. VP-R.

Red, rosé and white Côtes du Rhône are produced here. The red is particularly attractive – youthful and peppery, it can age well. The white is made from one third each Grenache Blanc, Bourboulenc and Clairette. The estate also produces a Vin de Pays de la Principauté d'Orange, which is a blend of Grenache and Syrah with 10% Cabernet Sauvignon. *Open: In working hours.*

Domaine de la Réméjeanne
Cadignac, 30200 Sabran. Vineyards owned: 24ha.
Produce: 25,000 bottles. VP-R.

A high proportion of Syrah (35%) in the blend of the red Côtes du Rhône from this estate gives considerable depth and a good ageing ability. The white Côtes du Rhône, which ferments for one month at a low temperature, is from Clairette, Bourboulenc and Ugni Blanc. Quality is good for both wines. Much of the wine from this estate is sold in bulk. *Open: Appointments preferred.*

Domaine de la Renjarde

84830 Sérignan du Comtat. Vineyards owned: 52ha.
Produce: 250,000 bottles. VP-R.

This newly planted estate is the only one in the Côtes du Rhône whose harvest is gathered entirely by machine. This does not seem to spoil the quality of the deep, peppery Côtes du Rhône Cuvée Henri Fabre, which has 60% Syrah. They also make a Côtes du Rhône Villages, Domaine de la Renjarde, which is 80% Grenache plus Syrah and Mourvèdre. Domaine de la Renjarde is in a more traditional style, for drinking younger. *Open: By appointment only.*

Domaine du Roure

St Marcel d'Ardèche, 07700 Bourg St Andéol. Vineyards owned: 11ha. Produce: 12,000 bottles. VP-R.

Vines more than 50 years old produce superb wine, full, rich and slow to mature. The Grenache dominates, with smaller amounts of Syrah, Cinsault and Carignan. While not all the wine is estate-bottled, there are plans to increase the amount up to around 80,000 bottles. *Open: Mon–Fri 8am–noon.*

Domaine Sainte-Anne

Les Celettes, St-Gervais, 30200 Bagnols-sur-Cèze. Vineyards owned: 26ha. Produce: 100,000 bottles. VP-R.

Red and white Côtes du Rhône are made here, the white with a little Viognier in the blend. There is also some Côtes du Rhône Villages. *Open: By appointment only.*

Château Saint-Estève d'Uchaux

Route de Sérignan, Uchaux, 84100 Orange. Vineyards owned: 55 ha. Produce: 300,000 bottles. VP-R.

An excellent estate on a sandy ridge north of Orange, giving a light style of wine. A full range of Côtes du Rhône wines is produced by the Français family, including a rare 100% Viognier Blanc de Cépage and a *méthode champenoise* Blanc de Blancs. Wines have both the Côtes du Rhône AC and the Villages AC – the Villages wine has 40% Syrah. There is a very fine Grande Réserve red, containing 50% Syrah. Other brand names include La Cuvée Friande, La Couloubrière and Cuvée des Deux Perdreaux. *Open: Mon–Fri 8am–noon; 2–6pm. Sat 8am–noon.*

André Vignal (Domaine de Saint-Georges)

Venejean, 30200 Bagnols-sur-Cèze. Vineyards owned: 30ha. Produce: 100,000 bottles. VP-R.

Red and white Côtes du Rhône are made on this estate, where the house dates back to the 12th century. The red Château de Saint-Georges is produced using carbonic maceration and matures quickly, with plenty of attractive fruit. there is a superior Cuvée Syrah, a rosé Côtes du Rhône Villages and a Côtes du Rhône Primeur. The white is fresh and fragrant, not a wine for ageing. *Open: By appointment only.*

Coopérative Vinicole La Suzienne

26790 Suze-la-Rousse. Vineyards owned: 1,000ha. Produce: 1m. bottles. Coop (937 members).

A huge cooperative in the heart of the Côtes du Rhône plain,

under the shadow of the Université du Vin. They make Côtes du
Rhône, Côtes du Rhône Villages and Coteaux du Tricastin
under the name of La Suzienne. Quality is variable but getting
better. All the bottling is done by the Union des Vignerons at
Tulette. *Open: By appointment only.*

Northern Rhône: Château Grillet

Neyret-Gachet (Château Grillet)

42410 Verin. Vineyards owned: 3ha.
Produce: 12,000 bottles. VP-R.

The one and only producer of Château Grillet from the smallest
AC in France, M. Neyret-Gachet actually lives in Lyons, where
he is a businessman during the week. At weekends, though, he is
down on his farm, where *maître-de-chai* A. Canet is in charge.
The wines, considered by some over-priced because of their
rarity value, are never to be forgotten once tasted. Almost
luscious, yet dry, they have the taste of ripe peaches or apricots
with a hint of sweet spice. The figure of 12,000 bottles per year is
at the top end of the scale – in 1978 only 3,800 bottles were
made. *Open: By appointment only.*

Northern Rhône: Condrieu

Pierre Dumazet

Limony 07340 Serrières. Vineyards owned: 0.6ha.
Produce: 2,000 bottles. VP-R.

M. Dumazet only produces tiny quantities of Condrieu from a
vineyard facing south and southeast on the terraces above the
river. Much of the wine goes to top restaurants in France, but a
little does get exported. He uses a mix of wood and stainless
steel and blends together wine made by both methods. These
are very fine wines, with all the apricot flavours of ripe
Condrieu are the result – if you can find a bottle. *Open: By
appointment only.*

Domaine du Château du Rozay

Le Rozay, 69420 Condrieu. Vineyards owned: Condrieu
2.3ha; Côtes du Rhône 1ha. *Produce: 10,000 bottles.* VP-R.

The Multier family make two styles of Condrieu. One, from old
vines, they call Château du Rozay, the second is a straight
Condrieu from younger vines. The wine is fermented in a mixture of stainless steel and wood. Those who admire the style of
the Condrieu will be delighted to know that more land has just
been planted. They also own a small plot of Syrah wines from
which they produce Côtes du Rhône. *Open: By appointment
only.*

Georges Vernay

1 Rue Nationale, 69420 Condrieu. Vineyards owned:
Condrieu 6ha; Côte Rôtie 2ha; St-Joseph 1ha.
Produce: 52,000 bottles. VP-R.

Traditional methods and modern equipment are sensibly
combined here to give wines of considerable style. M. Vernay is
certainly the big man of Condrieu, of which he makes about
30,000 bottles in a good year. He uses 10% new wood each
vintage for both red and white wines. *Open: By appointment
only.*

Northern Rhône: Cornas

Marcel Juge

Place de la Salle des Fêtes, 07130 Cornas. Vineyards owned: Cornas 3ha. *Produce: 15,000 bottles.* VP-R.

"My style never changes", writes M. Juge. And he is right. Heavy, tannic wine when young, his Cornas develops into rich, soupy wine full of herby fruit, with immense ageing ability. Not for the faint-hearted. *Open: By appointment only.*

Auguste Clape

07130 Cornas. Vineyards owned: Cornas 4ha; Côtes du Rhône 1ha. *Produce: 17,000 bottles.* VP-R.

Superb wines are produced by M. Clape in his small cellar on the main road of Cornas. His vineyards are high on the hill above. Although impenetrable wines when young, they still start life full of fruit lurking in the inky-black colour. With age – at least 10 years plus – they produce a rich, earthy, spicy wine, perfumed and surprisingly elegant. *Open: By appointment only.*

Robert Michel

Grande Rue, 07130 Cornas. Vineyards owned: 5ha. *Produce: 17,000 bottles.* VP-R.

M. Michel makes three styles of Cornas. The lightest comes from vineyards at the foot of the hill. The second in quality and depth comes from the hillside itself, while the third comes from old vines on the hill: this *cuvée* is called La Geynale. The wine is bottled un-fined, giving a very rich, earthy taste. Old-fashioned style. *Open: By appointment only.*

Alain Voge

07130 Cornas. Vineyards owned: Cornas 6ha; Saint-Péray 3ha. *Produce: 25,000 bottles.* VP-R.

M. Voge must be one of the few producers of Cornas who uses stainless steel in his cellar. This softens the tannin that can sometimes cover the fruit in Cornas, and his wines mature comparatively quickly. His Saint-Péray is made with Marsanne (98%) and Roussanne. *Open: By appointment only.*

Northern Rhône: Côte Rôtie

Albert Dervieux-Thaize

Ampuis, 69420 Condrieu. Vineyards owned: 3.1ha. *Produce: 15,000 bottles.* VP-R.

President of the local Syndicat des Vignerons, Albert Dervieux vinifies separately the grapes from the three parcels, in the Côte Blonde and Côte Brune and in another vineyard called Viaillère, that make up his small estate. Although he says his wine can take 15 or more years before maturity, others have found his wines tend to be on the lighter side. *Open: By appointment only.*

E. Guigal

Ampuis, 69420 Condrieu. Vineyards owned: 12ha. *Produce: 120,000 bottles.* VP-R and N.

The major force in Côte Rôtie, now that it owns Vidal-Fleury (q.v.). Happily, their size does not adversely affect their quality, which has a justified high reputation. Vinification takes place in stainless steel. They produce three styles of Côte Rôtie: a traditional blended Côte Brune and Côte Blonde; a lighter Côte Blonde La Mouline which has 12% white Viognier; and La Landonne, which is 100% Syrah, deep, well-structured and seemingly able to live for ever. *Open: By appointment only.*

Robert Jasmin

Ampuis, 69420 Condrieu. Vineyards owned: 3.5ha.
Produce: 12,000 bottles. VP-R.

One of the top producers in Côte Rôtie, M. Jasmin's tiny cellars in the centre of Ampuis are a delight to visit. He makes a blend of wines from the Côte Brune and Côte Blonde for his Chevalière d'Ampuis, pressing and then leaving the must to macerate for around 10 days. Everything is done in wood. The result, though, is surprisingly soft wines which are full of fruit even when young. He expects them to normally reach maturity after 10 years. *Open: By appointment only.*

Domaine de Vallouit

24 Avenue Désiré Valette, 26240 St-Vallier. Vineyards
owned: 13ha. Produce: 500,000 bottles. VP-R and N.

While the bulk of this firm's business is as a négociant for all the northern Rhône area, their principal vineyard holdings are in Côte Rôtie, where they have 10 hectares. They also own land in Crozes-Hermitage and Hermitage. As négociants they produce St-Joseph and a Côtes du Rhône. Their whites are a St-Joseph, a Hermitage and a Crozes-Hermitage. *Open: By appointment only.*

Vidal-Fleury

BP 12, Ampuis, 69420 Condrieu. Vineyards owned: 8ha.
Produce: 32,000 bottles. VP-R and N.

Now owned by Guigal (q.v.), Vidal-Fleury make Côte Rôtie from Côte Brune and Côte Blonde, both separately and together, using vineyard names like La Chatillonne, Le Clos, La Turque, La Pommière and Pavillon-Rouge. The firm is the oldest in the area, having been founded in 1781, and its reputation has remained high for much of that time. They still remain firmly committed to traditional ways. *Open: By appointment only.*

Northern Rhône: Crozes-Hermitage

Albert Bégot

Le Village, Serves-sur-Rhône, 26600 Gervans. Vineyards
owned: Crozes-Hermitage 5ha.
Produce: 15,000 bottles. VP-R.

Franck Bégot, who runs this estate with his mother, makes a red from Syrah and white from Marsanne, both AC Crozes-Hermitage. He uses organic methods in the vineyard and the minimum of treatment in the cellars. *Open: No.*

Cave des Clairmonts

Beaumont-Monteux, 26600 Tain l'Hermitage. Vineyards
owned: 79ha. Produce: 100,000 bottles. Coop (12 members).

Red and a small amount of white Crozes-Hermitage are made in this modern cooperative, using autovinification and temperature control. These techniques produce a modern, fresh white and a soft, young maturing red with plenty of colour and simple fruit. The red is more attractive than the white. *Open: Mon–Fri, in working hours.*

Charles-Jean Tardy and Bernard Ange

GAEC de la Syrah, Chanos-Curson, 26600 Tain l'Hermitage. Vineyards owned: Crozes-Hermitage 15ha. *Produce: 65,000 bottles.* VP-R.

Red and white Crozes-Hermitage are made, using traditional methods and ageing the wine in wood, with a proportion of new oak. The quality of their wines is very high indeed: a 1983 Domaine des Entrefaux tasted in 1986 was quite the best Crozes-Hermitage I have ever drunk. Other names (after portions of the estate) they use include Domaine des Pierrelles and Domaine de la Beaume. *Open: Mon–Sat 9am–noon, 3–7pm.*

Northern Rhône: Hermitage

M. Chapoutier

18 Rue du Dr. Paul Durand, 26600 Tain l'Hermitage. Vineyards owned: Hermitage 30ha; Crozes-Hermitage 5ha; Saint-Joseph 6ha; Côte-Rôtie 3ha; Châteauneuf-du-Pape 27ha. *Produce: 1 million bottles.* VP-R and N.

One of the largest firms in Hermitage, the family owned Chapoutier remains true to tradition, even down to pressing most of the grapes by foot-treading. They make the full range of northern Rhône wines, and have a major holding on the hill of Hermitage itself – from where they boldly display their name on the terrace walls. In some respects, their whites are more remarkable than their reds – especially the Hermitage Chante Alouette which ages a remarkable time. They have recently taken to blending vintages to produce top quality non-vintage wines under the name Cuvée Numerauté. As a négociant firm, they also make wine from Côtes du Ventoux, Coteaux du Tricastin, Tavel, Cornas and Gigondas. *Open: By appointment only.*

Domaine Jean-Louis Chave

Mauves, 07300 Tournon. Vineyards owned: 12ha. *Produce: 30,000 bottles.* VP-R.

One of the great names in Hermitage, Gérard Chave produces thoroughly traditional red and white wines which – certainly for the red – seem to live forever. His Hermitage is made from 100% Syrah – unlike some other Hermitage producers – and he carries out all the wine making in wood. The family has recently celebrated 500 years of winemaking from the same vineyard on the hill of Hermitage. *Open: No.*

Delas Frères

07300 Tournon. Vineyards owned: Hermitage 25ha; Cornas 12ha; Côte Rôtie 6ha; Condrieu 5ha. VP-R and N.

An old established firm of négociants who own vineyards in the main northern Rhône ACs, while buying in wine from the southern Rhône. They have maintained traditional standards while expanding their business. Now owned by the Champagne firm of Deutz. *Open: By appointment only.*

Desmeure Père et Fils

26600 Tain l'Hermitage. Vineyards owned: 17ha.
Produce: 33,000 bottles. VP-R.

A limited production of Hermitage and Crozes-Hermitage made traditionally and sold in bulk. *Open: By appointment only.*

Domaine Fayolle et Fils

Les Gamets, 26600 Gervans. Vineyards owned: Hermitage
1.5ha; Crozes-Hermitage 8ha.
Produce: 45,000 bottles. VP-R.

Fermentation of reds is in wood at this traditional family firm. They vinify the crop from each parcel of land separately: Le Dionnières for Hermitage; Le Pontaix and Les Voussères for red Crozes-Hermitage (Les Blancs for white). Of the Crozes-Hermitage wines, Le Pontaix is probably the best. Vinification takes place in a mixture of wood and cement tanks and the whole process is very traditional. *Open: By appointment only.*

Paul Jaboulet Aîné

BP 46, 26600 Tain l'Hermitage. Vineyards owned:
Hermitage 25ha; Crozes-Hermitage 36ha.
Produce: 1.5 million bottles. VP-R and N.

The most successful and most go-ahead firm in the northern Rhône, which has pioneered new, lighter styles of wines and has made the running in the increased reputation for the wines of the area. Their Hermitage La Chapelle is the most famous wine they produce, but they also make a full range from other areas of the Rhône. Their Crozes-Hermitage Domaine de Thalabert is generally considered one of the best wines of that AC. Négociant wines take in Châteauneuf-du-Pape, Côtes du Rhône (including the well-known Parallele 45), Côtes du Ventoux, Saint-Joseph and Côte Rôtie. A brand new plant outside Tain l'Hermitage is the outward symbol of their success. *Open: By appointment only.*

Marc Sorrel

128 bis, Avenue Jean-Jaurès, 26600 Tain l'Hermitage.
Vineyards owned: Hermitage 3ha.
Produce: 12,000 bottles. VP-R.

Old vines are behind the quality from this small vineyard, where traditional methods reign. M. Sorrel has vineyards exclusively in Hermitage: Le Méal, Les Bessards, Les Greffieux and Les Rocoules. He makes a red Hermitage: Le Greal, and a white (100% Marsanne): Les Rocoules. *Open: By appointment only.*

Cave Coopérative de Tain l'Hermitage

22 Route de Larnage, 26600 Tain l'Hermitage.
Vineyards owned: 650ha.
Produce: 500,000 bottles. Coop (500 members).

Besides having members with vineyards in Crozes-Hermitage, Saint-Péray, Saint-Joseph and Cornas, this cooperative controls two thirds of the Hermitage AC. Standards are good, if old fashioned, and quality is on the whole sustained. Their wines tend not to have the infinite ageing ability of the private Hermitage producers, but are attractive after nine or 10 years. Whites are made in a modern style, fresh and crisp. *Open: Mon–Sat, in working hours.*

Northern Rhône: Saint-Joseph

Pierre Coursodon

Place du Marché, Mauves, 07300 Tournon. Vineyards owned: 8ha. *Produce: 35,000 bottles.* VP-R.

Le Paradis, Saint-Pierre, L'Olivaie are some of the names that M. Coursodon uses for his red and white produced from vineyards in the southern part of the Saint-Joseph AC. The red is from 100% Syrah, fermented in wood; the white 100% Marsanne, made in lined tanks. *Open: By appointment only.*

Emile Florentin

Route Nationale, Mauves, 07300 Tournon. Vineyards owned: St-Joseph 4ha. *Produce: 16,000 bottles.* VP-R.

M. Florentin produces red and white Saint-Joseph on his small estate, called Clos de l'Arbalestrier. His vines are old and yields are low, resulting in complex wines. The red is perhaps a little too tannic for the fruit, but the white, from Roussanne, is very good indeed. *Open: By appointment only.*

Bernard Gripa

Mauves, 07300 Tournon. Vineyards owned: Saint-Joseph 4ha; Saint-Péray 1ha. *Produce: 25,000 bottles.* VP-R.

Wood fermentation is still the only way they make wine *chez* Gripa, and quality makes him probably the best producer of Saint-Joseph. His vineyards are actually in the heart of the AC, in the area known as Saint-Joseph. The red has the soft richness typical of the AC, the white, from Marsanne, is perhaps less exciting. M. Gripa's still (he does not make a sparkling wine) Saint-Péray is from a blend with 90% Marsanne and 10% Roussanne. *Open: By appointment only.*

Jean-Louis Grippat

La Sauva, 07300 Tournon. Vineyards owned: St Joseph 4.5ha; Hermitage 2.6ha. *Produce: 24,000 bottles.* VP-R.

A small yield from the terraces of Saint-Joseph gives M. Grippat an intense wine, but one whose fruit and life bring it round comparatively quickly – after five years. Part of his holding is in the area of Saint-Joseph. His white Hermitage (which, like the red Hermitage, is from Les Murets vineyard) is very highly regarded, and can age well for five or six years. M. Grippat and M. Gripa (see entry above) are cousins. *Open: By appointment only.*

Southern Rhône: Châteauneuf-du-Pape

Château de Beaucastel

Société Fermière des Vignobles Pierre Perrin, 84350 Courthézon. Vineyards owned: Châteauneuf 76ha; Côtes du Rhône 25ha. *Produce: 350,000 bottles.* VP-R.

This large family estate has pioneered organic methods, cutting out artificial fertilizers in the vineyard and adopting heat treatment of the grapes in the cellar before fermentation to give greater extract and avoid the need for sulphur. The vineyard has many old vines and yields are low. But the extra efforts are well rewarded by, to my mind, one of the top two or three

Châteauneuf available. They age superbly, full of rich vegetal fruit. In addition to the Château de Beaucastel which is Châteauneuf AC (and incidentally uses all 13 grape varieties permitted in the AC rules) they also produce a white Châteauneuf and an equally fine Côtes du Rhône Crû du Coudoulet on part of the estate which is outside the Châteauneuf AC. *Open: By appointment only.*

Domaine de Beaurenard

84230 Châteauneuf-du-Pape. Vineyards owned: Châteauneuf 30ha; Côtes du Rhône Rasteau 45ha.
Produce: 420,000 bottles. VP-R.

Domaine de Beaurenard is the name for both the Châteauneuf and the Côtes du Rhône wine produced here. It is one of the oldest concerns in the area, started in 1695, and Paul Coulon is the seventh generation. He uses a mixture of carbonic maceration and juice from pressed grapes to give a rich, fruity wine, low in tannin. The Côtes du Rhône Rasteau is a good, quick-maturing wine, which again is full of fruit. *Open: By appointment only.*

Domaine Berthet-Rayne

Route de Roquemaure, 84350 Courthézon. Vineyards owned: 6.7ha. *Produce: 15,000 bottles.* VP-R.

This small estate produces Châteauneuf and Côtes du Rhône, using thermovinification at controlled temperatures. They also make a small amount of Châteauneuf white. *Open: By appointment only.*

Domaine de Cabrières-les-Silex

84230 Châteauneuf-du-Pape. Vineyards owned: 60ha.
Produce: 150,000 bottles. VP-R.

One of the top estates of Châteauneuf, both because it is at the highest point of the AC area and because of the quality of the wine. The soil here consists almost completely of the large round stones so often seen in pictures of the Châteauneuf vineyards. They use traditional methods, fermenting and ageing in wood for their herby, meaty, spicy red. The white is also full and quite traditional in stlye. *Open: By appointment only.*

Domaine Chante-Cigale

84230 Châteauneuf-du-Pape. Vineyards owned: 40ha.
Produce: 80,000 bottles. VP-R.

Everything is done traditionally in wood here, and the intense colour of the wine is achieved by macerating the grapes for nearly three weeks. They only use Grenache, Cinsault, Mourvèdre and Syrah in the blend and the wine is kept for 18 months in wood. No white wine is made at present, but new plantings should change that. *Open: Mon–Fri 8am–noon; 2–6pm.*

Georges Pierre Coulon (Domaine de la Pinède)

84230 Châteauneuf-du-Pape. Vineyards owned: 10ha.
Produce: 38,000 bottles. VP-R.

Red and white Châteauneuf is made at this small estate, as well as a little attractive rosé vin de table called Réserve de la Pinède, and red Côtes du Rhône. *Open: Appointments preferred.*

Maxime Daumen (Domaine de la Vieille Julienne)

84100 Orange. Vineyards owned: Châteauneuf and Côtes du Rhône 23ha. *Produce: 20,000 bottles.* VP-R.

Very rich, heavy wines are the speciality of this estate, which goes back to the 17th century. Their production is split equally between Châteauneuf and Côtes du Rhône. *Open: Mon–Fri 8:30am–noon; 2–6pm.*

Diffonty et Fils (Cuvée du Vatican)

BP 33, 84230 Châteauneuf-du-Pape. Vineyards owned: Châteauneuf 16ha; Côtes du Rhône 6ha; Vin de Pays 16.5ha. *Produce: 215,000 bottles.* VP-R.

The sure-fire name Cuvée du Vatican is used both for the Châteauneuf and the Côtes du Rhône produced by this firm. The Châteauneuf has a long fermentation on the skins, giving it a very deep colour. The Vin de Pays du Gard is rosé and white, and sold under the name Mas de Brès. *Open: Mon–Sat 8am–noon; 2–6pm.*

Château de la Font du Loup

Route du Châteauneuf-du-Pape, 84350 Courthézon. Vineyards owned: Châteauneuf 15ha. *Produce: 80,000 bottles.* VP-R.

While fermentation has changed in recent years to stainless steel, ageing remains in wood. The red is elegant, less tannic than some Châteauneuf. The white is produced in small quantities, using a microvinification technique which gives considerable fruit and freshness and cuts down in the tannin. *Open: By appointment only.*

Château Fortia

84230 Châteauneuf-du-Pape. Vineyards owned: 28ha. *Produce: 75,000 bottles.* VP-R.

A traditional red and a modern-style white Châteauneuf are made at what is generally regarded as one of the top Châteauneuf estates. The family of Le Roy de Boisaumarié, the owners, are proud of the fact that their ancestor mapped out the best land in Châteauneuf and instigated what became the first AC area in France in 1923. *Open: Appointments preferred.*

Château de la Gardine

84230 Châteauneuf-du-Pape. Vineyards owned: Châteauneuf 53ha; Côtes du Rhône Villages 48ha. *Produce: 450,000 bottles.* VP-R.

The Brunel family have been *vignerons* since 1670, working on land to the west of Châteauneuf. They have recently increased the quantity of Syrah on the estate to 20% and cut down the amount of Grenache. This gives the wine greater ageing ability than some other Châteauneuf wines. The Côtes du Rhône Villages comes from near Rasteau and Roaix, and again Syrah is an important element in the wine. *Open: Mon–Fri 8:30am–noon; 1–5:30pm.*

Pierre Jacumin

Route de Sorgues, 84230 Châteauneuf-du-Pape. Vineyards owned: 12ha. *Produce: 40,000 bottles.* VP-R.

Cuvée de Boisdauphin is the name which M. Jacumin gives to

his Châteauneuf. He works traditionally, using wood, and produces an intense, deep-coloured wine that needs five or six years before it is approachable. *Open: In working hours.*

Lançon Père et Fils (Domaine de la Solitude)

84230 Châteauneuf-du-Pape. Vineyards owned: Châteauneuf 40ha; Côtes du Rhône 40ha. *Produce: 300,000 bottles.* VP-R.

A combination of traditional and modern techniques including carbonic maceration for the red wines. Interestingly, the Châteauneuf has a high (20%) percentage of Mourvèdre, which gives some power as well as an attractive perfume. M. Lançon makes white wines in both AC areas. The estate has been in the family since the 16th century. *Open: In working hours.*

Domaine Mathieu

Route de Courthézon, 84230 Châteauneuf-du-Pape. Vineyards owned: 15ha. *Produce: 70,000 bottles.* VP-R.

Full-bodied, aromatic Châteauneuf, made principally from Grenache in a traditional way. A white wine should be made soon from vines planted in 1985. Part of the production goes to négociants. *Open: By appointment only.*

Clos du Mont Olivet

15 Avenue Saint-Joseph. 84230 Châteauneuf-du-Pape. Vineyards owned: Châteauneuf 24ha; Côtes du Rhône 8ha. *Produce: 180,000 bottles.* VP-R.

Traditional Châteauneuf style, big, robust reds, with plenty of herby, spicy flavour. A small amount of white wine is also made, plus Côtes du Rhône red from vineyards to the east of Châteauneuf at Bollène. *Open: Mon–Wed 8am–noon; Thur– Fri 2–6pm; Sat 8am–noon.*

Domaine de Mont-Redon

84230 Châteauneuf-du-Pape. Vineyards owned: Châteauneuf 95ha; Côtes du Rhône 35ha. *Produce: 500,000 bottles.* VP-R.

One of the largest Châteauneuf estates – and also one of the best. The Châteauneuf vineyard is on the high plateau to the west of the AC area, looking north to Orange. They grow all 13 varieties of vines permitted under the AC rules, and also have small plantings of some which have virtually disappeared. Each variety is vinified separately and then blended. The Abeille family is highly serious in producing aromatic, very fruity wines, using some carbonic maceration. They have recently bought a Côtes du Rhône vineyard at Roquemaure to the southwest. *Open: By appointment only.*

Louis Mousset (Château des Fines Roches)

84230 Châteauneuf-du-Pape. Vineyards owned: Châteauneuf 200ha; Côtes du Rhône 100ha. *Produce: 10 million bottles.* VP-R and N.

A huge négociant firm centred on the mock-Gothic Château des Fines Roches (now a first-class restaurant), producing wines from all over the Rhône Valley, including vin de pays. Their own estates produce Château des Fines Roches Châteauneuf and Côtes du Rhône La Patrasse and Château du Prieuré. The négociant wines reach an acceptable standard, the Châteauneuf is much better. *Open: (Château) By appointment only; (Restaurant) Reservations only.*

Domaine de Nalys

Route de Courthézon, 84230 Châteauneuf-du-Pape.
Vineyards owned: 52ha. *Produce: 240,000 bottles.* VP-R.

All 13 grape varieties of Châteauneuf are planted in this large estate on the eastern side of the AC area, which has been in existence since 1778. They age the wine for 12 months in wood, producing a quick-maturing wine with a floral, perfumed bouquet and a soft texture. Smaller quantities of white are also made. *Open: Mon–Fri 9am–noon; 2–6pm.*

Château de la Nerthe

84230 Châteauneuf-du-Pape. Vineyards owned: 63ha.
Produce: 200,000 bottles. VP-R.

Now part of Burgundy négociants Richard and David Foillard, this estate has a great tradition on Châteauneuf. The wine is matured in wood, some of which is new. They make a white wine, Clos de Beauvenir, and also two reds, Cuvée des Cadettes and the superior Château la Nerthe. *Open: By appointment only.*

Nicolet Frères (GAEC Chante Perdrix)

84230 Châteauneuf-du-Pape. Vineyards owned: 20ha.
Produce: 60,000 bottles. VP-R.

Big, old-stlye wines are made on this estate on the western edge of the Châteauneuf AC area. They only make a red. *Open: By appointment only.*

Clos de l'Oratoire des Papes

Rue St-Joseph, 84230 Châteauneuf-du-Pape. Vineyards owned: 40ha. *Produce: 140,000 bottles.* VP-R.

Red and white Châteauneuf are produced from a vineyard whose centrepiece is an 18th century altar which probably has little to do with Popes and more to do with an insurance policy by a vigneron. Today, the owner Mme Amouroux runs the estate traditionally making classic wines. *Open: Mon–Fri 8am–noon; 2–6pm.*

Clos des Papes

84230 Châteauneuf-du-Pape. Vineyards owned: 32ha.
Produce: 110,000 bottles. VP-R.

Paul Avril, whose family has been making wine in the area for 300 years, produces traditional Châteauneuf using a long maceration and wood ageing for up to 18 months. His wines are well-structured, if tannic, and need a long time in bottle before drinking. 90% of production is red, with the remainder white. *Open: By appointment only.*

Père Anselme

BP 1, 84230 Châteauneuf-du-Pape. Vineyards owned: None.
Produce: 2 million bottles. N.

Père Anselme, owned by J-P Brotte, president of the local Syndicat, is one of the biggest firms in the area, acting as négociants for wine from all over the Rhône especially in Côtes du Rhône, Côtes du Rhône Villages, Coteaux du Tricastin, Côtes du Ventoux and Gigondas as well as Châteauneuf. A fascinating museum at their cellars in Châteauneuf is well worth a visit. *Open: Mon–Fri 8am–noon; 2–6pm.*

Domaine Pierre Quiot
Château Maucoil, 84100 Orange, Vineyards owned:
Châteauneuf 30ha; Gigondas 14ha; Côtes du Rhône 6ha.
Produce: 150,000 bottles. VP-R.

Four brand names are used at this estate: Château Maucoil and
Quiot Saint-Pierre for Châteauneuf; Pradets for Gigondas and
Patriciens for Côtes du Rhône. The Châteauneuf vineyard is
probably the oldest named land in the area and records date
back to the 16th century. The style is traditional in all three
estates. *Open: Appointments preferred.*

Château Rayas
84230 Châteauneuf-du-Pape. Vineyards owned: Châteauneuf
13ha; Côtes du Rhône 12 ha. *Produce: 00,000 bottles.* VP-R.

A small estate in Châteauneuf terms, but one which is highly
regarded for the quality of its traditionally made red
Châteauneuf, which, unusually, is made from 100% Grenache
and aged in wood for up to three years. They also make Côtes
du Rhône red and white from the estate of Château Fonsalette.
Open: By appointment only.

Domaine du Vieux Télégraphe
84370 Bedarrides. Vineyards owned: Chateauneuf 50ha.
Produce: 70,000 bottles. VP-R.

A very traditional estate, producing concentrated firm wines
which need many years for maturity. The Brunier family
vineyard is planted mainly with Grenache (80%) and also with
Cinsault, Mourvèdre and Syrah. The yields are low and the
complete bunches of grapes are fermented to give tannic wines.
Open: By appointment only.

Southern Rhône: Clairette de Die

Albert Andrieux
26340 Saillans. Vineyards owned: Clairette de Die 11ha.
Produce: 50,000 bottles. VP-R.

This estate produces a range of Clairette wines – from the still,
dry Domaine du Plot to the Brut *méthode champenoise* and
demi-sec *méthode dioise* sparkling wines. *Open: Mon–Fri
8am–noon; 2–6pm.*

Buffardel Frères
Boulevard de Cagnard, 26150 Die. Vineyards owned: None.
Produce: 300,000 bottles. N.

Sweet and dry Clairette de Die are the only wines produced by
this firm of négociants. Both are by the *méthode champenoise*,
using a number of different brand names: Buffardel Frères,
Albert Reymond, Leblanc Père et Fils, J. & R. Leblanc and
Jacques Leblanc. Their dry Blanc de Blancs is probably their
best. *Open: By appointment only.*

Union Producteurs du Diois
Cave Coopérative de la Clairette, Avenue de la Clairette,
26150 Die. Vineyards owned: 800ha.
Produce: 3.2 million bottles. Coop (530 members).

This cooperative controls 80% of Clairette de Die production,
and luckily does not do a bad job of it. Their Cuvée Tradition is

a very attractive, sweet, muscat wine made by the *méthode dioise*, while Voconces Brut is a dry *méthode champenoise* wine. They also make still Clairette de Die and Chatillon-en-Diois. *Open: In working hours.*

Domaine de Magord

Barsac, 26150 Die. Vineyards owned: 9ha.
Produce: 40,000 bottles. VP-R.

This small firm produces sweet Clairette de Die using the *méthode dioise* and a dry Brut using the *méthode champenoise*. *Open: Appointments preferred.*

Southern Rhône: Côtes du Rhône Villages

Romain Bouchard

Val des Rois, 84600 Valréas. Vineyards owned: Valréas
15ha. *Produce: 50,000 bottles.* VP-R.

The Bouchard family have been at this estate since 1681, and have commemorated the fact with a Cuvée de la 8ième generation, a blend of Grenache and Gamay. Their Côtes du Rhône Villages Valréas "Signature" is 75% Grenache and 20% Syrah, and can age well – up to 10 years. They also make Cuvée des Rois Côtes du Rhône red and rosé. *Open: Mon–Fri 9:30am–noon; 2:30–7pm.*

Cave des Vignerons de Chusclan

Chusclan, 30200 Bagnols-sur-Cèze. Vineyards owned: 750ha.
Produce: 2.4 million bottles. Coop (137 members).

Carbonic maceration and stainless steel produce youthful, fruity wines at this cooperative. They make standard Côtes du Rhône red, rosé and white as well as Côtes du Rhône Villages Chusclan rosé and red. Quality is reliable. *Open: Mon–Sat 8:30am–noon; 2–6pm.*

Daniel and Jean Couston

Route de Saint-Roman, 26790 Tulette. Vineyards owned:
Visan 50ha; Valréas 40ha. *Produce: 500,000 bottles.* VP-R.

There are two estates belonging to this company. The Visan estate is Domaine du Garrigon, where red Villages and white and rosé Côtes du Rhône are made. The Valréas estate is Domaine de la Grande Bellane, producing red and rosé. They also make a Côtes du Rhône Primeur. They prefer to use organic methods in the vineyards and stabilize the wine in the cellar with modern equipment rather than chemicals. *Open: By appointment only.*

Union des Vignerons l'Enclave des Papes

84600 Valréas. Vineyards owned: 2,000ha.
Produce: 3 million bottles. Coop (800 members).

They produce quick maturing wines at this huge cooperative, the bulk of which is Côtes du Rhône, with some Coteaux du Tricastin. There is also some Côtes du Rhône Villages Valréas. There have been big changes in the members' vineyards with an increase in Grenache and Syrah and a cutting down of Carignan. The Enclave of the Popes is a small area of land which remained Papal territory until the time of the Revolution and is now an enclave of the Vaucluse département in the middle of the Drôme. *Open: Mon–Fri 8am–noon; 2–6pm.*

Domaine des Lambertins

Vacqueyras, 84190 Beaumes de Venise. Vineyards owned: Vacqueyras 24ha. *Produce: 70,000 bottles.* VP-R.

A traditional family firm run by the Lambert brothers, producing Côtes du Rhône Villages Vacqueyras and Côtes du Rhône, both only in red. *Open: By appointment only.*

Domaine Martin

Plan de Dieu, 84150 Travaillan. Vineyards owned: 48ha. *Produce: 100,000 bottles.* VP-R.

Traditional techniques and stainless steel are used at this medium-sized estate. Reds are aged in wood, as is the Rasteau red Vin Doux Naturel which they make here from 100% Grenache. Other wines produced are red, white and rosé Côtes du Rhône and red Côtes du Rhône Villages. *Open: Mon–Fri 8am–7pm.*

Domaine du Moulin

26110 Vinsobres. Vineyards owned: Vinsobres 20ha. *Produce: 40,000 bottles.* VP-R.

A traditional producer, which makes only a Côtes du Rhône Villages Vinsobres – and a very good one at that. The red is cherry-fresh, attractive when young, but with the ability to age for three or four years. A white and rosé are also made. *Open: Mon–Fri 8am–noon; 2–7pm.*

GAEC Pelaquié

St Victor la Coste, 30290 Laudun. Vineyards owned: 14ha. *Produce: 20,000 bottles.* VP-R.

Red and white Côtes du Rhône Villages Laudun are produced at this small estate. Stainless steel is used for vinification, which gives a fruity, fresh red for drinking young. They also make white Côtes du Rhône and some red Lirac. The wines are attractive and well made. *Open: Mon–Sat 8am–noon; 2–6pm.*

Domaine Rabasse-Charavin

Coteaux Saint-Martin, 84290 Cairanne. Vineyards owned: 21ha. *Produce: 80,000 bottles.* VP-R.

A high-quality producer of Côtes du Rhône Villages from Cairanne and Rasteau and generic Côtes du Rhône red and white. They also make a 100% Syrah Côtes du Rhône, aged in wood, which is very good. The vineyards have a high proportion of 80-year-old vines. *Open: Mon–Fri 8–11:30am; 3–6pm.*

Cave des Vignerons de Rasteau

84110 Rasteau. Vineyards owned: 750ha. *Produce: 2.2 million bottles.* Coop (180 members).

One of the best cooperatives in the Rhône Valley, producing Côtes du Rhône and Côtes du Rhône Villages Rasteau, including a Cuvée Prestige which is matured in wood and a Côtes du Rhône Primeur. They are also the biggest producers of the sweet Rasteau Vin Doux Naturel, from 100% Grenache. One of the reasons for their success is that they pay members on the quality of the grapes, not the potential alcoholic content. Would that more cooperatives did the same. *Open: Mon–Fri 8am–noon; 2–6pm.*

Pierre Rosati

La Verrière, Route de Pègue, 84600 Valréas. Vineyards
owned: Valréas 18ha; St-Pantaleon-les-Vignes 2ha.
Produce: 26,000 bottles. VP-R.

Stainless steel vinification and then wood ageing for the reds
produces some smooth, clean-tasting Côtes du Rhône, both
generic and Villages from Valréas. M. Rosati also makes white
and rosé Côtes du Rhône. All the wines are sold under the name
Ferme La Verrière. *Open: Mon–Sun 8am–7pm.*

Château Saint-Maurice l'Ardoise

30290 Laudun. Vineyards owned: 96ha.
Produce: 450,000 bottles. VP-R.

Most of the production at this estate is of Côtes du Rhône
Villages or Côtes du Rhône, which is sold under a number of
different names: Château Saint-Maurice l'Ardoise, Château
Saint-Maurice, Domaine du Mont-Jupiter (there are ruins of an
ancient temple on the site) and Clos de Rossignac. M. Valat also
makes a small amount of Lirac from vineyards in Saint-
Laurent-les-Arbres, and Vin de Pays du Gard. *Open: In
working hours.*

Cave Coopérative St Pantaleon-les-Vignes

26770 St-Pantaleon-les-Vignes. Vineyards owned: Côtes du
Rhône 635ha; Coteaux du Tricastin 56ha; Côtes du Rhône
Villages 13ha; Côtes du Rhône Villages St-Pantaleon 47ha;
Côtes du Rhône Villages Rousset 35ha.
Produce: 180,000 bottles. Coop (220 members).

While half of the wine is sold in bulk to négociants, 20% is
bottled for the cooperative at Tulette. The main wines bottled
are Côtes du Rhône Villages St Pantaleon and Rousset and
some Villages Pantaleon which is aged in wood. *Open:
Appointments preferred.*

Domaine le Sang des Cailloux

Route de Vacqueyras, 84260 Sarrians. Vineyards owned:
Vacqueyras 18ha. *Produce: 85,000 bottles.* VP-R.

M. Jean Ricard makes a Côtes du Rhône Villages Vacqueyras,
which he ferments and matures in wood. The quality is high,
with herby, spicy fruit and touches of wood tannin which
suggest a good ageing ability. *Open: Mon–Fri 8am–noon;
1–6pm.*

Domaine la Soumade

Rasteau, 84110 Vaison la Romaine. Vineyards owned:
Rasteau 20ha. *Produce: 40,000 bottles.* VP-R.

Côtes du Rhône Villages Rasteau and Rasteau Vin Doux
Naturel are the estate's top AC wines. André Roméro also
makes generic Côtes du Rhône and an interesting Vin de Pays de
Vaucluse from a blend of Cabernet Sauvignon and Merlot.
Open: Mon–Sat 8am–noon; 2–8pm.

Domaine de Verquière

84110 Sablet. Vineyards owned: 50ha.
Produce: 100,000 bottles. VP-R.

M. Chamfort is a traditional producer, who uses wood for
maturing and is not afraid to leave the wine in cask for some

time. He makes red Côtes du Rhône Villages from Sablet, Vacqueyras and generic red and rosé Côtes du Rhône. There is also a high-quality Rasteau Vin Doux Naturel. *Open: Appointments preferred.*

Cave Zanti-Cumino (Domaine du Banvin)

84290 Cairanne. Vineyards owned: Cairanne 18ha.
Produce: 80,000 bottles. VP-R.

Some carbonic maceration is used at this estate. They make Côtes du Rhône red, white and rosé, plus Côtes du Rhône Villages Cairanne using a blend of Grenache, Syrah and Mourvèdre. The wines are all best drunk young. *Open: By appointment only.*

Southern Rhône: Côtes de Ventoux

Domaine des Anges

84750 Mormoiron. Vineyards owned: 8ha.
Produce: 25,000 bottles. VP-R.

A small estate owned by an Englishman, Malcolm Swann, who has planted Grenache, Syrah, Cinsault and Carignan to make a full fresh, easy-drinking Côtes du Ventoux which brings out all the attraction of this AC area. *Open: By appointment only.*

La Vieille Ferme

Route de Jonquières, 84100 Orange. Vineyards owned:
None. *Produce: 1 million bottles.* N.

The Perrin family, who own Château de Beaucastel in Châteauneuf-du-Pape (q.v.), also run this large négociant business which buys in grapes and wine from growers in Côtes du Ventoux (for red wines) and Côtes du Lubéron (for white). It is a modern firm, producing extremely good quality, ready-to-drink wines under the La Vieille Ferme label. There are plans to widen the business to produce wines from Gigondas, Vacqueyras and Muscat de Beaumes-de-Venise. *Open: By appointment only.*

Southern Rhône: Gigondas

Pierre Amadieu

84190 Gigondas. Vineyards owned: Gigondas 120ha; Côtes du Ventoux 35ha. *Produce: 990,000 bottles.* VP-R and N.

A traditional firm, with spectacular old cellars dug into the hillside of Gigondas. Their principal wines are Gigondas and Côtes du Ventoux from their own estates, but they also make Châteauneuf-du-Pape and Côtes du Rhône. Style is traditional as well, and none the worse for that. *Open: In working hours.*

Edmond Burle

La Beaumette, 84190 Gigondas. Vineyards owned: Gigondas 1.6ha; Vacqueyras 1ha; Côtes du Rhône 8ha; Vin de Table 5ha. *Produce: 30,000 bottles.* VP-R.

This is a small traditional firm which matures wine in wood, and whose pride and joy is their Gigondas Les Pallierondas, a rich and powerful wine. But M. Burle also makes Côtes du Rhône generic, Vacqueyras and Vin de Table. *Open: In working hours.*

Georges Faraud et Fils

Pres des Ecoles, 84190 Gigondas. Vineyards owned: Gigondas 13ha. *Produce: 40,000 bottles. VP-R.*

A small, traditional producer who only makes red and rosé Gigondas, under the name Domaine du Cayron. The red is big, beefy and needs time to mature. *Open: Mon–Sat 8am–noon, 2–8pm.*

Domaine de la Fourmone

Vacqueyras, 84190 Beaumes-de-Venise. Vineyards owned: Gigondas 9ha; Côtes du Rhône Vacqueyras 12ha; Côtes du Rhône 8ha. *Produce: 38,000 bottles. VP-R.*

A traditional producer, M. Combe makes a Vacqueyras full of deep fruit which sees at least eight months in wood. He also makes Gigondas under the brand name L'Oustau Fauquet, a big wine, but elegant, which needs at least seven years to begin to mature. *Open: Appointments preferred.*

Cave des Vignerons de Gigondas

84190 Gigondas. Vineyards owned: 250ha. *Produce: 500,000 bottles.* Coop (120 members).

This cooperative uses carbonic maceration to soften the tannins and increase the fruit in their Gigondas. As a result it is soft and quite quick to mature. The brand name they use is Cuvée du Président. They also make wines more traditionally under the names Signature and Tête de Cuvée. A smaller amount of Côtes du Rhône is also made. *Open: By appointment only .*

Domaine du Grand Montmirail

Gigondas, 84109 Beaumes de Venise. Vineyards owned: 30ha. *Produce: 66,000 bottles. VP-R.*

This estate, now owned by the merchant house of Pascal, is being revived by the energetic owner Denis Cheron. He has increased the proportion of Syrah in the blend, and restricted yields to produce concentrated wines with considerable ageing ability. Names used are Domaine du Roucas de St-Pierre, Domaine de St-Gens and Domaine du Pradas. *Open: By appointment only.*

Les Fils de Hilarion Roux (Domaine de Pallières)

84190 Gigondas. Vineyards owned: Gigondas 25ha. *Produce: 80,000 bottles. VP-R.*

A long-established (founded 1765) vineyard still in the same family. There is a traditional approach to winemaking, with long fermentation and ageing for up to three years in wood. The result is a red Gigondas of immense power, considerable tannin and a very long life. The estate also produces a rosé. *Open: By appointment only*

Le Mas des Collines

84190 Gigondas. Vineyards owned: Gigondas 15ha; Côtes du Rhône 38ha. *Produce: 60,000 bottles. VP-R.*

Mas des Collines is the name M. Detaxis uses for his Gigondas. His Côtes du Rhône he calls La Bruissière. Both are traditionally made wines, with good tannin and firm fruit. Much of the Gigondas vineyard is planted with old vines. *Open: Appointments preferred.*

Gabriel Meffre

84190 Gigondas. Vineyards owned: Gigondas 92ha; Châteauneuf-du-Pape 88ha; Côtes du Rhône 500ha; Côtes du Provence 60ha. *Produce: 2.5 million bottles.* VP-R and N.

The largest private producer of Gigondas, Gabriel Meffre has maintained good quality and has done much to help the reputation of the AC area. Modern, large-scale techniques are used, with stainless steel much in evidence. Many famous names come under the Meffre banner: Château de Ruth in Sainte-Cecile-les-Vignes; Château Raspail in Gigondas; and Château de Vaudieu in Châteauneuf. New plantations are currently under way to produce white Côtes du Rhône. *Open: By appointment only.*

Domaine du Pesquier

84190 Gigondas. Vineyards owned: Gigondas 15ha; Côtes du Rhône Sablet 15ha. *Produce: 30,000 bottles.* VP-R.

Most of the bottled wine that leaves this small producer of Gigondas – some of which goes to négociants. The estate is old – records go back to 1556 when it was associated with the Princes of Orange. *Open: Appointments preferred.*

Domaine Raspail-Ay

Gigondas, 84190 Beaumes-de-Venise. Vineyards owned: Gigondas 18ha. *Produce: 30,000 bottles.* VP-R.

Red and rosé Gigondas from the Domaine Raspail-Ay are made by Dominique Ay in a traditional style using wood for fermentation and maturation. A blend of Grenache, Mourvèdre and Syrah gives a big, complex, long-lasting wine. *Open: By appointment only.*

Domaine Saint-Gayan

84190 Gigondas. Vineyards owned: Gigondas 14ha; Côtes du Rhône Villages 16ha. *Produce: 70,000 bottles.* VP-R.

Roger Meffre produces firm, rich wines from his three estates. The Gigondas is powerfully tannic, a Côtes du Rhône Rasteau has a delightful perfumed flavour from the high (35%) proportion of Mourvèdre. Generic Côtes du Rhône from vineyards in Sablet comes in red, rosé and white. The estate has been in the family since 1400. *Open: Mon–Sat 9–11:45am; 2–7pm.*

Southern Rhône: Lirac

Domaine Assémat

30150 Roquemaure. Vineyards owned: Lirac and Côtes du Rhône 46ha. *Produce: 250,000 bottles.* VP-R.

Domaine Garrigues is the name of the Lirac estate, dominated by 60% Syrah. M. Assémat also makes a Rouge de l'Été from carbonic maceration, and white and rosé Lirac. On his other estate, Domaine des Causses et Steyres, he produces Côtes du Rhône white and red. The plantation of white grapes is a new development. *Open: Mon–Sat 8am–noon; 2–6pm.*

Domaine de Castel-Oualou

30150 Roquemaure. Vineyards owned: Lirac 52ha. *Produce: 250,000 bottles.* VP-R.

Red Lirac is the principal wine made at this estate by the Pons-

Mure family. The approach is traditional with long fermentation to produce a floral, violet-flavoured wine. The estate also produces small amounts of white and rosé Lirac. *Open: In working hours.*

<hr>

Domaine de Devoy
St-Laurent-des-Arbres, 30126 Tavel. Vineyards owned: Lirac 40ha. *Produce: 200,000 bottles.* VP-R.

Traditional and modern techniques mix, with stainless steel being used for fermentation and no wood ageing. The Lombardo brothers make red, rosé and white Lirac. *Open: Mon–Fri 8am–noon; 2–6pm.*

<hr>

Château de Ségriès
30126 Lirac. Vineyards owned: Lirac 20ha. *Produce: 20,000 bottles.* VP-R.

The Comte de Régis, one of the pioneers of the Lirac AC, makes traditional, quite tannic reds and rosés and a softer white at this estate, whose château dates from the 17th and 18th century. *Open: By appointment only.*

<hr>

Domaine de la Tour de Lirac
30150 Roquemaure. Vineyards owned: 33ha. VP-R.

The wine produced at this estate is red and rosé Lirac, and is specifically made to be drunk young. *Open: By appointment only.*

<hr>

Domaines Verda (Château Saint-Roch)
30150 Roquemaure. Vineyards owned: Lirac and Côtes du Rhône 60ha. *Produce: 250,000 bottles.* VP-R.

There are two estates owned by the Verda family in Lirac. The original is Château Saint-Roch which produces red, rosé and white Lirac. The reds include a special *cuvée* which has two years in wood and two in bottle before sale. The other estate is Domaine Cantegril-Verda, acquired in 1983, where they make a lighter style of wine for more immediate drinking, and where they also make Côtes du Rhône. All their wines reach a high standard. *Open: Mon–Fri 8am–noon; 2–6:30pm.*

Southern Rhône: Tavel

<hr>

Château d'Aquéria
31026 Tavel. Vineyards owned: Tavel and Lirac 55ha. *Produce: 300,000 bottles.* VP-R.

The 17th century property has been owned by the Olivier family since 1920. The bulk of production here is of Tavel rosé, with smaller quantities of red Lirac. They combine traditional and modern techniques to produce a classic Tavel, full of raspberry fruit and with a good balance of acidity and fruit. The vineyard is being expanded. *Open: Mon–Fri 8am–noon; 2–6pm.*

<hr>

Domaine de la Genestière
30126 Tavel. Vineyards owned: Tavel 30ha; Lirac 11ha. *Produce: 200,000 bottles.* VP-R.

The owners of this estate, the Bernard family, mainly produce Tavel rosé, but they also make some Lirac red and white. They use traditional methods to make their wines. *Open: Appointments preferred.*

Domaine Jean-Pierre Lafond

Route des Vignobles, 30126 Tavel. Vineyards owned: Tavel 30ha; Lirac 10ha; Côtes du Rhône 10ha.
Produce: 150,000 bottles. VP-R.

This old-established family estate works with modern methods to make a deliciously fruity, fresh Tavel. M. Lafond also makes red Lirac and Côtes du Rhône. Brand names include Roc-Amande and Cuvée Lafond as well as Domaine Pierre Lafond. *Open: Mon–Fri 9am–noon; 2–6pm.*

Domaine Maby

BP 8, 30126 Tavel. Vineyards owned: Tavel 40ha; Lirac 30ha; Côtes du Rhône 30ha.
Produce: 500,000 bottles. VP-R.

The Maby family has owned vineyards for several generations. They use stainless steel for the Tavel and for a white Lirac, while wood is preferred for the red Lirac and Côtes du Rhône. The styles reflect the vinification, with fresh rosés and whites, and reds which need at least four years in bottle. *Open: Appointments preferred.*

Prieuré de Montézargues

30126 Tavel. Vineyards owned: Tavel 32ha.
Produce: 100,000 bottles. VP-R.

The Priory dates back to the 13th century. Tavel is the only wine made here, using stainless steel to give freshness. *Open: Appointments preferred.*

Les Vignerons de Tavel

BP3, 30126 Tavel. Vineyards owned: Tavel 400ha.
Produce: 1 million bottles. Association of VP-R (130 members).

Modern techniques – cold temperature fermentation, centrifugation – plus the traditional cold maceration on the skins which avoids the problem of tannin which can affect some Tavel rosés, are employed by this grouping of producers. The wine is designed to be drunk young and fresh. This is not a cooperative but more of a marketing organization. *Open: Mon–Sun 9am–noon; 2–6pm.*

Château de Trinquevedel

30126 Tavel. Vineyards owned: Tavel 26ha.
Produce: 100,000 bottles. VP-R.

Carbonic maceration for 72 hours is used to make this Tavel quite a deep rosé colour. It is fresh, attractively fruity and one of the most refreshing Tavels around. *Open: By appointment only.*

Southern Rhône: Côtes du Lubéron

Château de Canorgue

84480 Bonnieux. Vineyards owned: 15ha.
Produce: 60,000 bottles. VP-R.

Red, rosé and white Côtes du Lubéron in a fresh style for the white and rosé and with some ageing in wood for the red. The style is attractive and easy to drink. *Open: Mon–Fri 9am–noon; 3–7pm.*

Cellier de Marrenon

Quartier Notre-Dame, 84240 La Tour d'Aigues. Vineyards
owned: Côtes du Lubéron 11,000ha; Côtes du Ventoux
3,000ha.
Produce: 9.9 million bottles. Coop (5,000 members).

This huge cooperative dominates the Côtes du Lubéron, and has
done much to bring the quality of the wines from the area up to
an acceptable level. Red, rosé and white Côtes du Lubéron and
Côtes du Ventoux is made; the red made for drinking young by
carbonic maceration. They also produce Vin de Pays de
Vaucluse, a little Côtes du Rhône and Châteauneuf-du-Pape
and vin de table. *Open: By appointment only.*

Château Val-Joanis

84120 Pertuis. Vineyards owned: 170ha.
Produce: 500,000 bottles. VP-R.

This brand-new model estate produced its first wine in 1982,
and has set new standards for the whole of the Côtes du
Lubéron. The Chancel family has invested a fortune in top class
equipment for the vineyard and the winery. The wines
themselves are improving year by year: they have planted
Chardonnay and Sauvignon as well as Ugni Blanc for whites.
Reds are made from Cinsault, Grenache and up to 60% Syrah.
Gamay is used for rosés. *Open: In working hours.*

Château Turçan

84690 Ansouis. Vineyards owned: 20ha.
Produce: 50,000 bottles. VP-R.

Red, rosé and white Côtes du Lubéron are all made on this
estate. The vineyard operations are run organically, and great
care seems to be taken in the selection of the fruit. They use
carbonic maceration for the red, making an attractively fruity
wine. *Open: Mon–Fri 10am–noon; 2–4pm.*

Southern Rhône: Côtes du Vivarais

Union des Producteurs

07150 Orgnac l'Aven. Vineyards owned: 450ha.
Produce: 350,000 bottles. Coop (83 members).

This cooperative dominates the VDQS of Côtes du Vivarais,
producing red, rosé and white. The red has 30% Syrah and 40%
Grenache, the white 50/50 Clairette and Grenache Blanc. The
brand name is Vins d'Orgnac. *Open: By appointment only.*

Domaine de Vigier

Lagorce, 07150 Vallon Pont d'Arc. Vineyards owned: 35ha.
Produce: 70,000 bottles. VP-R.

Côtes du Vivarais VDQS is made from 100% Syrah. The estate
also produces varietal Merlot and Chardonnay Vin de Pays des
Coteaux de l'Ardèche. *Open: Mon–Fri 8am–noon; 2–6pm.*

Les Chais du Vivarais

07700 Saint-Remeze. Vineyards owned: 270ha.
Produce: 80,000 bottles. Coop (120 members).

Much of the wine produced by this cooperative goes in bulk.
They make red, rosé and white Côtes du Vivarais. *Open: Mon–
Sat 8am–noon; 1–6pm.*

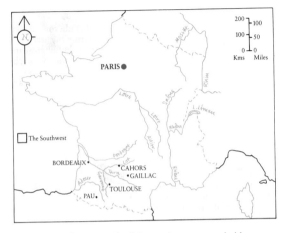

PARIS ●

The Southwest

BORDEAUX ●

● CAHORS
● GAILLAC
● TOULOUSE
PAU ●

Producers in the vineyards of the southwest are probably pretty
tired of being described as "forgotten" or of being told that
their wines are being "rediscovered". Yet there is something
about this secret countryside in the hinterland of Bordeaux and
in the foothills of the Pyrénées that sets this area apart from the
rest of French wine.

The southwest vineyards, wedged between the great ex-
panses of Bordeaux and the Midi, are tiny by comparison. Not
so long ago they were still struggling to survive the effects of
phylloxera which almost wiped out the whole area. What was
left was disappearing through indifference. Yet, gradually, life
has returned through the efforts of cooperatives who, in the
southwest, have performed a vital role in bringing together tiny
plots of land to make commercial sense. Life has returned
through the determination of a few private estates, some
newly established, some ancient, which have provided a quality
standard to emulate. And we must not forget the intrepid travel-
lers who went on wine buying trips to the southwest and came
back with tales – and samples – of wines that refused to die.

There are really two distinct wine traditions here. Histori-
cally, the northern vineyards of the region – Bergerac, Côtes du
Marmandais, Côtes du Duras, Cahors – were closely linked to
Bordeaux. At one time their wine was more famous than the
wines of Bordeaux itself, later they were used to beef up insipid
wine from the vineyards of the Gironde. Some of these areas
today make Bordeaux look-alikes at lesser prices, while
Cahors, for example, has moved along a distinct path of its
own. But even now, they all have a recognizable link with
Bordeaux.

That is not true of the wines from further south. Here we get
into strange territory indeed. Grape varieties from a dim,
almost mythical, past, with difficult Basque names, yield up

wines with a range of tastes that is found nowhere else. There
are sweet white wines and impenetrable red wines, there are
sparkling wines made by methods unique to the area. Increasingly there are some excellent dry white wines.

All the vineyard areas in this section are in the hilly land
between the mountains of the Massif Central and the Pyrénées.
I've already called it secret countryside. There are quiet valleys
and deep rivers and miles of woods, and small, ancient towns
and villages perched on hilltops or hanging to the side of river
valleys. Part of the southwest is called Gascony, home of one of
the richest gastronomic traditions in France – home, too, to
Armagnac brandy.

The region enjoys an Atlantic rather than a Mediterranean
climate, but one protected from the rigour of the ocean storms
by the vast pine forests of the Landes, which stretch from the
edge of the Bordeaux vineyards to the Pyrénées. The summers
are cooler than they are in Languedoc and Roussillon, the
winters often harsh. The rainfall is higher, too. The consequence for the wines is apparent immediately in tasting: they are
lower in alcohol than the wines of the Midi, they tend to have
more complex, varied flavours. The whites, while full bodied,
often also have good acidity; the reds, when deep and tannic,
can age well, while lighter reds, made sometimes to be drunk
chilled, can be as fresh as Loire reds. Vintages: Most dry whites
and rosés should be drunk young, as should many of the reds.

The Appellations
AC

Béarn: Red, rosé and dry white wines from a large area of the
département of the Pyrénées-Atlantiques. The Béarn AC
surrounds the smaller, superior ACs of Madiran and Pacherenc
du Vic-Bilh as well as Irouléguy and Jurançon. Reds and rosés
come from Tannat to a maximum of 60%, Courbu Noir, Fer,
Manseng Noir, Pinenc and Cabernet Sauvignon and Cabernet
Franc. Whites are a similar mix of local and Bordeaux grapes:
Gros Manseng, Petit Manseng, Courbu, Baroque, Lauzat, plus
Sémillon and Sauvignon.

Bergerac: The area-wide AC for the Bergerac region. Red and
rosé are made from Cabernet Sauvignon, Cabernet Franc,
Merlot, Malbec and the local Fer. Generally light wines, which
should be drunk young. Vintages: '82, '83, '85, '86.

Bergerac Sec: The white equivalent of Bergerac. Wines can be
made from Sémillon, Sauvignon, Muscadelle, Chenin Blanc
and the local Ondenc. A number of new-style wines, made with
Sauvignon, are of high quality.

Cahors: Red wine only from vineyards on the slopes and the
valley floor of the Lot river between the towns of Puy l'Evêque
and Cahors. Its history as a vineyard is distinguished: established before the Romans, and highly regarded by Avignon
Popes and the Russian Tsars. Grapes are Malbec (known
locally as Auxerrois) up to 70%, Merlot, Tannat and Jurançon
Noir. The wine at its best is deep coloured, with high tannins,
but also good fruit which needs a good four years before
softening out. Lighter wines of lesser quality are also made.
Prices for the wines have been good, but are likely to rise now
that they have become popular in France. Production is up to 10
million bottles a year. Vintages: '76, '78, '79, '81, '82, '83, '85.

Côtes de Bergerac: Red wine from the Bergerac region with a higher alcoholic content (11% instead of 10%) than straight Bergerac. Around two million bottles are produced. Grapes are the same as for Bergerac: Cabernet Franc, Cabernet Sauvignon, Merlot, Malbec, Fer. Vintages: see Bergerac.

Côtes de Bergerac Moelleux: Sweet white wine from the general Bergerac AC, made from Sémillon, Sauvignon and Muscadelle. Soft, at their best clean and fruity, but generally rather dull.

Côtes de Buzet: Vineyards on the left bank of the Garonne, between Agen and Aiguillon, producing red, rosé and dry white wines. Reds come from Cabernet Franc, Cabernet Sauvignon, Merlot and Malbec. The small amount of white made comes from Sémillon, Sauvignon and Muscadelle. Most of the wine is produced by the cooperative, which, luckily, has high standards. Vintages: '78, '79, '81, '82, '83, '85.

Côtes de Duras: Dry and sweet white and some red wine from an area immediately adjacent to the Bordeaux Entre-deux-Mers AC area. Whites are from Sémillon, Sauvignon, Muscadelle, Mauzac and Ondenc, plus Ugni Blanc. Dry whites are better than the sweet, which tend to be sulphured. Reds are from Cabernet Franc, Cabernet Sauvignon, Merlot and Malbec, and have attractive fruit and some depth.

Côtes du Frontonnais: Red and rosé wines only from a small area north of Toulouse on the east bank of the River Garonne. The grapes are up to 70% Négrette, plus Cabernet Sauvignon, Cabernet Franc, Cinsault, Malbec, Merlot, Syrah and Gamay. Excellent wines at good prices, with fresh, soft fruit and great quaffability. The commune of Villaudric is allowed to add its name to the AC. Vintages: '82, '83, '85.

Côtes de Montravel: Small amounts of sweet white wine from within the general Bergerac area. Certain hillside slopes in certain communes are allowed to use the Côtes de Montravel AC, whose wines are generally of higher quality than simple Montravel (q.v.). Sémillon, Sauvignon and Muscadelle are the permitted grape varieties.

Gaillac: a range of white, medium white, red, rosé and sparkling wines from the valley of Tarn, betwen Albi and Rabastens. Over half the production is of white wine, made from Mauzac Blanc and Len de l'El, with Ondenc, Sauvignon, Sémillon and Muscadelle. Much of the white wine is dull – especially the slightly sparkling Perlé. Reds come from a variety of grapes: Fer, Duras, Gamay, Négrette and Syrah up to 60%, with smaller amounts of Cabernet Sauvignon, Cabernet Franc, Jurançon Noir, Merlot, Portugais Bleu (the German Blauer Portugieser), and the white Mauzac. Occasional reds can be superb. Vintages: (red) '78, '79, '81, '82, '83.

Gaillac Doux: Sweet white wines made from Mauzac Blanc, Len de l'El, Ondenc, Sauvignon, Sémillon and Muscadelle.

Gaillac Mousseux: Sparkling Gaillac made by the *méthode gaillaçoise* (a form of *méthode champenoise* which involves a second fermentation in the bottle, but, unlike champagne, without added sugar or yeast). Some of it can be very good. Other sparklers are made by the classic *méthode champenoise*. Grapes used are the usual Gaillac selection: Mauzac Blanc, Len de l'El, Ondenc, Sauvignon, Sémillon, Muscadelle.

Gaillac Premières Côtes: Rare dry and medium sweet white wine from the Gaillac region, reaching a higher alcohol level than simple Gaillac.

Haut Montravel: Sweet white wines from the Montravel region of Bergerac. The rules are similar to Côtes de Montravel (q.v.). Grapes used are Sauvignon, Sémillon, Muscadelle.

Irouléguy: Red, rosé and white wines from the foothills of the Pyrénées in the valley of the Nive, between St-Jean-Pied-de-Port and Bidarray. Most of the production is of rosé, and both rosés and reds are made from Tannat, Fer, Cabernet Sauvignon and Cabernet Franc. The tiny production of white comes from Gros-Manseng, Petit-Manseng, Courbu, Lauzat, Baroque, Sauvignon and Sémillon.

Jurançon: Sweet wines from an area between the rivers Gave de Pau and Gave d'Oloron, southwest of the town of Pau. Grapes are Gros-Manseng, the better quality Petit-Manseng and Courbu. For this increasingly rare – but outstanding – sweet wine, grapes are picked as raisins, with concentrated sugars, which gives a spicy wine, with a lemony tang and golden in colour. Examples, when found, can be a revelation. Vintages: (sweet) '75, '78, '79, '82, '83.

Jurançon Sec: A dry, and much duller, version of Jurançon (see previous entry). Grapes are the same: Gros-Manseng, Petit-Manseng and Courbu.

Madiran: Red wine from an area on the southern edge of the Armagnac region, around the village of the same name. The principal grape is the Tannat, which lives up to its name to make a hard, tough, tannic wine when young, which has to spend 20 months in bottle. It needs at least five years before it begins to open out with some elegance, but much more rough power. Other grapes used are Cabernet Sauvignon, Cabernet Franc and Fer. The more Cabernets are used, the more sophisticated (but less typical) the wine becomes. The white wine of the area is called Pacherenc du Vic-Bilh (q.v.). Vintages: '75, '76, '78, '79, '81, '82, '83.

Monbazillac: A famous name in sweet wines, coming from the Bergerac region, but one which has fallen on bad times. The wine can be as good as Sauternes, but almost never is because it is sulphured and not enough attention is paid to the degree of botrytis in the grapes. But the few producers who do it well make wines that are even richer than Sauternes, developing faster and fading more quickly. Grapes used are Sémillon, Sauvignon and Muscadelle. Vintages: '71, '75, '78, '79, '83, '85.

Montravel: A range of white wines – from dry to sweet – made at the western edge of the Bergerac region, along the lower slopes bordering the road to St-Emilion, and, strangely enough, west of the town of St-Foy-la-Grande whose vineyards are in the Bordeaux region. Wines are made from Sémillon, Sauvignon, Muscadelle, Ugni Blanc, Chenin Blanc and Ondenc.

Pacherenc du Vic-Bilh: White wine from the same area as Madiran (q.v.). It can be dry or slightly sweet, but whatever the style it has an intense fruit, seemingly luscious to smell, sometimes likened to ripe pears. Grapes are Ruffiac (or Pacherenc), Gros-Manseng, Petit-Manseng, Courbu, plus Sauvignon and Sémillon. Small production, which is almost all consumed locally, although a little slips out.

Pecharmant: The best red wines of Bergerac come from a small area on the right bank of the Dordogne river, east of the town of Bergerac. Grape varieties are Cabernet Sauvignon, Cabernet Franc, Malbec and Merlot. The wines, higher in alcohol than simple Bergerac, are also aged longer in wood, and mature well: five or six years would be a good time for such wines. Quality is better than any simple Bordeaux AC. Vintages: '78, '79, '82, '83.

Rosette: Medium sweet wine from the slopes north of the town of Bergerac. Production is small, most of the white in the area going as Bergerac Sec. Grapes used are Sauvignon, Sémillon and Muscadelle.

Saussignac: A white wine, normally dry, made in the communes around the village of Saussignac, which is west of Monbazillac. The wines need an alcohol level of 12.5%, making them richer and fuller than ordinary Bergerac Sec. Grapes are Sémillon, Sauvignon, Muscadelle, Ondenc and Chenin Blanc. Wines from this AC are rare.

VDQS

Côtes de Brulhois: Vineyard area just south of the Côtes de Buzet, lying on both sides of the Garonne river. Red and rosé only, made from Cabernet Sauvignon, Cabernet Franc, Merlot, Tannat and Malbec. Quality is improving, and they were elevated to VDQS status from Vin de Pays in 1984.

Côtes du Marmandais: Soft, attractive reds and somewhat less interesting whites from vineyards adjoining the Bordeaux region, lying on both sides of the Garonne river. The grapes cover both the Bordeaux varieties – Cabernet Franc, Cabernet Sauvignon and Merlot – with local southwest varieties – Fer, Abouriou, Malbec – one from the south of France – Syrah – and Gamay. The small production of white comes from Sémillon, Ugni Blanc and Sauvignon.

Côtes de Saint-Mont: Red, rosé and white wines from the southwestern corner of the Armagnac region. Reds come mainly from Tannat, with Cabernet Sauvignon, Cabernet Franc and Merlot, and are attractive, simple, slightly rough at the edges. Whites are from Meslier, Jurançon, Picpoul and Sauvignon. The main producer is the local Madiran cooperative.

Tursan: Red, rosé and dry white wines from the eastern Landes, touching on to the AC area of Madiran and Pacherenc du Vic-Bilh. As such, the style is like a minor version of these wines. Reds and rosés are made from Tannat, Cabernet Franc, Cabernet Sauvignon and Fer. White comes from the local grape, the Baroque.

Vins d'Entraygues et du Fel: Red, rosé and dry whites from the southern slopes of the Massif Central. A tiny production for such an imposing-sounding wine. Reds and rosés come from a whole range of grapes: Cabernet Sauvignon, Cabernet Franc, Jurançon Noir, Fer, Gamay, Merlot, Négrette, Pinot Noir. Whites are, more soberly, from Chenin Blanc and Mauzac.

Vins d'Estaing: Another tiny area – producing no more than 1,000 bottles or so a year, from the same area and grape varieties as the Vin d'Entraygues et du Fel.

Vins de Lavilledieu: Almost exclusively red wines from another small area on the Garonne river to the north of the Côtes du Frontonnais. Virtually every local grape variety seems to be thrown into the vat, but the principal ones are Négrette, with Fer, Gamay, Jurançon Noir, Mauzac Noir and Picpoul added in smaller proportions.

Vins de Marcillac: Sound, simple red and rosé wines from just north of the town of Rodez in the Aveyron département. The grape varieties include Cabernet Franc, Cabernet Sauvignon, Gamay, Jurançon Noir and Merlot, on top of at least 80% of Fer.

Southwest: Béarn

Les Vignerons de Bellocq
64270 Bellocq. Vineyards owned: 120ha.
Produce: 600,000 bottles. Coop (150 members).

The most important source of Béarn wine, this cooperative makes a range of rosé (the vast majority), red and white wines, using controlled temperature techniques and eschewing any use of wood. Reds include a 100% Cabernet Franc and Cabernet Sauvignon wine, and two top red *cuvées*, Cuvée des Vignerons and Cuvée Henri de Navarre. *Open: By appointment only.*

Southwest: Bergerac

Domaine de l'Ancienne Curé
Colombier, 24560 Issigeac. Vineyards owned: 20ha.
Produce: 35,000 bottles. VP-R.

M. Christian Roche makes a range of Bergerac wines: Monbazillac, Bergerac Sec (100% Sauvignon), a sweet Côtes de Bergerac Moelleux and red and rosé Bergerac. Temperature controlled fermentation is used for the whites, but reds are vinified in wood. *Open: By appointment only.*

GAEC du Bloy (Guillermier Frères)
Bonneville, 24230 Vélines. Vineyards owned: 33ha.
Produce: 70,000 bottles. VP-R.

Red Côtes de Bergerac is this company's mainstay, using Merlot, Cabernet Franc, Cabernet Sauvignon and a little Malbec. The Guillermier brothers also make Rosé Bergerac, dry white Montravel and Bergerac as well as some sweet Côtes de Bergerac. *Open: Mon–Fri 8:30am–1pm; 2:30–5:30pm.*

Château la Borderie
24240 Monbazillac. Vineyards owned: 63ha.
Produce: 400,000 bottles. VP-R.

Two estates make up the family property of Château la Borderie. On the larger estate, which bears the château name, the Vidal family makes Monbazillac, red Côtes de Bergerac, dry white Bergerac (from 100% Sauvignon) and Bergerac Rosé. The smaller, 10-hectare Château Treuil de Nailhac estate produces the Monbazillac, the red and the dry white. *Open: Mon–Fri 8:30am–noon; 2–6:30pm.*

Comte de Bosredon (Château de Belingard)
24240 Pomport, Sigoulès. Vineyards owned: 85ha.
Produce: 500,000 bottles. VP-R.

This ancient family estate is home to some Celtic remains as well as the Bosredon family. However, their wine production has moved with the times and they use some carbonic maceration on the red Côtes de Bergerac so that they can be drunk young. Some of the sweeter Monbazillac and Côtes de Bergerac is matured for a time in wood. A modern-style Bergerac Sec is attractive. *Open: Appointments preferred.*

Michel Brouilleaud
24240 Monestier. Vineyards owned: 8ha.
Produce: 15,000 bottles. VP-R.

M. Brouilleaud's main production is of a full, rich Bergerac

Rouge, made from 60% Cabernet Sauvignon and 40% Merlot. He makes much smaller quantities of Bergerac rosé and sweet and dry Bergerac white. He uses the brand name Clos de la Croix Blanche. *Open: Mon–Sat 8am–noon; 2–7pm.*

Château Champerel

Pécharmant, 24100 Bergerac. Vineyards owned: 6.6ha.
Produce: 26,000 bottles. VP-R.

A very fine, intense red Pécharmant, made from 50% each Merlot and Cabernet Sauvignon, is the only wine from this small vineyard. It is fermented in stainless steel, and aged for at least a year in new *barriques. Open: By appointment only.*

Château Corbiac

Pécharmant, 24100 Bergerac. Vineyards owned: 11ha.
Produce: 50,000 bottles. VP-R.

This château and its estate has belonged to the same family since the Middle Ages. They make full, rounded Pécharmant, normally deeply coloured and full of fruit. *Open: Mon–Sun.*

Château Le Fagé

Pomport, 24240 Sigoulès. Vineyards owned: 40ha.
Produce: 120,000 bottles. VP-R.

A traditional estate, which has been in the Gerardin family for 200 years, making white Bergerac Sec, Monbazillac and a Côtes de Bergerac red, which is matured in cement tanks and normally bottled in the year after the harvest. They also use the name Château de Géraud. *Open: Mon–Sun.*

Domaine du Haut Pécharmant

Pécharmant, 24100 Bergerac. Vineyards owned: 23ha.
Produce: 150,000 bottles. VP-R.

The Pécharmant made on this estate, owned by the Roches family, is a blend of 40% Cabernet Sauvignon, 20% Cabernet Franc, 30% Merlot and 10% Malbec. The wine is designed for ageing with deep, tannic fruit initially. Good, if austere. *Open: Mon–Fri 8am–noon, 2–7pm.*

Château de la Jaubertie

Colombier, 24560 Issigeac. Vineyards owned: 46ha.
Produce: 300,000 bottles. VP-R and N.

Modern techniques, inspired by Australian winemakers, have produced a range of wines from this estate which have been a great success in the UK market – helped by the fact that the owner, Henry Ryman, is himself English. His whites, especially a 100% Sauvignon, are characterized by excellent fruit and good varietal character. Reds are also well made: the barrel-aged réserve is especially good. The approach may not be typical Bergerac, but it works. *Open: Appointment necessary.*

Domaine de Libarde

Nastringues, 24230 Vélines. Vineyards owned: 20ha.
Produce: 60,000 bottles. VP-R.

A traditionally run estate, right at the western end of the Bergerac region, just before it turns into Bordeaux. Bergerac rouge, Montravel dry white and Haut-Montravel sweet white are all produced. The Haut-Montravel is especially worth seeking out. *Open: By appointment only.*

Jean Louis Molle
Moulins de Boisse, 24560 Issigeac. Vineyards owned: 8ha.
Produce: 60,000 bottles. VP-R.

M. Molle makes red Bergerac (40% Merlot, 30% Cabernet
Franc, 30% Cabernet Sauvignon) and a white dry 100%
Sauvignon Bergerac Sec high up on an exposed slope above the
Dordogne. *Open: Mon–Sat 8am–noon; 2–7pm.*

Cave Coopérative de Monbazillac
Monbazillac, 24220 Sigoulès. Vineyards owned: 876ha.
Produce: 5.5 million bottles. Coop (150 members).

The largest producer of Monbazillac, and owner of the
showpiece Château de Monbazillac, a 20-hectare estate surrounding a superb mediaeval castle. But they also make red and
dry white Bergerac, Pécharmant and vin de table. Quality could
be better, but the wines are reliable. The cooperative forms part
of the giant Unidor group of cooperatives (q.v.). *Open: Mon–
Fri 9am–noon; 2–5pm.*

René Monbouché
Gendre Marsalet, 24240 Monbazillac. Vineyards owned:
26ha. Produce: 45,000 bottles. VP-R.

Three estates comprise the domaines of M. Monbouche:
Gendre Marsalet, which produces Côtes de Bergerac red;
Grand Conseil, producing dry white Bergerac Sec; and Theulet
et Marsalet which makes Monbazillac. The reds and the
Monbazillac are matured for a time in wood. *Open: Appoint-
ments preferred.*

Château Michel de Montaigne
24230 Vélines. Vineyards owned: 15ha. VP-R.

This is the country estate of the Mähler-Besse family, part-
owners of Château Palmer in the Médoc and major Bordeaux
négociants. At this former home of the philosopher Montaigne
they produce a red Bergerac, a blend of Merlot and both
Cabernets. *Open: By appointment only.*

Château de Panisseau
Thénac, 24240 Sigoulès. Vineyards owned: 50ha.
Produce: 300,000 bottles. VP-R.

This large estate surrounds a very pretty little 13th century
château. The Becker family produces two whites, from 100%
Sauvignon and 90% Sémillon (with only a touch of Sauvignon).
They also make a classic Bergerac rouge, and a rosé from 100%
Cabernet Sauvignon. The Sémillon dry white is particularly
worth seeking out. *Open: Mon–Fri 8am–noon; 2–6pm (not the
château).*

Clos Peyrelevade
Pécharmant, 24100 Bergerac. Vineyards owned: 10ha.
Produce: 40,000 bottles. VP-R.

Only Pécharmant is produced on this estate – a blend of 55%
Merlot, 20% Cabernet Sauvignon, 16% Cabernet Franc and
9% Malbec. They make a wine which, although it is not
matured in wood, needs some time in bottle. They specialize in
half bottles and magnums – three-quarters of their production
is bottled like this. *Open: Appointments preferred.*

Château la Raye

24230 Vélines. Vineyards owned: 15ha.
Produce: 60,000 bottles. VP-R.

Itey de Peironnin has a charming château from where he produces a very fine red Bergerac (a blend of 50% Merlot and 50% Cabernets) and a sweet Côtes de Montravel. *Open: By appointment only.*

Château Thénac

Thénac-le-Bourg, 24240 Sigoulès. Vineyards owned: 15ha.
Produce: 120,000 bottles. VP-R.

Modern techniques with stainless steel have been introduced to the vineyard around this old château, which is being gradually reorganized by new owners. They make a red Bergerac, using one third of Merlot, Cabernet Franc and Cabernet Sauvignon, with 1% of Malbec, and a clean tasting dry Bergerac Sec. *Open: By appointment only.*

Château de Tiregand

Creysse, 24100 Bergerac. Vineyards owned: 33ha.
Produce: 175,000 bottles. VP-R.

The Saint-Exupéry family have owned this estate with its 17th century château since 1830. It is the largest producer of Pécharmant, which makes up almost the entire production. It is aged in wood for anything up to two years. A little dry white Bergerac Sec is also made. *Open: Mon–Sat 8am–noon; 2–6pm.*

Unidor

Unions des Coopératives Vinicoles de la Dordogne, 24106
Saint-Laurent des Vignes. Vineyards owned: 4,009ha.
Produce: 5 million bottles. Coop (8 coops as members).

This is an amalgamation of cooperatives in Bergerac, controling nearly 40% of all Bergerac. It also takes in wine from Côtes de Duras and the eastern edges of the Bordeaux vineyard at Ste-Foy-le-Grande. They do the maturing of the wine and its bottling and the whole plant is run on very modern lines. Few excitements. Brands include: Monsieur Cyrano, Domaine de la Vaure, L'Océanière, Fort Chevalier, Les Trois Clochers, Selection Unidor, Château Septy. *Open: By appointment only.*

Southwest: Cahors

Domaine de la Caminade

Ressès et Fils, 46140 Parnac. Vineyards owned: 19ha.
Produce: 150,000 bottles. VP-R.

Some stainless steel is used for vinification on this family estate, and the grapes are de-stalked before fermentation. The results are wines that are not too austere. Plans are to make a wine aged in new wood. *Open: By appointment only.*

Château de Cayrou

46700 Puy l'Évêque. Vineyards owned: 40ha.
Produce: 200,000 bottles. VP-R.

M. Jouffreau owns two estates: the 16th century Château de Cayrou and the smaller 10-hectare Clos de Gamot. He uses organic methods in his vineyards, while employing stainless steel in the *caves*. His wines, austere while young, age well. He uses the brand names Comte de Guiscard as well as the estate names. The family has owned the Cayrou estate for 300 years. *Open: Appointments preferred.*

Château de Chambert

Floressas, 46700 Puy l'Évêque. Vineyards owned: 55ha.
Produce: 300,000 bottles. VP-R.

This estate was restored in the 1970s by a local négociant, Caves Saint-Antoine, and the first vintage of any size was in 1979. Vinification takes place in stainless steel, followed by wood ageing in *barriques*. Although the vines are still young, the quality is impressive, and the estate is one to watch. *Open: By appointment only.*

Domaine de Garrigues

Vire-sur-Lot, 46700 Puy l'Évêque. Vineyards owned: 17ha.
Produce: 100,000 bottles. VP-R.

M. Roger Labruyére makes his Cahors using stainless steel and aiming at a lighter style, with plenty of fruit. Unusually, he has a little Jurançon in the blend which typically is dominated by 70% Malbec (Auxerrois). *Open: Mon–Sun.*

Les Côtes d'Olt

Parnac, 46140 Luzech. Vineyards owned: 1,400ha.
Produce: 100,000 bottles. Coop (500 members).

The largest cooperative in Cahors, using a number of brand names: Côtes d'Olt, Comte André de Monpezat, Marquis d'Olt and the wood-aged Impernal. Much of the wine is sold in bulk to merchants and négociants. *Open: By appointment only.*

Domaine de Paillas

Floressas, 46700 Puy l'Évêque. Vineyards owned: 27ha.
Produce: 210,000 bottles. VP-R.

A young vineyard, producing soft wines using stainless steel vinification. The Lescombes family bought the estate in 1978 and have replanted on the slopes above the valley floor. Although the wine can be drunk reasonably young, it does repay some ageing in bottle. *Open: Appointments preferred.*

Domaine de la Pineraie

Leygues, 46700 Puy l'Évêque. Vineyards owned: 25ha.
Produce: 200,000 bottles. VP-R.

Stainless steel vinification and wood maturation are combined to produce wines with good fruit but also some ageing ability. The blend is simply Auxerrois (Malbec) 85% and Merlot 15%, and the long maceration of 15 days brings intense colour to the wines. *Open: Mon–Sat 8am–noon; 2–7pm.*

Domaine de Quattre

Bagat en Quercy, 46800 Montcuq. Vineyards owned: 53ha.
Produce: 300,000 bottles. VP-R.

The three estates owned by the Heilbronner family include the 19-hectare Domaine de Quattre, the 16-hectare Domaine de Guingal and the 18-hectare Domaine de Treilles. Most of the wines from the three estates are produced to be drunk young, although some *cuvées* from Domaine de Treilles are aged in wood. The Domaine de Guingal wines are 100% Malbec (Auxerrois). *Open: Appointments preferred.*

Clos Triguedina

46700 Puy l'Évêque. Vineyards owned: 42ha.
Produce: 300,000 bottles. VP-R.

This large and important estate produces two qualities of wine. Clos Triguedina is designed to be drunk young, while Prince Probus, aged in new oak and from 100% Malbec (Auxerrois) needs some bottle age. The Baldès family have owned the estate since 1830, and in the last few years have invested large sums putting in stainless steel for vinification. *Open: Appointments preferred.*

Georges Vigouroux

9 Place de la République, 46500 Gramat. Vineyards owned: 67ha. Produce: 4 million bottles. VP-R and N.

Georges Vigouroux, one of the big names in Cahors, owns the Château de Haute-Serre and the small Château de Mercues (the château is now a four star hotel). The Haute-Serre wine, produced in a vineyard which was reclaimed from scrub in the 1970s, is rich in fruit and tannin when young, needing time to become enjoyable; the Mercues ages more quickly. *Open: Mon–Sun 10am–noon; 3–6pm.*

Southwest: Côtes de Buzet

Les Vignerons Réunis des Côtes de Buzet

Buzet-sur-Baïse, 47160 Damazan. Vineyards owned: 1,000ha.
Produce: 6.6 million bottles. Coop (430 members).

The cooperative controls the vast proportion of the production of the Buzet AC, and very well they do it, too. They use a number of different labels, but their best wine is the Cuvée Napoleon, a ripe, rich wine which comes from older vines. But the standard generic Buzet is good, too, as an easy-to-drink wine. Other labels they use for red wines are Château de Gueyze, Château du Bouchet and Domaine Roc de Caillou. They also make small amounts of rosé and white. *Open: (Summer) Mon–Fri. Appointments at other times.*

Southwest: Côtes du Duras

Domaine des Cours

Ste Colombe, 47120 Duras. Vineyards owned: 10ha.
Produce: 30,000 bottles. VP-R.

The Lusoli family make a white 100% Sauvignon and a red which is 50% Merlot and 50% of the two Cabernets. The white is particularly attractive, made from free-run juice with temperature controlled fermentation, giving plenty of fruit. The red is more traditional. *Open: Appointments preferred.*

Société Coopérative Agricole les Vignerons des Coteaux de Duras

47120 Duras. Vineyards owned: 315ha.
Produce: 500,000 bottles. Coop (83 members).

As with so many of these smaller AC areas in the southwest, it is the local cooperative which takes much of the production and keeps the area ticking over. Production is divided equally between red and white, but interestingly, they make varietal reds – 100% Cabernet Sauvignon (designed for a little ageing) and 100% Merlot (to be drunk young) and a 100% white Sauvignon, as well as a more normal blend including Sémillon and Muscadelle as well as Sauvignon. The brand name they use is Berticot. *Open: By appointment only.*

Southwest: Côtes du Frontonnais

Domaine de Baudare

Campas, 82370 Labastide St-Pierre. Vineyards owned: 27ha.
Produce: 120,000 bottles. VP-R.

A typically Frontonnais fruity style is achieved on this estate. Controlled fermentation brings out the colour and flavour of the Négrette in the red and rosé, both of which are bottled under the Domaine de Baudare name. The estate also produces Vin de Pays Comté Tolosan – red, and sweet and dry white. *Open: By appointment only.*

Château Bellevue la Forêt

D 49, 31620 Fronton. Vineyards owned: 105ha.
Produce: 800,000 bottles. VP-R.

A newly developed estate which has revived the area. It has been planted with the traditional varieties – 50% Négrette, with Cabernet Franc, Cabernet Sauvignon, plus Gamay and Syrah. The standard wine is called André Daguin, while the wine that goes under the name of the château is red or rosé. They are also experimenting with small amounts of red aged in new wood, a Cuvée Spéciale. *Open: Appointments preferred.*

Domaine de la Colombière

31620 Villaudric. Vineyards owned: 20ha.
Produce: 170,000 bottles. VP-R.

Baron François de Driésen makes a wide range of red and rosé wines on his estate. He uses carbonic maceration for Négrette and Gamay, and the Gamay goes into a rosé Vin Gris. Baron de D Rouge is 50% Négrette, 10% Gamay and 40% of Cabernets, while the longer-lasting Villaudric Réserve is 5% Gamay, 60% Négrette and 35% of Cabernets. The style is attractively forward and fruity. *Open: Appointments preferred.*

Southwest: Gaillac

Domaine des Bouscaillous

81140 Castelnau de Montmirail. Vineyards owned: 18ha.
Produce: 100,000 bottles. VP-R.

Yvon Maurel makes a range of Gaillac wines. In the reds, there is a 100% Gamay Primeur as well as a wine designed for some ageing, in which the Duras grape predominates. There is also a rosé, a blend of Jurançon and Gamay. Whites include a dry white with 80% Len de l'El and 20% Sauvignon, and a sweet white made from Mauzac. Mauzac is also the grape in a delicious low alcohol Pétillant de Raisin. *Open: Appointments preferred.*

Jean Cros Père et Fils

Mas des Vignes, 81140 Cahuzac-sur-Vère. Vineyards owned: 10ha. *Produce: 60,000 bottles.* VP-R.

High quality is everywhere at this small family concern. They own two vineyards: Domaine Jean Cros and Château Larroze, from which they produce a full range, including a white from 100% Mauzac, and reds from Duras plus Syrah and Braucol. The reds are very fine. *Open: Mon–Sat 11am–7pm.*

Domaine de Labarthe
Castanet, 81150 Marssac. Vineyards owned: 22ha.
Produce: 120,000 bottles. VP-R.

The Albert family has been making wine at this estate since the 17th century and now produces a full range of Gaillac wines. They make a Primeur from Gamay, and a soft, warm vin de garde from the local Duras and Braucol plus the Bordeaux Cabernets and Merlot. Rosé comes from Gamay and Syrah. Len de l'El is balanced with Sauvignon in a dry white, while 100% Mauzac is used for the sweet white. They also make a *méthode champenoise* wine from Mauzac and Len de l'El. *Open: By appointment only.*

Cave de Labastide de Levis
81150 Marssac sur Tarn. Vineyards owned: 1,644ha.
Produce: 7 million bottles. Coop (521 members).

The cooperative dominates the Gaillac AC area, producing on the whole wines that are sold ready for drinking. Their semi-sparkling Gaillac Perle can be quite attractive, and the Gaillac primeur red is full of fresh fruit. They also make a sweet, low-alcohol Pétillant de Raisin. *Open: Appointments preferred.*

Domaine de Moussens
81150 Cestayrols. Vineyards owned: 14ha.
Produce: 15,000 bottles. VP-R.

Syrah dominates the wines from this estate – and the more there is the better they seem to be, as in the 1984 vintage. Duras and Braucol are the other grapes. A rosé is made from Gamay and Syrah, and Pétillant de Raisin from 100% Mauzac. Plans are afoot to make a dry white from Len de l'El and Sauvignon. *Open: By appointment only.*

Domaine de Pialentou
Brens, 81600 Gaillac. Vineyards owned: 12ha.
Produce: 25,000 bottles. VP-R.

The red is the best wine from this small estate, in good vintages having enough tannin to keep for three or four years in bottle, but with enough fruit to be drunk younger. M. Ailloud also makes a dry white and a rosé. *Open: Appointments preferred.*

Mas Pignou
81600 Gaillac. Vineyards owned: 20ha.
Produce: 80,000 bottles. VP-R.

Dry white and red are produced at this estate, owned by Jacques Auque. His red, using Braucol, Duras, Merlot and the two Cabernets, has some wood maturing which gives it good ageing ability without losing fruit. The white is a 50/50 Sauvignon and Len de l'El. *Open: Mon–Sun 8am–noon; 2–6pm.*

Robert Plageoles (Domaine de Tres Cantous)
81600 Gaillac. Vineyards owned: 21ha.
Produce: 50,000 bottles. VP-R.

One of the best producers in Gaillac, M. Plageoles owns two estates – the 10-hectare Domaine de Tres Cantous and the 11-

hectare Domaine de Roucou Cantemerle. His wines are sometimes a blend of both estates. His reds are made from the Duras and Gamay grapes. In whites, he makes sparkling Gaillac Mousseux and delicious Sauvignon dry and Mauzac sweet white still wines, and a rare AC Gaillac Premières Côtes, the Sherry-like Vin de Voile, from Mauzac, which stays in cask for six years. He also makes a sweet wine from Ondenc, a style not seen for around a century. *Open: By appointment only.*

Southwest: Iroulégy

Cave Coopérative des Vins d'Irou[ég]y et du Pays Basque
64430 St-Etienne-de-Baigorry. Vineyards owned: 8oha.
Produce: 300,000 bottles. Coop (60 members).

This cooperative virtually controls the whole of Irouégy production and has gone some way towards saving the appellation for posterity. The aim is to increase the area under vine to 200 hectares by the turn of the century. They make various qualities of red and rosé, the top wines being called Cuvée des Maitres Vignerons. In good years, they also make a red Cuvée Réserve. *Open: By appointment only.*

Southwest: Jurançon

GAEC Barrère
64150 Lahourcade. Vineyards owned: 15ha.
Produce: 80,000 bottles. VP-R.

Clos Cancaillau is the name under which wines are produced on this small estate. They make dry, medium-dry and sweet Jurançon, using blends of Gros Manseng, Petit Manseng and Courbu (for the sweeter wines only). *Open: Mon–Sat.*

Clos Guirouilh
Route de Bélair, Lasseube, 64290 Gan. Vineyards owned:
8ha. *Produce:* 50,000 *bottles.* VP-R.

An ancient estate, in the Guirouilh family since the 17th century, which specializes in a traditional sweet Jurançon from dried grapes and aged in oak. Most of their production, inevitably, is of the less interesting dry white. *Open: Appointments preferred.*

Caves des Producteurs de Jurançon
63 Avenue Henri-IV, 64290 Gan. Vineyards owned: 400ha.
Produce: 2 million bottles. Coop (300 members).

Jurançon dry and sweet in different qualities are the only AC wines from this cooperative. By far the bulk is of dry Jurançon, made from Gros Manseng, in three styles: Selection Viguerie Royale, Primeur and Millèsime. The same styles apply to the sweet Jurançon. They also sell wine from two small estates: Château les Astous and Domaine Lasserre. *Open: Mon–Sat 9am–noon; 2–6:30pm. Open Sundays in the summer.*

Cru Lamouroux
La Chapelle de Rousse, 64110 Jurançon. Vineyards owned:
6ha. *Produce:* 30,000 *bottles.* VP-R.

Jean Chigé and Richard Ziemek produce only sweet Jurançon Moelleux from their small vineyard which has been in the Chigé family since 1880. The wine, made from 60% Petit Manseng and 40% Gros Manseng, is vinified in stainless steel and matured in wood for 18 months. The result is a classic sweet wine with intense flavours of pineapple and honey. *Open: Appointments preferred.*

Clos Uroulat
64360 Moncin. Vineyards owned: 5.5ha.
Produce: 18,000 bottles. VP-R.

Charles Hours, the owner of this small property, makes a classic style of sweet Jurançon Moelleux, ageing the wine in *barriques* for 12 months, using 100% Petit Manseng. He also makes Jurançon Sec, using stainless steel for vinification and a blend of Gros Manseng and Courbu. Quality for both wines is high. *Open: By appointment only.*

Southwest: Madiran and Pacherenc du Vic Bilh

Domaine Barréjat
Maumusson, 32400 Riscle. Vineyards owned: Madiran 14ha; Pacherenc 2ha. *Produce: 90,000 bottles.* VP-R.

The Capmartin family has owned this estate for three generations. They make a traditional style of Madiran, using a slow maceration to get maximum colour, and the finished wine needs some years in bottle. The blend is 50/50 Tannat and Cabernets. The Pacherenc du Vic Bilh is vinified in stainless steel. *Open: Mon–Sat 8am–noon; 2–7pm.*

Alain Brumont
Maumusson, 32400 Riscle. Vineyards owned: Madiran 77ha.
Produce: 500,000 bottles. VP-R.

M. Brumont owns three estates, all producing Madiran. Domaine Bouscassé is the largest with 36 hectares; Château Moutus has 29 hectares; and Domaine Meinjarre has 12 hectares. The Domaine Bouscassé spends a year in wood, while Château Moutus spends time in new wood. He also makes Rosé de Béarn and dry and sweet Pacherenc from a newly-bought property. *Open: Mon–Sat 8am–8pm.*

Pierre Laplace
Haute Biste, Aydie, 64330 Garlin. Vineyards owned: 40ha.
Produce: 300,000 bottles. VP-R.

The Madiran from Château d'Aydie, M. Leplace's estate, is dominated by Tannat (up to 60%) with 20% each of Cabernet Franc and Cabernet Sauvignon. It is made traditionally and aged in wood, giving initially quite a tough wine, but one that mellows with time. A new wine is made from 100% Tannat, aged in new wood. He also makes smaller amounts of white Pacherenc du Vic Bilh, using stainless steel, to give a fresh, crisp wine. *Open: Mon–Fri, in working hours.*

Lucien Oulie (Domaine du Crampilh)
Aurion-Idernes, 64350 Lembeye. Vineyards owned: 20ha.
Produce: 132,000 bottles. VP-R.

Red Madiran and white Pacherenc du Vic Bilh are both produced at M. Oulie's vineyard. He uses the full range of local grape varieties in both his wines. The Madiran needs four or five years ageing, the white Pacherenc should be drunk young and fresh. *Open: By appointment only.*

Château Peyros

Corbères, 64350 Lembeye. Vineyards owned: 23ha.
Produce: 140,000 bottles. VP-R.

Stainless steel is used for vinification in this carefully run estate which M. de Robillard purchased in 1967. He only makes Madiran, using 50% Cabernet Franc, 5% Cabernet Sauvignon and 45% Tannat. The result is a wine which is lighter and less tannic than some from this AC. Plans include a new cellar for wood ageing of the wines. *Open: Appointments preferred.*

Domaine Pichard

Soublecause, 65700 Maubourguet. Vineyards owned: Madiran 12ha; Pacherenc 0.6ha. *Produce: 84,000 bottles.* VP-R.

M. Vigneau makes what is locally considered a fine Madiran, using 45% Tannat, 40% Cabernet Franc and 15% Cabernet Sauvignon. He ages the wine in wood before bottling. His small production of Pacherenc du Vic Bilh is bottled young. *Open: Mon–Sun.*

Union de Producteurs Plaimont

32400 Saint-Mont. Vineyards owned: 1,860ha.
Produce: 6 million bottles. Coop (1,350 members).

This large cooperative brings together three smaller cooperatives to produce Madiran, Côtes de Saint-Mont and Vin de Pays des Côtes de Gascogne. Their white Vin de Pays has been a runaway success for its clean, perfumed taste, given especially by the Colombard grape. Some Madiran and Côtes de Saint-Mont (known as the Collection Plaimont) are aged in new wood, while their standard range is known as Plaimont Tradition. *Open: Appointments preferred.*

Les Vignerons Réunis du Vic-Bilh-Madiran

Crouseilles, 64350 Lembeye. Vineyards owned: 496ha.
Produce: 3 million bottles. Coop (210 members).

By far the largest production from this cooperative is of Madiran (almost half the production for the AC), but it produces Béarn red and rosé and Pacherenc du Vic Bilh dry and sweet. *Open: Mon–Fri 8:30am–noon; 2–6pm.*

Domaine de Teston

Maumusson, 32400 Riscle. Vineyards owned: 20ha.
Produce: 157,000 bottles. VP-R.

Madiran, Pacherenc du Vic Bilh and the VDQS wines of Côtes de Saint-Mont are all made by M. Laffitte. He uses stainless steel and modern technology, but then matures the red in new wood. He says he is particularly proud of his newly acquired Côtes de Saint-Mont vineyard, which is planted with 70% Tannat, 20% Cabernet Sauvignon and 10% Fer Savadou. *Open: By appointment only.*

The following is a list of VDQS producers in the Southwest: Henri Avallon; Cave Coopérative du Canton d'Auvillar; Cave Coopérative de Cocumont; Pierre Lacombe; Laurens-Teulier; Société Coopérative Vinicole des Côtes du Marmandais; Les Vigérons de Tursan; Cave des Vignérons du Vallon; Cave Coopérative La Ville Dieu du Temple.